CHRIST'S HOSPITAL

First published 1984

ISBN 086364 005 2

Published by Ian Allan Ltd, Shepperton, Surrey;
and printed by Ian Allan Printing Ltd at their works
at Coombelands in Runnymede, England.

Contents

For Angus Ross

Scholar, Donation Governor and Chairman
of the Council of Almoners

The Worshipful the Treasurer of Christ's Hospital

Preface

The late George Allan was a boy at Christ's Hospital from 1897 to 1902, the seismic years which saw preparations for the move of the Boys' School from its ancient home in Newgate Street to Sussex. For most of his adult life he served the Foundation, from 1933 to 1946 as Clerk.

The book was first published in 1937 and appeared again, as revised by George Allan himself, ten years later.

It was at the invitation of the original author's son Ian, himself an Almoner of Christ's Hospital, that I undertook the preparation of this new, and necessarily much-amended, edition. This invitation I accepted with much reluctance for there must be some suspicion of impertinence in tampering with the work of a man, as was George Allan, deeply immersed in the history and administration of the Foundation and, as was George Allan, unshakeably committed to the perpetuation of its spirit of charity. But, onerous as it has been in some respects, the task has also been a delight for in its performance I am able to repay some small part of the great debt which I owe to Christ's Hospital.

Such difficulties as there have been have been eased – and my pleasure enhanced – because, as always is the case in Christ's Hospital affairs, my pleas for assistance have been answered eagerly and efficiently.

David Young, of the Christ's Hospital Office, prepared the index; for that both the publisher and I owe him gratitude; but my thanks go to him also for his enthusiastic and scholarly assistance in resolving several historical conundrum.

Many of the illustrations in this volume are evidence to Alan Hollingsworth's skill as a photographer.

It is a rare and amiable feature of the Christ's Hospital community that so often the wives of Old Blues take to themselves voluntarily the loyalty and affection for the Foundation that their husbands owe out of duty and gratitude. My wife, herself a Donation Governor, has assisted me with much more than moral support in the preparation of all my books but I suspect that never before has she felt such deep involvement as has been hers whilst I have been working on this volume.

Another Old Blue wife, my dear friend, Elaine Barr, has helped me in various ways. To her and to her colleague at the Victoria and Albert Museum, Michael Snodin, my thanks are particularly due for notably expert advice about the silver which forms such a handsome part of C.H. treasures.

The dedication to Angus Ross is no mere dutiful formality. His wisdom and care as Christ's Hospital approaches the second metamorphosis of this century, the re-unification of its two Schools, must secure for him a place among the greatest of all Treasurers but I honour him also for many decades of friendship and – to me more surprising – for the fact that he read part of the typescript without battering with me so much as one of his customary caustic comments.

My thanks go also to my secretary, Deborah Brown. After typing and re-typing from the manuscript she must now know as much as do I about the Foundation, and almost as much as did George Allan. I owe much to her accuracy and more to her unshakeable good humour.

J. E. Morpurgo
Scholar, Donation Governor
and Almoner of Christ's Hospital

The

Religious, Royal, and Ancient Foundation

of

CHRIST'S HOSPITAL

May those prosper who love it,

and

may God increase their number

CHAPTER ONE

Origin and Growth

Christ's Hospital boasts a literature richer than that of any other school. It could be no more than happy coincidence but, more likely, it has been the unique traditions of the Hospital and their profound sense of community and of gratitude to the Foundation which, over the centuries, have persuaded Blues in all generations to set to print their tributes and their recollections of school-days in poem, essay and book. Certainly – and this too may be either accident or inherited respect for the literary arts – Christ's Hospital has been unusual among schools in the number of its sons who have made their adult careers in literature or in journalism or who, though passing their lives in some other calling, have shown nevertheless by occasional exercise a rare gift as writers. Of these, the professionals and the skilled amateurs, almost every one has at some time saluted Christ's Hospital.

In this plush literary record the glorious conjunction of Coleridge, Lamb and Leigh Hunt – three who stand close to the summit of English literary achievement – has enshrined the ethos of the Hospital forever firm in the minds of readers far outside the intimate circle, but they had their noble precursors – George Peele and David Baker among them – their articulate contemporaries – W. P. Scargill, T. S. Surr and the first great editor of *The Times*, Thomas Barnes – and they have had a host of brilliant successors. In this century, for example, Edmund Blunden, one of England's finest writers, devoted a whole book to Christ's Hospital and supplemented it with several poems, with essays and with a myriad of allusions. Middleton Murry, Philip Youngman Carter, Graham Hutton, Sydney Carter, Michael Swan, Keith Douglas, Percy Young, Barnes Wallis (seemingly from a world quite other than the literary but in this patently a man of letters) and (in a brave attempt to bowl on an unfamiliar wicket) the England cricketer, John Snow: all have written on Christ's Hospital.

This outpouring of praise, reminiscence and explanation has been so various and so continuous that, in 1953, it was possible to put together, exclusively from the writings of those who had been educated in the school or who had served the Foundation, a representation of the four hundred years of Christ's Hospital history and of the panoply of its traditions. Such too is the world-wide interest in the mysteries of this unique institution that *The Christ's Hospital Book* was bought everywhere, even in the United States, Canada, Australia and New Zealand, and was, by the crudest commercial measure, successful as no other similar act of piety.

There have been also many formal histories but of these most were too detailed, too obviously written for those who understood already the eccentric nature of the Hospital – and many too turgid – to arouse much attention from a public outside the ever-interested parochial audience.

It was with the intention of explaining to this larger constituency the idiosyncratic purposes, the peculiar organisation and the especial characteristics of Christ's Hospital that the late G. A. T. Allan, himself a devoted Blue and the much-loved and much-respected Clerk of Christ's Hospital, prepared the first version of this book for publication in 1937.

George Allan was commissioned to write his book as one in a series on the Great Public Schools of Britain. Set in that context the invitation was an anomaly, a blatant demonstration of a contradiction which must be resolved from the outset if the true nature of the Foundation is to be understood. Except by the meanest and most legalistic definition – by the presence of the Head Master of the Boys' School as a member of the Headmasters' Conference – Christ's Hospital is not a public school at all, as generally the world understands that term. Indeed, the principles upon which the school was established and has been continued for almost four-and-a-half centuries are close to being antithetical to those which prevail in most public schools.

Christ's Hospital is an independent school, and jealous of its independence, but it is, first and above all else, a charity.

So also, it may be argued, were many of the great public schools in their origins and so also are they all to this day by the nice (and convenient) measure of legal status. But Christ's Hospital stands virtually alone in that it has remained true to the charitable intentions of its sixteenth century Founders and alone in that its charitable purposes transcend all others. More even than that: by the oldest and most generous interpretation of the word, Christ's Hospital is the quintessential charity, the product of a 'dede of pittie', the continuing consequence of acts of love. The words of the Schools Inquiry Commissioners ring as true to-day as they did when first they were written in 1867:

Christ's Hospital is a thing without parallel in this country, and *sui generis*. It is a grand relic of the medieval spirit – a monument of the profuse munificence of that spirit, and of that constant stream of individual beneficence which is so often found to flow around institutions of that character.

We have always been a school for both boys and girls. The Christ's Hospital Girls' School is, in fact, the oldest school for girls in the country ('a poor young maiden child' is recorded in the earliest extant record of admissions – for 9th December, 1554 – and another girl is, if only by the accident of the alphabet, the first whose name appears in the Registers, unbroken since 1563). But there are many public schools for girls and now many public schools that are co-educational, as soon we will be also, and it is not this concession to equal opportunities for the sexes which sets Christ's Hospital apart from the public schools. The fundamental, and patently charitable, distinction is evidenced most surely by contrasting the principles which control the Hospital's conditions for the admission of children with those which influence the governing bodies of the public schools at large.

With only limited exceptions parents who look to educate their children in a public school must first 'enter' them – register them as candidates – and then, once the child has passed the appropriate examination, that child is enrolled, *providing always that the parents can pay the required fees.*

Christ's Hospital works in contrary fashion. The first and, for most prospective Blues, the all-important stipulation is "that no child will be admitted whose parents or next friends are not, in the opinion of the Council of Almoners, in need of assistance towards his education and maintenance."

From this over-riding consideration there stems a consequence which creates another and no less significant difference between the community at large which is Christ's Hospital and the communities – children and former pupils – of the public schools. As 'need' is the prime criterion a parent must meet before entering his child as a Scholar of Christ's Hospital (and in this usage, too, the Hospital is unique: all its children are 'scholars', at least by the courtesy of

nomenclature) so also, by definition, are those parents unable to offer to their children the benefits of financial support, family influence or powerful contacts to help them on their way after they leave school. It has therefore been imperative upon the Hospital that, if it is to carry out to the full its charitable purposes, it must continue the care of its children even after they complete their formal education.

This part of its self-imposed responsibility it has fulfilled faithfully from the sixteenth century until to-day but the fraternity (what one irreverent member of the community has called 'the Old Blue Mafia') has always shown itself to be an effective substitute for family patronage.

In all it is the manner in which Christ's Hospital's men and women have consistently overcome the initial handicap of poverty and the inhibition of lack of influence – the phenomenally high "success-rate" – which, in an age dedicated to equal opportunity for all, makes Christ's Hospital precepts and methods much more than merely fascinating. The Hospital must be a model, to be imitated, cherished – and never to be destroyed.

There is one more characteristic which demands attention even thus early in the narrative, a characteristic which differentiates if from the public schools, and which re-inforces the boast that it is, above all else, a charity and the active heir to the noblest of charitable instincts. For more than three hundred years parents gave nothing towards the costs of education and maintenance and even in this century their contribution has been minimal. Therefore the Hospital has depended for its financial stability entirely on generous benefactors. Happily, there have been many such and among their number a goodly proportion have been sons and daughters of the House. In a manner that is almost a miraculous justification of the School's Christian ethos and proof that it is, in every sense, a charity, Christ's Hospital has been throughout its history largely self-perpetuating. The response to Appeals launched since the Second World War has demonstrated that it is not only Blues who have prospered who have answered the call to make some financial recompense for the benefits received in youth for, to-day as in the past, the weight of this duty must fall upon those who can bear it and these are the very men and women who are debarred from entering their own children into the Hospital. They have never failed to carry this burden and there can be no other school in the world which educates the children of other men and women at the expense of those who, by their own skills and exertions, have worked themselves out of the possibility that they can confer upon their own offspring the privileges which they themselves enjoyed in youth.

Henry VIII wrought better than he intended when he took from the Grey Friars their properties close to St. Paul's Cathedral and bestowed them on the City of London "for the relief of the poor". For six years this gift lay dormant. Then it was that Bishop Ridley's strident sermon on Charity moved the heart of Henry's young son and stirred Edward VI to seek further and more practical advice from Ridley. King, Bishop, the Lord Mayor and Aldermen conferred and, in 1552, settled for the establishment of three Royal Hospitals: Christ's (in the Grey Friars), for the education of poor children; St. Thomas's, for the care of the sick; and Bridewell, for the correction of "the idle and vagabonds".

The learned writer of the 1837 "Report of the Commissioners for Inquiring concerning Charities" says, in his own inimitable style, that

it was not a refounding or extension of any charitable foundation of a similar nature already endowed and existing on the same spot previously to the dissolution of the monasteries, but a new foundation owing its commencement to the active benevolence of some distinguished citizens of London, stimulated perhaps in the first instance by the extreme distress to which the suppression of the religious houses had reduced many of the mendicant poor, but eventually directed into a more beneficial channel than that of mere eleemosynary distribution.

The earliest history of the Foundation is contained in a precious manuscript, the work of John Howes, citizen, grocer and at one-time apprentice and servant to our first Treasurer, Richard Grafton, whose printing-press produced (within the Hospital's precincts) his own edition of the Bible. Howes became Renter of the Hospital (collector of rents) and as such it was one of his duties to attend upon the scrutineers of the Hospitals, for they had at first a common chest, and to "inquire and search out for all the legacies so given, and make thereof rehearsal to the scrutineers or gatherers of them, who shall receive the same". Howes was paid on commission: "He shall have of every £ received two pence and none other fee or wages."

The Howes manuscript is in the form of "a familiar and friendly discourse dialoguewise setting forth the first order and manner of the erection of the Hospitals of Christ, Bridewell and St. Thomas the Apostle". Bound in white vellum, mystic, wonderful, the document was produced in the Court of Chancery a century later and duly endorsed as an exhibit. Like the Ark of the Covenant it then disappeared from history; but unlike the Ark it was re-discovered after two hundred years amongst the lumber of a disused store-room.

See how the good seed germinated. A committee of thirty was appointed which did commonly meet every day in the inner chamber of the Guildhall. In counting the cost of their undertaking they first thought good to begin with themselves, and each gave his contribution of £10 or £20 according to his ability. Then they exhorted the preachers, ministers, churchwardens and sidesmen to obtain from their parishioners a frank benevolence and weekly pension. And to that effect they delivered therewith a very fine, witty, and learned oration, being printed, which they gave to every preacher and minister, the better to instruct and persuade the people in every parish to give liberally.

The Annual Accounts for 1552 – and we possess still an unbroken series of accounts from that day to this – show that this witty oration, added perhaps to the solicitations of interested friends, was not without tangible result. The heading of the first page runs as follows:

A perfect and full declaration of all such sums of money as have been from time to time given not only of the free and liveral disposition of divers Aldermen and Commoners, Governors of this House, and of the several gifts of other, but also received by a monthly collection throughout the Wards of the City of London towards the relief and sustentation of the poor of Christ's and St. Thomas's Hospitals and the members and parts thereof as hereafter more plainly shall appear.

And, having run for two years, the account ends:

Summa totalis of all the charge of Christ's Hospital sythen the time of the erection thereof unto the last day of the month of June anno 1554 as well as in building beds and other furniture as may particularly appear by the account amounteth £4641, 6s. 9d.

Civic benevolence was thus the first stone in our structure. After the spontaneous contributions of the Committee of Thirty came an application to the Aldermen, then to the City Companies, whose subscriptions are set out in detail by Howes. The first gift in kind came from one of the thirty, who took upon himself to provide 500 feather beds, 500 pads of straw to lay under them, as many blankets, and a thousand pair of sheets. The King, acceding to the suppliant Ridley, gave his palace of Bridewell, a truly royal gift – on paper. But Howes says naively that "it was not without an infinite charge, and the situation thereof was such that all the cost was cast away, there was no coming to it but through sinking lanes or over a filthy ditch which did so continually annoy the house that the King had no pleasure in it'. Edward also handed over the Savoy and its lands. The account includes money received from the sale of such articles as "one dozen of silver spoons weighing 34 oz. at 4s 8d. the oz., £7, 18s 8d.''. By royal warrant, all the linen belonging to the churches in London – save only sufficient for their own needs – was brought to the Governors for the use of the poor, this being of especial service to St. Thomas's.

The City itself was not slow to do its share in meeting the increasing expenditure of its healthily-growing nursling. The Common Council in 1548 had granted to St. Bartholomew's Hospital 500 marks out of the profits of Blackwell Hall, the common market-place for woollen and linen goods. In 1557 the profits surplus to these 500 marks were "wholly bestowed to the relief and support of the poor sick and indigent persons in the Hospitals of Christ and St. Thomas for evermore and to no other use". The Hospital eventually became the managers of Blackwell Hall, and as such had to concern itself with discoveries such as are recorded in the following minute: "By the report of Edward Towney, a cardmaker dwelling in Southwark, at a town in Yorkshire called Osset beside Wakefield the best cardwire to make cards is there made, and is to be bought for 9s 0d. the stone after 12 lb. to the stone at the hands of one John Robinson. . . and for the wire made in Gloucestershire one Hill of Gloucester hath the trade of it."

In 1582 the Corporation, which had exercised an immemorial jurisdiction over all persons working carts within the liberties of the City, transferred authority to Christ's Hospital. A carroom (the right to have a cart marked by the Governors) brought the Hospital an annual rent of 17s. 4d., with an entrance fee of twenty shillings. Carts were brought to the Hospital each July for branding, except during those periods when the Woodmongers Company enjoyed the privilege in exchange for an annuity of £150.

As early as 1577 the Governors appear to have evolved another scheme for supplementing income. Persons who desired to be buried with some pomp and circumstance might, from this date and for nearly two hundred years, hire a number of boys and girls to attend and sing at their funerals or to act as mutes. The larger the donation, the more the attendants; and the matter might be arranged by legacy, though the Governors would almost certainly have found some means to insure against an obvious risk.

Gifts of money, houses and lands were quickly and liberally bestowed by those who saw the good work that was being done by the Hospital, and who had an opportunity of noting the intense interest taken by the Governors in their charges and the conscientiousness with which they fulfilled their trust. So impressive was the high standard of integrity displayed by the Governors that a great many persons appointed them trustees corporately, not always with a *quid pro quo* for the Hospital. Many of these sixteenth century trusts are even to-day carried out, to the letter, by the Foundation.

So much for the beginning of the endowments, which continued to increase.

What of the children? Most were taken in for shelter, either from the streets or from homes that were no homes at all. The street-keepers and the beadles were constantly engaged in rounding up those who, without their services must have become in time idlers, vagrants – or worse. There was in those early days no age-limit; during the first twenty years the Hospital opened its charity to babies one day old and to men and women of "forty years and upwards". Some few of the children were foundlings but there was no basket outside the Hospital's gates such as later Captain Coram set before his and, indeed, the most diligent search was made for the parents of children abandoned in the streets – and woe betide them if they were found, as may be seen from this minute:

Wednesday being Embring Day and the 16th December, 1556. Where by the Lord Mayor and his brethren the Aldermen it was adjudged that a woman named Norton dwelling in Southwark for leaving and forsaking of a child in the streets should be whipped at Bridewell and from there sent unto the Governors of Christ's Hospital for a further reformation, which thing being done she was sent unto the pillory in Cheap with a paper on her head wherein was written in great letters Whipped at Bridewell for leaving and forsaking her child in the streets and from thence carried into Southwark and banished for her offence out of the city.

Yet that the Foundation was an educational establishment from the beginning is clearly proven. This is no mere personal opinion, but the mature decision of the Judicial Committee of the Privy Council, which in a judgment delivered in 1889, found that, almost immediately after the foundation, the original site and the large gifts made to it had been applied to education, and that Christ's Hospital's Governing Body, acting separately from 1557 onwards, had been concerned with educational funds. To this conclusion they were drawn above all by the words of the King's indenture of 1553, where the Royal Founder insisted that he graciously considered:

the good and godly endeavours of his most humble and obedient subjects the mayor and commonalty and citizens of London, who diligently by all ways and means do travail for the good provision of the said poor and every sort of them, and that by such sort and means as neither the child in his infancy shall want virtuous education and bringing up, neither when the same shall grow into full age shall lack matter whereon the same may virtuously occupy himself in good occupation or science profitable to the commonweal.

Such was the quality of the education provided in the Hospital that some, even from the first generation of Blues, were sufficiently learned to make their way to Oxford or to Cambridge and many had been so well-trained that they could pass out of school into service as clerks and scriveners.

Many did not remain for long humble servants to the great. A little more than a century after the foundation Daniel Defoe wrote:

What City Knights and Aldermen we know from Bluecoat Hospitals and Bridewells flow

Soon the excellent reputation enjoyed by boys reared in Christ's Hospital attracted attention far outside the boundaries of the City of London. In 1616, the Court of Common Council appointed two Deputies to go to Ireland to report on the progress of the plantations in Londonderry and Coleraine. They were "to have special care that those children which were lately sent over for servants and apprentices out of the Hospitals in London, to be employed in both the towns may be well bestowed and placed with honest tradesmen and housekeepers for their better breeding". The Deputies reported in due course that "the twelve children sent over from Christ's Hospital arrived all safe and well at Londonderry and are placed ten of them there and two of them at Coleraine, and these indentures we will deliver to the Treasurer of Christ's Hospital, to be there kept for their use."

This pioneering venture was commemorated by a stained-glass window in Londonderry's Guildhall, with, in one light, a group of boys in their familiar blue-coats and, in another, the Hospital's arms.

Further afield even than Ireland: already almost a decade before the Pilgrim Fathers set foot on Plymouth Rock (and thereby set in train the fallacy, which still persists in popular fable, that they were the creators of the first permanent British settlement in North America) the first Blue had arrived in the well-established Virginia Colony.

The proficiency shown by Thomas Sexton and his many seventeenth and eighteenth century successors so impressed the leading planters of Virginia that the custom of sending "back to the Hospital for a boy who can read well, write clearly and cast accounts" persisted until well after the United States had become an independent nation and, because there too many of these boys stayed on and prospered after their indentures were completed, many prominent families in the Southern States – but particularly in Virginia – can claim a Blue as founding-father.

During the seventeenth century – after the streets had been fairly well cleared and the "City was now in its beauty" – the Governors were much occupied with the age of admission of children and the type of child to be taken in. One of the earliest regulations is to confine admissions to the City.

No foreigner's child, born without the liberties of this City, nor any others, though their parents be free of this City, being born without the said liberties, shall be admitted children of this House, except it be upon very great consideration.

In 1664: "no child under the age of 4 years shall be admitted from any great Personage by letter or otherwise except the same be the child of a freeman of London and born within the said city". Fifteen years later: "no child shall be admitted into this House at the suit of any parish or person whatsoever, except it be of the age of 3 years or more". In 1652 it was ordered that no children be taken in but "such as be freemen's children", and shortly afterwards those were barred who were "lame or otherwise infirm in the body".

By 1676 these various regulations had crystallized. Candidates for admission must be children of freemen, living within the City, not under seven years of age, orphans wanting either father or mother or both; none to be taken in that are foundlings, that have any probable means of being provided for in other ways, "or that are lame, crooked, or deformed, or that have any infectious disease, as the leprosy, scald head, itch, scab, or that have the evil or rupture". Nor might any child be admitted whose brother or sister had already entered.

The progress of the Hospital in its first century was not without hindrances. The Founder King lived but a short time after he set his signature to the Charter, and his sister, Queen Mary I, looked with devout Catholic disfavour upon an institution which made emphatic its essentially Protestant origins by its continued occupation of the Grey Friars. It was her inclination to put an end to this heretical impertinence, but she was engrossed with other burning issues – close to Christs's Hospital in Smithfield – and the Foundation was protected by the affection of the citizens of London.

There survives from the Marian interlude one story which deserves to be authentic. The Founder King, it is said, had conferred upon the Hospital the right to greet the Monarch on the occasion of his first visit to the City. (The origins may be legendary but the privilege undoubtedly exists – and is still exercised.) Queen Mary showed her disdain for the Hospital by turning her back on the boy chosen to present to her its Loyal Address. That boy, so runs the tale, was St. Edmund Campion!

Divine retribution and divine intercession, perhaps, but more likely the Accession of sturdy and Protestant Queen Elizabeth I, saved the Hospital and in her reign it continued to grow and to develop its functions as a school. But growth brought with it new difficulties. The care, spiritual, physical and educational, of so many children created financial anxiety – a burden from which the Governors have seldom been freed. Expenses soared and many City parishes failed to pay their due subscriptions. The Governors borrowed: £1500 from the City Companies and £500 from the Corporation. Even this was not enough and so the Common Council decreed that all fines and forfeitures incurred by Billingsgate porters be made over to the Hospital. (It is not stated if the forfeitures could be paid in kind!) Further, the Common Council called upon the Master and Wardens of the Woodmongers "to shew

Cyttie the Aldermen of

every Companye broug

every of the sortes of th

Dignitie.

It is not to be doubte

Dutie.

The nomber was grea

Of ffatherles childr

Of Sore & sicke ps

Of poore men over

Of aged persons   -

Of decayed househo

Of ydell vagabonde

The whole nomber

all sortes wch requ

A page from John Howes MS, 1582.

y Warde & the Wardeines of

n theire reportes severallye of

ore.

t the nomber was greate.

ıdede as shall appeare, viz. :—

-    -   -   -   -   300

-    -   -   -   -   200

ened wth theire children   350

-    -   -   -   -   400

rs   -   -   -   -   650

-    -   -   -   -   200
                              ———

as yt appeareth to be of

ed present relefe   -   - 2160 (sic)

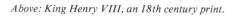

Above: King Henry VIII, an 18th century print.

Above right: King Edward VI.

Right: Nicholaus Ridley, Bishop of London in 1550.

Below: Queen Mary I, an 18th century print.

Below right: Saint Edmund Campion.

Right: Samuel Pepys.

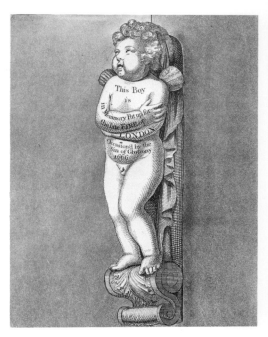

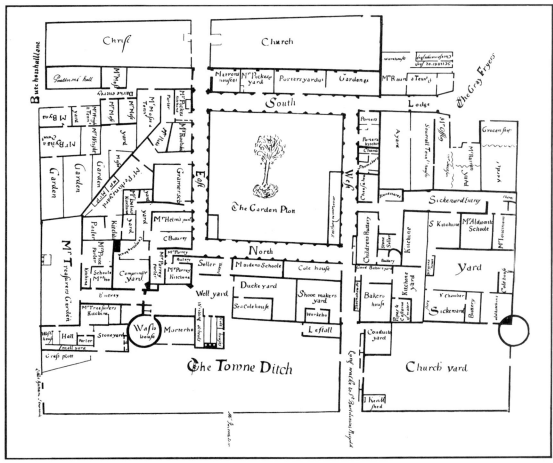

cause why they pay not the money they owe to Christ's Hospital''

Not unnaturally the City wished to know where it stood with regard to certain rights of patronage which such generosity might be expected to confer. From 1630, and for more than two hundred years, there was an undercurrent of ill-feeling between the Corporation and the Hospital Governors, as may appear by such notes as these from Corporation Records: 1630, Committee appointed to consider the particulars presented touching Christ's Hospital; 1697, Committee appointed to examine the constitution of Christ's Hospital; 1720, Committee appointed to inform themselves of the rights and privileges of the Court in relation to admitting poor children of Christ's Hospital; 1772, Reference to enquire as to the right of the members of the Court to be Governors of the Royal Hospitals.

By way of a *modus vivendi*, an Act of Parliament was passed (*22 Geo. III, c. 77*) in 1782 to render valid and effectual certain articles of agreement.

Whereas Disputes have arisen between the said Mayor and Commonalty and Citizens, and the Persons acting as Governors of the said Hospitals, touching their respective Right, Powers, and Privileges, in the Ordering, Management, Government, and Disposition of the said Hospitals, and the Estates, Possessions, and Revenues thereof; And it is conceived to be for the mutual Benefit of the said Mayor and Commonalty and Citizens, and of the said Hospitals, that all such Disputes should cease, and be finally and amicably settled, adjusted, and terminated, . . .That, in order to effectuate the salutary Purposes hereinbefore mentioned, it is agreed as follows: (1) That the list of Governors be presented to the Lord Mayor on the 21st September every year; (2) That the Governors might describe themselves, for the purposes of litigation, &c., as the Mayor and Commonalty as Governors; (3) That the Seal be kept by the Chamberlain; and (4) That the Court of Common Council should nominate twelve Governors.

Since the passing of this more than usually verbose piece of legislation, only minor differences have arisen between these two great bodies.

The names of many of those individual benefactors who, in its first two centuries, followed the example of Crown and City, are recorded only in Christ's Hospital's archives and in its more detailed histories but one name, that of Erasmus Smith – he whose generosity was largely responsible for the great building-programmes of the late seventeenth and eighteenth centuries – has rare currency. Still to-day as they make their way up the School, progressing from form to form graced according to Christ's Hospital's unique nomenclature, most Blues would echo the mystification expressed more than a century ago by Leigh Hunt in his *Autobiography*.

The Upper Grammar School was divided into four classes or forms. The two under ones were called Little and Great Erasmus; the two upper were occupied by the Grecians and Deputy Grecians. [Leigh Hunt, himself never greater than a Deputy Grecian, should have known better and should have put these two forms in their proper ascending order.] We used to think the title of Erasmus taken from the great scholar of that name; but the sudden appearance of a portrait among us, bearing to be the likeness of a certain Erasmus Smith, Esq., shook us terribly in this opinion and was a hard trial of our gratitude. I believe he was a rich merchant and that the forms of Little and Greater Erasmus were really named after him.

The name of Erasmus Smith has vanished long-since from public recognition and even within Christ's Hospital, if he is remembered at all, it is not from any sense of thanksgiving for his many benefactions nor yet out of respect for his vigorous personality and his intellectual energy, but only because of that antique quirk which made his Christian name the eponym for two rungs in the academic ladder climbed by generation after generation of the Hospital's boys. But among Smith's contemporaries there was one whose fame is imperishable in the Hospital, no less substantial in the history of the Royal Navy and who, beyond all other diarists, has won the affection of readers everywhere.

The school-days of Samuel Pepys we must concede. with courtesy and gratitude to St. Paul's, our erstwhile neighbour in the City but, from his early manhood (the period of the *Diary*) and for the rest of his days, Pepys's interest in the Hospital was intense.

It was, indeed, in his last years, when he was tired, dispirited by loss of public office and nearly blind, that Pepys's demonstrated most forcefully the wisdom, perspicacity and zeal which already for three decades he had given to his task as a Governor. By that time the administration of the Hospital was in some disarray. Pepys decided upon a thorough investigation, launched it on his own initiative, carried it through virtually without assistance, paid for it from his own pocket, and unaided wrote the consequent report. Faced at first with reluctance, and even obstructionism, from the Officers his persistence won the day, but only after several years of prodding and persuading. The situation he uncovered was truly deplorable and that he did not hide his dismay and disquiet is clear in the opening paragraphs of the report, signed in his own hand and dated from York Buildings, March 23rd, 1697-8:

I shall not offer at any other Introduction to what I am now presenting you with, than this short Reflection; viz. That if the bestowing all his Goods (and those all his own Goods) to feed the Poor, was not Warranty sufficient with St. Paul himselfe, against ye Supposition even of his Want of Charity; how much less reason have We to regret ye Doubts now stirring both without doors and within, touching the Perfection of Our Managements, who (some few excepted) bring nothing hither of our Own to merit by, saving that of Our Service, As Accomptants for the Goods, and Executors of the Benefactions, of Others?

And in this Enquiry it is, that Duty to God; to the Poor; to ye Memory and Wills of our Royal Founders, and Other Our Religious Benefactors; to this Court; and to my own Obligations as Your Fellow Servant in this Trust; I have for some time been exercized, and now come with all Respect to give you ye Effects of. Entring on it with ye observing; That ye Points of principal Trust in all Societys of Charity, seem to be those, which relate either to the Revenues, or to the Ends, of those Societys. And that governing myselfe by this Division, and assigning to each its particular Section; the part which first offers itselfe for Your Entertainment upon this Subject, is the Considering of the Present State of that Revenue, which by the Piety of our Founders and Benefactors, Ourselves stand entrusted with; viz. How far the same (as Loans to God Almighty) have been on our part attended, with such a measure of Vigilance and Sincerity in ye Collecting Sollicitousness in ye Improving; Uprightness, Circumspection and Thrift in ye Dispensing; Method and Truth in ye Accounting-for; Strictness of Controll in ye Auditing; Fidelity, Frequency, and Fulness in our Reporting; and lastly, Application and Uninterestedness of Conduct through ye Whole; as not to have exposed ye same to any Impairments by Neglect of Unfaithfulness on one hand, or to an Overweight of Charge by any Improvidence on ye other; in prejudice to the Honour or Support of the Foundation, or Both.

After such a proemium it is hardly to be wondered at that the Report itself forced the resignation of the Treasurer who (we regret to have to record) had to be ejected from his official residence by the Sheriff. It is, however, more pleasing to note that ''in acknowledgment of his great zeal and concern for the interest of Christ's Hospital'' Pepys was presented with the Freedom of the City.

Pepys's strident denunciation of maladministration made the way clear for reforms and thus for some of the great developments in the eighteenth century but already, some twenty years before he presented his scathing report, Pepys had made his most substantial and most enduring contribution to the story of the Hospital.

In 1672 Pepys became Secretary of the Admiralty but before achieving this, the senior post occupied by a civilian in the administration of British marine power, he had served the Navy in high office for many years and he and his Royal Patron James, Duke of York, had been for all that time much perturbed by the poor quality and scant supply of sailors both for the Royal Navy and the Merchant Marine and particularly by the inefficiency of officers as navigators. Pepys saw a means whereby he could further the cause of Britain's sea-power and at the same time add something of abiding significance to the Hospital and it was the conjunction of these two ideals that led him to play a leading part in the establishment with Christ's Hospital of the Royal Mathematical School. He did not strive alone to this purpose. The list of his allies reads like a roll-call of the great of British science at a time when British science was plush with greatness, a roll-call too of members of the newly-formed Royal Society (an institution with which the Hospital maintains links to this day). Flamsteed, Newton, Wren: all were Governors and all Pepys's partners in the grand design of establishing the Royal Mathematical School.

The King was less enthusiastic. Charles II was not a seaman as was his brother James and, if he liked to see himself – and to be seen – as patron of the sciences and the arts his reluctance to part with money, even with money that belonged properly to others, was more potent than his interest in the improvements of the sea-service. However, such were the persuasive powers of Pepys and his friends that Charles at last conceded to the Hospital a legacy to which it was already entitled, and so won for himself the glory of being considered our second Royal Founder. (The original grant, conferred by Letters Patent in 1675 was later converted to an annuity of £370, 10s. 0d. A slightly-amended Patent was granted in 1858, and the annuity is to-day represented by a capital sum in Consols.)

According to the custom of the times, the foundation of the Royal Mathematical School, *Auspicio Caroli Secundi,* was celebrated by striking a medallion. On one side is a handsome bust of Charles II; on the reverse side a Christ's Hospital boy being patted on the head by Arithmetic, Astronomy and Commerce. Overhead are two cherubs, and zephyrs blowing upon some fine ships.

The reverse of ''this rare and glorious medallion'' is said to have been designed by Isaac Newton (who certainly presented the die to the Hospital). It is almost identical with the badge worn on their shoulder ever since by the forty "Mathemats".

The Royal Mathematical School went through some vicissitudes in its early days and for a century and more Mathemats were the bully-boys of the Hospital and the terror of townees, but the R.M.S. inspired both Peter the Great (with the aid of two lads straight out of the Hospital) and Louis XIV to set up similar institutions in their own kingdoms, and before long Mathemats were proving their worth not only in the Royal Navy (our admiral of the time was not a Mathemat but then Cloudesley Shovell's navigation was, to say the least of it, dubiously efficient for he landed his fleet and himself on the rocks off Cornwall) but also in the Maritime Service of the East India Company and as captains of "Bombay Buccaneers". However, the greatest glory of the R.M.S. is in the history of exploration. A Mathemat surveyed the Dividing Line between Virginia and North Carolina, there were Mathemats – and the man who became eventually the greatest Master of the R.M.S. – with Cook when he circumnavigated the world. Mathemats helped to open up the American West. Mathemats explored the interior of Australia.

Isaac Newton's services to Christ's Hospital were not confined to designing or presenting medals. He had helped to create a school for navigators; almost 20 years later he produced, especially for them and for their fellow-scholars in Christ's Hospital, a reformed system for mathematical study.

The Treasurer of the time wrote to thank the great man:

Your letters and paper by the carrier and post, are safe come to hand, wherein you have taken so great pains and care, and expressed so great kindness withal, as could not have been expected from anybody of less candour and ingenuity than Mr. Newton, nor could anything less than so great an advantage to our House and the public as your advice will amount to have animated you with so much courage and patience.

The author of this fulsome letter was that same Treasurer who, only three years later, was to be hustled out of office and home by the investigative energy of Samuel Pepys!

Not infrequent chicanery and squabbles – not only with the Crown and City but also with Peterhouse, Cambridge and our neighbour, St. Bartholomew's

Hospital – all are episodes in the early history of the Hospital but generally the Governors acted in what they thought to be the best interests of their charges, and generally progress was wondrous.

There were disasters, too, and not all of them created by any defect in the Hospital's administration.

Thirty-two children died in the Plague of 1665, and the Great Fire in the next year destroyed most of the buildings.

We have our own eye-witness account of the Fire, recorded in the Minutes for 2nd September 1666.

It pleased Almighty God by a dreadful fire, which began at a house in Pudding Lane near to New Fish Street, to burn and consume the third part of the City of London with some part of the freedom to Temple Bar. Of all the 97 parishes within the walls but 12 are standing, and St. Sepulchre's and St. Bride's were burnt without the walls. This terrible fire began at the place before mentioned on Sunday morning, being the 2nd day of September, 1666, and continued about four days. By which fire this Hospital of Christ's was almost consumed with the two great Churches adjoining, excepting the four cloisters to which the fire hath done no hurt, and about three wards towards the sick ward and several other rooms there, as also to the wardrobe of this Hospital over the south cloister, the glazed windows of the Church on that side being very little damnified.

Tuesday night, 4th September, saw more than two hundred of the children

carried away to the Nag's Head at Islington belonging to the Hospital, which then stood void, and after the night's lodging there they were received into the new corporation near Clerkenwell, and there were dieted for four days at 5d. a day apiece.

The destruction of the buildings had happy consequence for there followed the great re-building programme in which Wren and Hawksmoor played their miraculous part. There followed also the first substantial migration.

Not a fortnight after the Fire more than fifty children were sent to Ware and a similar number to Hertford.

Thus begins the substantial connection between Christ's Hospital and Hertfordshire and with its county town.

CHAPTER TWO

Hertford

The association between Christ's Hospital and Hertford has lasted for 300 years and, in this century, the name has become among Blues of both sexes, virtually a synonym for the Christ's Hospital Girls' School. Even so it cannot be denied that, although in this same century, Christ's Hospital, Hertford has earned a handsome reputation as one of the finest schools for girls in Britain, still to-day it comes often as a surprise even to persons who are otherwise generally well-informed when they are told that Christ's Hospital educates both sexes.

And the fault lies not with the Governors, past and present, most certainly not with the girls of recent school-generations who – for example, by the measure of university successes – have acquitted themselves no less admirably than their brother-Blues, but rather with the disdain for the education of women which prevailed, in Britain as elsewhere, for the first three centuries and more of the Christ's Hospital's history, perhaps also – a consequence of that disdain – with the absence of a feminine equivalent to that continuity of literary tribute which has enshrined the Christ's Hospital Boys' School firm in the sentiments of a vast congregation of readers, and it could be also because, in this unlike the boys, the girls of Christ's Hospital have for more than a century had no unique uniform to make them immediately identifiable and to set them apart from the girls of other more conventional girls' schools.

As has been seen the two schools are coeval. We are, in a very real sense, but one Foundation, sharing one Council, identical traditions, identical conditions for admission, and imbued with the same spirit of affection and loyalty to the Foundation. For more than 360 years, first in London and then at Hertford, all of Christ's Hospital's girls were reared on the same site as all or some of Christ's Hospital's boys and it is only in this century that the girls have had exclusive possession of Hertford.

The first girls admitted to Christ's Hospital were housed above the Library which Richard Whittington had built for the Grey Friars. Their formal education was minimal but soon – remarkably soon – enlightened benefactors were giving money expressly for the purpose of teaching the girls to read, and soon too they were given over to the care of an usher who was to teach them also to write, in the Writing School – when it was not being used by boys.

However, already in the sixteenth century, our first historian, John Howes, set down aggressively masculine opinions of the futility of school-learning for women such as were repeated a hundred years later by John Evelyn – Pepys's fellow-diarist and fellow-Governor – when he wrote in a passage that contains one word that is, for us in our generation, an unfortunate *double-entendre* "the girls [of the Hospital] are instructed in all such works as becomes their sex and may fit them for good wives, mistresses, and to be a blessing to their generation".

This, if in less lofty terms, was a view shared by most of those responsible for educating girls and among them the Governors of Christ's Hospital and so it was that, for those first three centuries Christ's Hospital girls spent a little time on learning to read and write, rather more on the Catechism but most of their school hours mending and sewing. Though it is notable that the girls were never condemned to master spinning – then considered to be the lowliest of feminine crafts – the Governors saw to it that their education must serve the domestic economy of the Foundation. As late as 1784 the Upper Mistress was told to ensure that her girls were capable of knitting all the yellow stockings needed by the boys. Her charge continued:

> You shall teach the girls to work so that they may be able to make up all the linen worn or used by the Hospital in Town or Country, and with the Undermistress you shall take care that the same needlework be continued to be done under the usual instruction.

The great migration into Hertfordshire after the Fire

followed a route already trodden, before they moved to the school in London, by many of the Hospital's children, both boys and girls. From its earliest days the Foundation had taken in infants too young to receive instruction, too young even to fend for themselves. These it had "put to nurse" in families living in the country close to London, most of them in Essex or Hertfordshire. No qualifications were required of these foster-parents, save that they be of good reputation, and for their services they were paid anything from 8d. to 1s. a week for each child – with a bonus for every child who had small-pox.

After the Fire some sixty girls were boarded in a house at Hoddesdon and their mistress was magnificently rewarded with £1.08d. a child. The actual site of the Hoddesdon house cannot be identified but in 1687 a gallery was erected in Broxbourne Church (then in the parish of Hoddesdon) "for the use and benefit of the Bluecoat children belonging to Christ's Hospital then harboured in the parish".

Much more is known about the boarding-school at Ware which was acquired at about the same time and which housed 200 of the smaller boys until, in 1760, they were removed to Hertford. Some of the buildings stand still in Bluecoat Yard where a memorial plaque has been placed by one of our Governors but it is no longer possible to imagine the site as it once was, "a fine building like a college, making a large quadrangle and containing a school house and a Master's house and twenty houses for nurses to keep children".

As a nursling-academy for the Hospital Hertford had probably preceded both Hoddesdon and Ware for already by 1653, although he did not live or teach on Hospital premises, the Governors were describing one Aaron Peters, the proprietor of a local day-school, as its Headmaster in Hertford, and were paying him 2d. a head for each child he taught.

The second Headmaster, appointed in 1674, Samuel Goodman, was a prominent Quaker. Two years after his appointment, when he was prosecuted for teaching without a licence, he entered as part of his defence the good work that he and his wife were engaged upon in instructing the "Blewe Coat" children in reading, writing and arithmetic. The plea served him little with the magistrates for he was fined, but the Governors stood by him and he held his office as Headmaster until 1682.

During the régimes of these two headmasters the children continued to live with nurses and perversely it was one of the magistrates who had condemned Goodman who opened the way to the purchase of the first Hertford site.

Sir Henry Chauncy of Yardley Bury was a barrister of some distinction and a notable antiquarian but he was also notably unfriendly to the Society of Friends. His interest in the Hospital was alert and on 14th June 1680 he wrote to the Clerk:

When I returned from London I was informed that some of the Governors of the Hospital had been at our town and were inquisitive after a purchase of half an acre of ground to build an house and a school for their children and their master for his habitation, and I, having a great respect for so good and charitable a work, have enquired out a very convenient purchase for you in an open airy place at that end of the town next to London, where you may have that quantity of group with a dwelling house built of timber upon the same for about 15 or 16 years purchase, which is the usual rate of selling houses in our town, and the price I presume will come to about £120. Sir, if this may be a convenient purchase for the Hospital, I pray be pleased to make it known to the Governors, and I will wait on you at your house on Friday, between two and three of the clock in the afternoon, to know their answer, for the owner of the house has promised me that the Governors shall have the refusal of it at the price another will give for it. Sir, I know of another purchase in our town, but I conceive it not so convenient for your use as this will be.

On the 24th June Chauncy writes again, this time from Middle Temple:

I received an account from one of your servants that, if the house I proposed to you was not sold, you and two of the Governors would go to Hertford on Monday next and see the same; but I doubt whether your appearing there may not rise the price. Wherefore I think if you should employ some person to treat with Mr. Seward, who is the owner of the house, and to beat down the price as low as may be, and then for you to go down and conclude, will be the better way, or if you think it convenient that I should write to Mr. Seward to send me a particular of the house and land, and the rent at which it is now let, and what his lowest price is, and upon the return of that you may please to go thither and see it.

There followed, on the 26th, another letter enclosing the "particular" written by Seward. Chauncy writes:

As for the house and orchard, it may be very convenient for you, and this he has sold to Smart for 15 years purchase, and as I conjecture by his particular he asks 16. But as for the mead, his copyhold, and common at Lammas are not convenient for you in regard you may have no use for it; but if you shall purchase both house and mead together I suppose you may have it the cheaper, and I know two at Hertford will gladly take the mead off your hands, and I presume it will make near twenty years purchase. Sir, I conceive it will not be convenient for you to take a journey thither till you shall receive an answer both from Seward and Smart, for that there has been some contract between them about the house. I am informed that

Seward is in a great fright for his money for that he has made a purchase elsewhere, and part of the purchase money he paid on midsummer day and the other part he is obliged to pay very speedily, which is the reason he would not discharge Smart till he was sure of another purchaser.

Chauncy soon became himself a Governor but already, in this correspondence he had shown that general amity for the Foundation which has persisted throughout its history and that readiness to serve the Hospital which still animates its Governors. ("If I may be serviceable to you herein, I have my aim, for what I offer is merely out of kindness to your House".)

The site suggested by Chauncy was bought by the Governors, and was thus seminal to the history of the Hospital – much more so than would have been the purchase of the suggested "half acre" – but the plan drawn in 1682 is additionally interesting for it bears the first-known example of the Hospital's arms, blazoned precisely as we have them to-day – though we cannot trace any grant from the College of Heralds:

Argent a cross gules; in the first quarter a sword of St. Paul proper; on a chief azure, between two fluer-de-lys or; a Tudor rose argent.

The land secured by the Hospital through Chauncy's intervention – together with a small field acquired almost immediately thereafter – covered an area which is almost coincidental with all that to-day a casual observer can see when looking through the front gates at Hertford but for ten years after the purchase the Hospital continued to use the buildings that it had bought with the land. Children were still boarded-out but as the Master now lived in a Hospital building on the site, it was to his house that they came for their lessons. Then in the headmastership of Robert Devall (himself an Old Blue) which lasted for 19 years from 1685, the brave plan was launched which was to create, for the first time, what would now be called a purpose-built school.

Most of the existing buildings were pulled down and in their place the Governors raised a school-house, cottages to house 320 children and two houses for masters. And, if that curious observer who looks through the gates of twentieth century Christ's Hospital, Hertford could somehow transport himself back to the last years of the seventeenth century or the first of the eighteenth, he would discover a general conformation of the school not so very different from that which he sees with his twentieth century eyes. True, the buildings were not red-brick but faced with white plaster but the rectangular lay-out was already as it is to-day. To each side of a playground there were ten cottages behind a row of lime-trees. At the north end of the rectangle stood the Writing School – large enough to hold all the children when at their lessons – and two houses for masters. At the south end, the

pillars of the entrance-gates onto Fore Street, were pedestals for figures of Bluecoat boys.

As ever, when embarking upon a daring new venture the Governors appealed to royalty, to the City and to private benefactors and, as ever, the summons was answered with great generosity. Princess Anne headed the subscription-list having been encouraged so to do by her close friend, a Governor and close friend to the Hospital, the Bishop of London, Henry Compton. (Himself an ex-naval officer, Compton had particular affection for the Royal Mathematical School. Educational schemes, both in England and in America, found him always encouraging. It was he who, in 1680, composed the Hospital's Special Graces and Prayers – in use to this day.) The City, City Companies, the citizens of Hertford, many Governors and, for the first-time on record, several Old Blues, added their contributions but even so (as once more has happened not infrequently in the Hospital's history) the cost of an ambitious building-programme outstripped both the original estimates and the proceeds of the public appeal and for six years, from 1698-1704, the Hertford site was rented to tenants.

It was at that time a Hospital regulation that no boy could be transferred to London until he could read easily and it is, perhaps, a significant comment on changing educational standards that, when Devall was ordered to send to London the hundreds of boys in his charge that he reported on 10 "dyslexic" children and "not above six which are not yet entered into the Bible".

It is from the years immediately after the re-occupation of the Hertford premises that we have the first unequivocal record of girls in the school-buildings that were to become eventually their unique preserve. Hitherto, apart from the short-lived Hoddesdon experiment, they had occupied their one Ward in London, their one table in the London Dining Hall (when they were not crowded-out by the boys) and, when the boys' time-table allowed, the Writing School, but in 1707 one cottage on the east side of the playground was reserved for the exclusive use of "maiden children". There girls, like their male contemporaries, were largely in the care of unqualified nurses but now a Schoolmistress was appointed to teach them – and, of course, to supervise their sempstress duties – and in 1742, when the girls already occupied four cottages, at Hertford if not yet in London, Christ's Hospital became for girls, as it had been for boys from its Foundation, truly a school even by modern definition, for then it was, for the first time, a Schoolmistress was appointed who had previous experience of the class-room.

Even so, though the Governors never ceased to proclaim, and generally to demonstrate, concern for the girls in their care, the interests of female Blues were always subordinate to those of their privileged male contemporaries. (The one dubious privilege which they shared without hindrance was subjection to severe discipline, including not infrequent beatings.)

When the Ware School was closed finally in the mid-eighteenth century, place had to be found at Hertford for some 200 small boys. Then, as many times before and since, the Governors were tempted to abandon altogether what seemed to them the thankless task of educating girls for these "maiden children" would never bring credit to the Hospital by their academic, nautical, literary or business progress, would never become benefactors of the Hospital and never join the ever-increasing number of Old Blues who sat around the Court Room governing the Foundation. But the temptation had to be resisted, largely because several substantial legacies (and notably the Gift of John and Frances West bequeathed to the Hospital in 1720) stipulated that they must be dedicated to the education of both boys and girls. So instead, all the girls were shipped from Hertford to London.

Change-of-heart followed quickly. In 1778 the girls – and this time all of them – were moved back to Hertford, to new buildings built specially for them.

It could well be that the date of this move, which later generations of Christ's Hospital girls view with pride, may nevertheless explain in part the lack of knowledge about the Girls' School which is, in notable contrast to awareness of the Boys' School, general in the public at large. Two of the three most articulate and best-known laureates of the Christ's Hospital tradition, Coleridge and Lamb, entered the school four years later, the third, Leigh Hunt, not until 1791. Of the three only Coleridge was ever a schoolboy at Hertford, and he for only a few weeks. In all their many references to the Hospital in essays, letters and poems not one of the three so much as gives a casual mention to a Christ's Hospital girl.

But even had Clio been less mischievous; even if she had not played this sharp trick of chronology; it is unlikely that the writers of the Golden Generation – or their successors for more than a hundred years – would have paid much attention to the girls. Even after comparatively commodious accommodation had been provided for the girls – a two-storeyed building, containing two 'flats' for staff, a Ward and a schoolhouse built on a site adjoining the Boys' School, and soon after an additional Ward – the two sexes were separated, as much by strict regulation as by high walls and locked gates. The only glimpse ever caught by girl of boy or boy of girl came each afternoon when they joined together for "Duty" (prayers) in the Dining Hall that had replaced one of the staff-houses to the west of the Writing School, and on Sunday when both sexes attended Morning Service in the Parish Church, and it seems likely that the reasons for this strict segregation were more subtle than concern for morality. Many of the girls were adolescents but none of the boys more than 10 years old and with such disparity in their ages not even the most prurient Victorian could have feared for the virtue of the girls

(or the boys). In truth, certainly until the middle of the nineteenth century, the Governors remained ambivalent about the Girls' School. Inherited obligations persuaded them to retain it, and flickerings of conscience and charity brought from them an occasional outburst of spending but not until the last half of the nineteenth century could they, or for that matter parents of girls who might be entered into Christ's Hospital, regard the education of girls as in any real sense a powerful call upon the Foundation. The Boys' School had its distinguished alumni, its vast constituency of well-educated and generally prosperous Old Blues, and though the Governors had never abandoned the intentions of the Founders, already by the beginning of the eighteenth century (and increasingly as that century progressed) a place in the Boys' School for its children was much coveted by highly-educated if indigent parents. (Coleridge, for example, was the son of a scholarly country parson, the headmaster of a grammar-school, Leigh Hunt of a Tory Philadelphia lawyer turned popular preacher.) The Girls' School was still in reality an orphanage.

So it was that, in the early years of the nineteenth century the number of girls declined. At one time, when there were upwards of 1,000 boys at Hertford and London, there were but 18 girls – the precise number decreed by West's Gift.

The ambiguity in the Governors' attitude is nevertheless evidenced by one proud gesture. When the new buildings were finished, as complement to the figures of Bluecoat boys on the gates, the Hospital placed statuettes of two girls in their lovely seventeenth century costume in niches overlooking Fore Street.

Perversely, one of the first reforms adopted by the Governors in their latter-day effort to revise the Girls' School, to give it some genuine equivalence with the Boys' School and some real possibility of participating in the crusade for female education, was the abolition of this ancient uniform. Since 1874 the girls of Christ's Hospital have been dressed sensibly, which is to say, much as the girls of any other school, and therefore generally in a fashion which, though some decades behind the times, is not sufficiently antique to be distinctive. And paradoxically this well-intentioned reform has in time created one of the few persisting disparities between the Hospital's two schools, has fostered among the girls one of the last genuine causes for the belief that they are, in the Christ's Hospital community, second-class citizens, and among the boys the remnant of conviction that, in that same community, they are superior beings.

It was, it must be admitted, as much outside pressure, from the Press, Parliament and the women's suffrage movement, as any awakening of conscience that brought about the true beginnings of Christ's Hospital as one of Britain's greatest schools for girls. Already in the middle years of the nineteenth century the Governors had on occasion paid for a particularly

Right: Richard Whittington's Library at Grey Friars from a print c. 1763

Below: The School at Hertford as it was c. 1900

'Part of Chrifts Hofpital taken from the Stewards Office 1763.'

Above right: 'Girls in niches overlooking Fore Street' 1983

Right: 'The Playground', 1983

Right: The Assembly Hall at Hertford, 1983.

Below right: Playing fields and Chapel, Hertford 1983.

Left: 'Susannah Holmes' — a painting by A. J. Oliver R. A.

Below: 'The Presentation of the Charter' — a photograph c. 1901.

promising girl to finish her schooling at some other institution but, until the furore over women's education became strident, most girls left for humble employment before they were sixteen. Then, however, with such as Lord Lyttleton castigating the Hospital in the Lords for its undeniably preferential treatment of boys and with *The Times* (ever-interested in the Hospital since an Old Blue, editor Thomas Barnes, first added thunder to its voice) enquiring pointedly of the Governors of Christ's Hospital why it was that they excluded girls from its benefits, action was inevitable.

In 1875 the Hospital advertised for a Principal Mistress who most have "a thorough acquaintance with all subjects embraced in an ordinary English education, together with French, Drawing and Instrumental Music".

Three years later, for the very first time, the existence of the Girls' School won recognition from a source more resolutely masculine and much loftier than *The Times* or the House of Lords. *The Blue*, the school magazine published in Newgate Street, commented (still somewhat condescendingly) that the Girls' School had "been increased to seventy little maidens", and that the Governors were looking soon to add another 130.

That same number of *The Blue* remarked on another change in the Hospital's affairs of no less portentous significance. Hitherto the Queen herself had been the only female Governor; now eight ladies were added to the Governing Body.

At about the same time the school year for both boys and girls was divided into the three terms conventional to other schools, with a four-week vacation at Christmas and Easter, and seven weeks in the Summer (a system that persisted at all the Hospital's establishments until, in 1964, Hertford opted for the awkward four-term year). This relief from school, which must have been much-welcomed by the boys and girls, was also virtually the first time in the Hospital's history that the authorities conceded explicitly that the children in its care were entitled to family-life. In the previous three centuries all that had been allowed to them was an occasional leave-day, brief and irregular holidays at home. Some boys (and presumably some girls) had been re-united with their parents only two or three times in six or seven years.

To give credence to their more generous intentions the Governors built a new class-room block, but still the highest academic possibility open to the girls who occupied it was the College of Preceptors Examination. In 1889 some girls were entered for the Cambridge Local and in 1898 *The Blue*, this time almost unabashed in its brotherly pride, announced that "The Girls' School at Christ's Hospital, Hertford, has passed a greater number of girls in honours than any other girls' school that entered for the Junior Cambridge Local last December".

Even so, the bias of teaching at the Girls' School was still predominantly non-academic – indeed it was not until 1919 that the girls were relieved of their last domestic responsibility for the boys. Only then were they freed from the duty to turn the heels of the yellow stockings worn at Horsham.

The revision of "The Scheme" in 1891 (of which more later) greatly affected the whole Foundation. Immediately, for the girls, it spelt an enlargement of the curriculum to include History, Geography, Mathematics, some Natural Science and a choice between French and German. Girls could now study at school until they were seventeen; some to the advanced age of nineteen.

By that time the great debate about the move from Newgate Street to the country was already intense and also the number of small boys at Hertford was much reduced. The conjunction of these two circumstances led to another debate: either Hertford would be closed and the girls, like the boys, moved to the new site, or else Hertford would be preserved and given over entirely to girls. (The heretical suggestion that Christ's Hospital abandon altogether the education of girls was once more and happily dismissed.)

The verdict having gone to an all-female school at Hertford, the first concession was the ceding to the girls of some part of the now ancient site and when, in 1902, Horsham was ready for the boys, Hertford became the Christ's Hospital Girls' School.

It was by then tacitly accepted by the Governors (now, under the new Scheme represented for administrative purposes by the Council of Almoners) that, so far as was practicable, the Girls' School must be treated in all things as equal to the Boys' School and so, to rhyme with the grandiose building-programme at Horsham, Hertford was rebuilt.

The two ranges of Wards on each side of the central space were demolished and eight new separate blocks took their place. Two over-large class-rooms were converted into one Assembly Hall worthy to be called a Hall; a Chapel and new class-room blocks were erected, as well as a swimming bath, gymnasium, and sanatorium. The new buildings were formally opening by H.R.H. George, Prince of Wales, in 1906, and instead of the stereotyped proceedings on such an occasion, when everyone knows beforehand exactly what is going to be said and done, there was an unexpected thrill.

The arrival at school of the Prince and Princess of Wales, [says the *City Press*] in a carriage and pair lent by the Marquess of Salisbury, was marked by a somewhat exciting incident, as, on entering a short avenue lined by trees and leading to a red-carpeted dais, on which the Lord Mayor and Sheriffs were standing ready to receive the royal visitors, the horses attached to the carriage took fright. Finally one of them collided with the trunk of a tree, and the excited animals were brought to a standstill by some sturdy constables. The Lord Mayor [an Old Blue] and Sheriffs left the dais and went to the assistance of the Prince and Princess, who alighted without displaying any sign of alarm.

There have been in this century many additions to the Hertford site. A handsome octagonal Library, an Art School, a new Science Block and Squash Court. The Dining Hall is one of the two-hundred-year-old buildings, though altered beyond recognition. It is decorated with a frieze from the Newgate Street Hall consisting of the armorial bearings of Presidents and Treasurers, intersected by busts of King Edward VI. There is a large picture by Frederick Goodall, R.A., entitled "By the Sea of Galilee", as well as a full-length portrait of Susannah Holmes, a more charming picture of whom hangs in the School Hall.

Susannah was a girl in the school in the eighteen-twenties, selected for portrayal by A. J. Oliver, R.A., on account of her beautiful eyebrows. In later life she fell on evil days and, it is rumoured, into an evil profession. She visited the Counting House, and with little persuasion induced the Treasurer to buy the two portraits and to get her elected to a small annual pension.

There is hint of paradox in the statement that once our girls were rid of the overweening presence of our small boys and allowed to occupy unhindered the enlarged Hertford site so also did they enter more and more into their proper inheritance as part of an indivisible Christ's Hospital community, but the paradox is certainly less obvious to those who are of the community than it may be to even the most perspicacious onlooker.

Many interwoven influences contributed to the developing integration of spirit. As the excellence of the Girls' School advanced, as for example, the number of girls gaining academic honours in the universities increased phenomenally and the career achievements of Old Girls began to match the successes not only of any other schools for girls but also came to be at least decently comparable to the age-old magnificence of the Boys' School, so also did the girls – and the Old Girls – shake off most of that sense of inferiority which for centuries had been forced upon them by the reality of circumstance.

The Council was no longer in any way hesitant about its Girls' School. Buildings, money, prizes, grants from the Exhibitioners Fund and the Advancement-in-Life Fund went readily to girls

Of equal significance in a Foundation which holds its products within the community for the whole of their lives, some Old Blue organisations have come at least to accept Old Girls into membership. Already in the years between the Wars, when the Club-rooms at Great Tower Street were much-used, the ladies of the Hospital were admitted but Old Girls were not accorded full membership of the Christ's Hospital Club until 1981.

In 1977, for the first time, Old Girls (and the Head Girl) joined in the annual Founder's Day Dinner.

The Old Blues Dramatic Society, on the other hand, embraced Old Girls (literally and figuratively) from its beginnings and in its hey-day (also in the 'twenties and 'thirties) did as much to enhance the sense of a unified community as it did for the theatre arts, and more than any of the larger societies. It was this Society which was, above all others, responsible for a surprisingly large proportion of the surprisingly large number of marriages of Old Blues and C.H. Old Girls.

The senior and most exclusive of Christ's Hospital organisations, the Amicable Society of Blues, remains obstinately sexist as it was at its foundation in 1629 but on this tender subject – and beyond boasting that three times in more than 350 years the Amicables have relented by holding a Ladies' Night – this book must remain discreet for both authors and publisher have served in their turn as President of the Amicables.

But the most palpable contribution to the identification of Christ's Hospital's girls with the totality of the Foundation was the inclusion of girls in all of the major ceremonies of the Hospital and the transposition to Hertford of most of the traditional exercises which had long been practised at Newgate Street and which had been transferred without amendment to Horsham.

In the handsome painting (hanging in the Library at Horsham) which celebrates the Foundation, both girls and boys kneel in gratitude to the Founder King. Since that time, however, and until the beginning of this century, girls had generally been excluded from state occasions. Both girls and boys were present at the formal opening of Horsham and at the royal inauguration of the new Hertford buildings. When, in 1911, George V became king (and for the very first time) girls assisted in the presentation of the Loyal Address. Girls joined the boys in the St. Matthew's Day visit to London and actually marched with them through the City.

Still, as late as 1983, there are many Old C.H. Girls who have never seen Horsham and many Old Blues who know not Hertford, but throughout this century First Parting Grecians have attended Hertford's Speech Days and Monitresses the Speech Day at Horsham, and at Hertford the Head Girl delivers, without benefit of script, an English Oration just as has the Senior Grecian for more than 300 years.

Symbol to this ever-increasing integration: on several great occasions – the Quatercentennial Service in St. Paul's Cathedral, the Services in Westminster Abbey – to celebrate the presentation of a memorial to Edward VI and to honour the third centenary of the Royal Mathematical School – girls played a part equal to that played by the boys. And, most vigorous of all demonstrations of advanced unity, when in 1980, again in St. Paul's Cathedral, the Hospital led the nation in honouring the life and work of that great and devoted Blue, its much-loved Treasurer, Barnes Wallis, the orchestras and choirs of the two schools were merged for the occasion.

Perhaps the most substantial influences upon the emotional integration of the two schools have been also the most subtle. When, for example, that first Principal of Hertford was called upon to make public the school's motto the answer that she gave "Perseverance" was a meek acceptance of second-class status. Now the girls use, as firmly as have the boys for centuries, the proud sonority "Fear God, Honour the King, Love the Brotherhood". With minor, necessary, and sometimes embarrassing consequence, the school song sung by the girls is that sung by the boys (though Hertford calls it the *Carmen* and Horsham the *Votum)*. So also, if again for the time being with minor amendment, is the school hymn. Monitresses say Bishop Compton's graces before and after meals in the Hertford Hall just as do Grecians at Horsham. Blues and Old Blues of both sexes join in the same toast to the Foundation:

The Religious, Royal and Ancient Foundation of Christ's Hospital, may those prosper who love it, and may God increase their number.

And, though by some etymological quirk the affectionate nickname for the school is at Hertford reserved for references to Horsham, when that Toast is drunk in mixed company feminine voices are raised as fervently as male in its inevitable amen, the unanimous shout "Housie".

Middleton Murry wrote in his autobiography that when he entered Christ's Hospital he was "endowed with ancestors". That rich inheritance is now the property entire as much of the girls as of the boys and if inevitably, until this century, most of the ancestry in the female line is anonymous, Christ's Hospital's girls have come to accept as theirs by right the totality and the richness of the heritage. The long list of Christ's Hospital's heroes belongs as much to them as to their brothers.

There have been in recent years changes at Hertford which are, as it were, independent of the spirit of the Foundation but, save in the opinion of a few sturdy conservatives, in no way antipathetic to it.

In 1963 Hertford followed the example set by Horsham in 1902 and substituted for the age-old word "Ward" the term "House" as used in most schools, but held to numbering Houses – in this unlike Horsham which gave to its houses the names of distinguished Old Blues.

Girls are now permitted more social freedom than was formerly the case and are even allowed to wear on occasion their own clothes.

Academically, in sporting and other extra-curricular activities, and most obviously in drama and music, Christ's Hospital Girls' School has become at least the equal and in many fields the superior to any other school for girls in the country.

All these advances but above all in the overt and subtle re-unification of a common identity the endeavours of this century have heralded a conclusion that most of those who were responsible for them never foresaw: the physical, practical and entire re-unification of Christ's Hospital. The events and circumstances which led to the decision to amalgamate the two schools on the Horsham site – and the plans for that amalgamation – will be rehearsed later in this book. For this moment all that needs to be said is that there is in truth only one Christ's Hospital, established and continued with but one charitable purpose, enriched by commonly-held traditions and imbued with a spirit that is shared by all its children, by the young in its immediate care and by all those of us, men and women alike, who can never "forget the great benefits . . . received in this place".

CHAPTER THREE

London

The late George Allan served the Foundation for most of his life, as a member of the Counting House staff, as Steward at Horsham, and as Clerk of the Hospital. His school-days (1897-1902) coincided with the last years in Newgate Street and consequently the chapter that follows is both history and spirited reminiscence. Therefore, it is appropriate that this section of the book is re-produced almost as Allan wrote it, with only a few minor editorial amendments.

The besetting sin of Old Blues is an inordinate affection for relating reminiscences of their school-days. In early manhood such stories tend to the Rabelaisiean, in middle life they become apocryphal, while age at times transcends the inventive faculties of a Munchausen. The boredom of our juniors is politely, though often imperfectly, concealed; and, having learned my lesson, I am constantly fighting against the temptation to begin sentences with "When I was in the school". May I be forgiven if in writing some account of the London school, especially as it was in my time, I sometimes show an inclination to stress the personal aspect of school life. My experiences are those of hundreds, nay thousands, of others.

And first, to be utterly egoistic, a word about ourselves. We do not call the school the Blue Coat School, nor the boys Bluecoat boys. These are expressions used by outsiders to the community who are apt to forget that there is only one Christ's Hospital but that there were at one time many Bluecoat schools, most of them established in the seventeenth century as provincial imitations of the City of London's Foundation (and that some survive to this day). For us the school is C.H. *tout court* or, in a usage that has become customary in the last sixty or so years, Housie (as a noun spelt by convention in this way to differentiate it from the much older and exclusively adjectival form Housey). So a boy in the school is a C.H. boy or a Housey boy, his dress Housey uniform and the cheer raised on the touch-line, like the response to the Housey Toast, "Housie".

Now let me try to take you on a spirit walk round the London buildings. It is possible from plans of various dates to trace the development from a colony of tenements, small houses and shops, yards, and public walks, to a great coherent whole covering an area of five acres, bounded by Newgate Street, Giltspur Street, St. Bartholomew's Hospital, and King Edward Street. Nothing now remains – we may not even claim the preserved bastion of the Roman wall – save a commemorative tablet on the front of the Post Office building.

One part of the old Grey Friars monastery was incorporated by Wren in his rebuilding of the south façade, and remained to the end. This was the cloister know as The Giffs, rather below ground level, a place of monastic calm – during school hours; at other times it was a favourite hockey pitch, though games were frequently interrupted for a "mull", our primitive method of settling differences, which elsewhere might be seen by the vigilant eye of authority. The entrance, in Christ Church Passage, with its figure of the Founder, was removed brick by brick and re-erected at Horsham, complete with inscription:

Edward the Sixth, of famous memory, was the Founder of Christ's Hospital: and Sir Robert Clayton, Knt. and Alderman, sometime Lord Mayor of this City of London, erected this statue of King Edward, and built most part of this Fabric, Annon Dom. 1682.

When, a few years ago, several coats of plaster were chipped off the statue an undercoat of gilding was discovered. The King was returned to his original glory (and is now behind Big School at Horsham).

On another building a statue of Sir John Moore (not the hero of Corunna) by Grinling Gibbons carried a tablet recording that in 1694 "this Writing School and stately building was begun and completely finished at the sole cost" of this former Lord Mayor, who was President at that time and had "been otherwise a liberal benefactor".

One relic of an even older and pre-C.H. past survived until the beginning of the nineteenth century, the Whittington Library, founded in 1429 by Richard Whittington "and furnished with books at the expense of £556.10s., of which £400 were given by the Founder and the remainder by Dr. Thomas Winchelsey, a Brother of the House".

In 1795 (as we have seen) the Governors embarked on a comprehensive rebuilding scheme which was not completed for thirty years. The most important work of that period consisted of new ranges of Wards, Grammar School, Mathematical School, and Dining Hall. This last, the work of John Shaw, was the familiar building seen from Newgate Street through those railing which seemed to have a peculiar fascination for the passer-by. I have a very spirited sketch of the laying of the Foundation Stone by the Duke of York in 1825, drawn by Pugin when a C.H. boy. His natural talent is as evident as his sense of humour, which leads him to depict figures crowding the house tops, even flag-staffs, in a way that would never be sanctioned to-day. The Hall was reputed to be the largest in London, except Westminster Hall, with a roof unsupported by pillars. On the staircase hung a very Victorian painted glass window, which was illuminated from the outside on Public Supper nights, and looked – to us – very pleasing. We used the Hall for meals, of course, for a Sunday evening service, and once a year for an examination in drawing attended by the whole school. For Speech Days and concerts a huge stage was put up at one end for the Choir and some of the boys, while the rest sat on a temporary platform at the sides. The handsome oak panelling (decorated with the frieze later moved to Hertford) added greatly to the dignity of the Hall without relieving its gloom. Stained glass windows contained the arms of benefactors; Verrio's enormous painting – "this monumental picture" – took up almost the whole of one side; the so-called Holbein Charter picture hung over the western gallery; and the organ at the east end was flanked by *Moses receiving the Tablets of the Law* by W. Brockeden and *St. John in the Isle of Patmos* by Sir Robert Ker Porter. All the pictures were so begrimed with smoke and dust that little could be seen of the subjects. The "Holbein" was always invisible.

The Grecians' Cloister, the central arch of which was moved to Horsham and re-erected in separate halves, dated from 1836, yet sixty years later it was still "the New Cloi". Its claim to fame is that it formed the background to most of the annual photographic groups of Grecians, but it provided also a pleasing foreground for a view of Christ Church spire and the dome of St. Paul's.

The dormitories were large and airy, but although we had no day-rooms, studies, or any other place to keep our belongings or spend our time, they were places from which we were sternly banished all day long. During the longer periods of leisure we played "Housey rugger" in the Hall playground, all the players – several hundreds of them – using the same pitch, the same goals, the same touch-lines, but playing sixteen separate games. The game was like rugger, except that instead of a scrum the ball was knocked forward with the fist. Ward matches, however, in which there was the keenest rivalry, were the genuine Rugby Football, scrums and all, but played on asphalt and in plimsolls. Concussions and broken limbs were not unknown. When there was not time for a more or less organized game we knocked about or "spadged" (a word probably derived from the German *spazieren,* meaning "to walk aimlessly backwards and forwards over a straight course, two or three or more abreast, arm in arm"); and this was our principal spare-time occupation on Sundays, for even on that day of days we were not allowed in the Wards.

The Warden had supreme control of out-of-school discipline. He was not a Master, but a retired military man. He it was who granted rare leave to pass the gates, and who, by means of patrolling Beadles, kept us from fighting, from going out in the rain – on wet days our spadging was confined to the Cloisters – from playing with hard balls, from kicking footballs in the Cloisters, from doing any of those mischievous things which normal boys might be expected to do. Punishment for such grave misdemeanours was extra drill before breakfast. Drill was a punishment which could also be meted out by monitors, though the lesser disciplinary offences were met by ten or twenty minutes' "standing on" our settles – iron boxes kept at the foot of the bed to hold all our gear. For such a purpose we *were* allowed to enter the dormitory.

Canings in my time had risen from matters of routine to stately ceremonial functions, in which one of the two principal roles was taken, not by a Master, but by a Beadle. My clearest recollection of one where I participated – I speak feelingly – is of the Head Master, watch in hand, calling out at intervals all too short: "Go on . . . Go on", until the tale [*sic*] was finished. There were occasional "brushings" (birchings), reserved for offences so heinous that they were usually followed by expulsion.

Masters were doubtless much the same as masters always are. I do not propose to deal with them as individuals nor to weigh up their merits and demerits. Nor do I attempt any estimate of the relative greatness of our Head Masters. Not all my contemporaries think as I do of my own Head Master, but none of them can have forgotten the haunting jingle of the notice that used to hang on his study door:

Call upon a man of business
In the hours of business
Only on business
Transact that business
And go about your business
To give the man of business
Time to go about his business

The C.H. uniform is, to-day as it has been for centuries, a curiosity to many, but to those who wear it or have worn it in their youth a symbol of continuity, and to the Christ's Hospital ethos a powerful influence in assuring that entire classlessness which is of supreme sociological significance in a community which (as one Head Master put it) takes in ''the burglar's son and the Bishop's grandson'', and gives to them both, as their prime social conceit, only the glory of being Blues.

In historical terms there can be little doubt that it is a modified survival of the ordinary dress of the Tudor period. Our predecessors before 1865 wore a long yellow petticoat under their blue coat, and it has been supposed that the yellow linings of the coats, as still worn, are rudimentary petticoats. This is not the case. In 1638 it was solemnly decreed that the linings of the coats should be dyed yellow ''to avoid vermin, by reason the white cottens is held to breed the same''.

In spite of rumours which crop up occasionally, I find no record of any recent discussion by the Governors as to changing the dress. It is evidently a fixed idea that to alter the dress would be to alter the School, and I for one am extremely glad that no attention was paid even to John Howes, who, in his zeal for reformation of the House, told his imaginary interlocutor that he

> would have all the boys that are above eight years of age to have doublets, breeches, and short coats made according to the fashion of the time, the better to set forth the children: for as the Lord hath made them perfect in their creation, so let there be no imperfections in their outward actions that may any way hinder their preferment, for apparel shapeth and manners maketh, and the eye must be pleased, always observing and keeping your colours of watchet and blue.

Even the iconoclastic Commissioners of 1837 shrank from what the old Duke of Cambridge would have described as ''a needless outrage on traditional sentiment'', and sheltered themselves by reporting with reference to

> the ancient pecularities of the school [that] in particular, we are in favour of leaving it to the Governing Body to consider whether any change should be made in the ancient dress now worn by the scholars, or any relaxation of the rules regarding it. Several critics, *ab extra,* are more or less against it; but Dr. Haig Brown appears to be the only person connected with the school who would do away with it. Mr. Trollope, Mr. Wilson, and Charles Lamb, speak of the abolition with horror, and as a kind of sacrilege.

There are many explanations of why the boys wear no head-gear, but caps did not disappear from the costume until 1857. They must have been too small to be comfortable, and being in general rather a nuisance than a protection they were probably stowed away for convenience in the capacious pocket of the coat. To correct a popular fallacy I assert here that *some* Old Blues *do* go bald.

The girdle of red or plum-coloured leather is stamped with stars and roses, with the head of the Founder, and with a full-length figure of a C.H. boy. For some obscure reason the silver buckle of the broad girdle has to be purchased at the expense of the wearer. Hardship in this instance is more apparent than real, for the wearing of a broad girdle is a privilege accorded to boys on reaching what is called the Upper School. The length of the girdle requires fine adjustment: if too tight it marks the new boy; if too loose to cover the join between the body and skirt of the coat it looks slovenly. The award of a ''Travers'' buckle, for proficiency in mathematics, ceased shortly before the exodus.

The Office of the foundation, known as the Counting House, was only visited by boys on admission and on discharge, when they had an opportunity of seeing the handsome and stately Court Room, furnished with Chippendale chairs and magnificent period tables and buffets, lined with pictures of benefactors, shrouded in mystic gloom and acoustically malevolent. In the past medical and educational examinations were held in the Court Room, and on leaving school a parent had to accompany each child to the Office to sign the Register ''discharging the House of him (or her) for ever''.

To the boys much more familiar was the Tuck Shop, presided over for fifty years by Johnnie. Time was when the Beadles kept the Shop; to them was granted a monopoly by making boys change their cash into ''Housey money'' – copper tokens specially struck for the purpose. The effect of this regulation was that whatever money a boy had could only be spent at the school shop, from which the Beadles sucked no small advantage. On the abolition of this somewhat undesirable practice a lease of a small room was given to Johnnie at a rent of £80 a year. Trade was always brisk, and profits must have been good. I know that a grocer's assistant in Ivy Lane offered at the time of the removal to run the shop at Horsham on the same lines and, for that privilege, to pay a rent of £200 a year. Johnnie, in spite of many rumours, was not an Old Blue, though Tommy (Andrews), his ofttimes assistant, was.

William Trollope, in his *History* (1834), draws a lurid picture of burials in the cloisters by torchlight, with a procession of boys singing a dirge as the coffin was borne to its last resting place. Such melancholy rites ceased when the Governors bought a plot in the City Cemetery at Ilford, whither were moved all the human remains disinterred at the demolition. In one of the Cloisters was a simple and touching mural tablet, still bricked up in the porch of Christ Church, saying only "Here lyes a Benefactor. Let no one move his bones". Strange to say, the body-snatchers who dug around the spot with intent to disregard his pious wish found no bones at all. On the subject of funerals, D'Arcy Thompson recalls that the Burial Anthem was always sung on Sunday nights. It seems curious that this should ever have been discontinued, for every night at bedtime we listened to a prayer, which began, "Lord, let the rest that we are going to mind us of the hour of death, and now that we are going to lie down let us consider that it may be we shall rise up no more". It could only have been the natural and healthy exuberance of boyhood that prevented us from becoming the morbid introverts that the worthy author of the prayer would have made us.

Indeed, many of the religious observances of the School in London must have been handed down from the heyday of Puritanism, but all our special prayers were written by Bishop Compton of London, and we used them before breakfast and before tea, kneeling upright on the bare boards of the Dining Hall while our food and drink got gradually colder and colder. Sunday morning services at Christ Church were no better. Again we knelt upright on bare boards, through all the prayers, and on alternate Sundays all through the Litany. Small wonder if such hardening of the body was not without its effect on the tenderness of the soul. The fortunate ones were the Grecians occupying huge armchairs in the galleries of the Church and using a wooden kneeler.

Food was, of its kind, good, even if not too plentiful. Like Cleopatra, it was apt to make hungry where it most satisfied, but there was about it no infinite variety. Bread, dripping, and coffee or cocoa, was breakfast daily; bread, butter (of sorts), and milk (of sorts) was tea or supper – the six o'clock last evening meal. Dinner was meat and potatoes only. Revolutionary changes were made in 1893, and a meat breakfast was served four days a week; pudding twice a week, on other days cheese; variety of dishes was introduced, such as haricot, stew, hash, steaks, mince; and the evening drink was strengthened into tea. When "fish and duff" was served the pudding came first; the plates were then scoured with bread – which was then thrown under the table – and the same plates were used for the fish. Boys had the option of a piece of bread and cheese or a mug of milk instead of cheese, served in the Wards at 8 p.m. It is hard to understand why so few boys availed themselves of this addition, but the fact remains that after the first rush of enthusiasm late suppers were never popular.

From the days when it first seemed good to authority to keep some kind of check on the boys' comings and goings in the City those who were allowed out wore a brass ticket tied to their coats. The use of these tickets ceased in 1721, yet nearly two centuries later masters were distributing imaginary "tickets" to boys wanting leave. Getting a ticket meant having his name put on a

Plan of Christ's Hospital, London c. 1901.

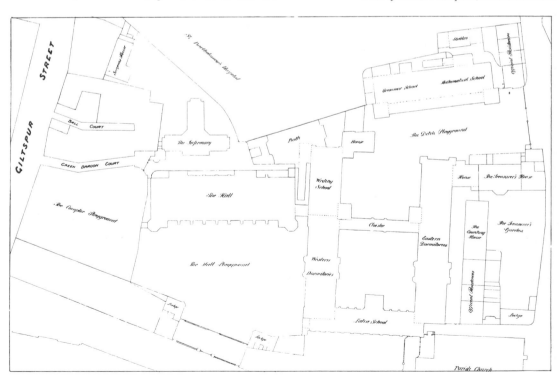

Above: An etching of the building, c. 1720.

Left: The Lodge, Christ Church Passage, c. 1900.

Below: The Founder's Statue, resplendent in gilt, at Horsham, 1982

The Great Hall — from a 19th century print.

The Hall as it was in 1901.

The Garden and the Grecians Cloister as it was in 1901.

The Central Arch in its new location at Horsham, 1982

*Left: Dormitories in London —
1823 and 1901.*

*Right: The Hall playground
c. 1901*

Above: The Band in the Hall playground c. 1901.

Below: The Travers Buckle.

Right: The Country House door, c. 1901.

The Court Room, c. 1901

The Giffs and Johnnies in the 19th century.

Above: The Arches under the Writing School, c. 1901.

Right: The Porter's Lodge, East Side, c. 1901.

Below: The same Christ's Hospital boy safe in his niche at Horsham

list to be sent to the Steward – later, the Warden, who took over many of the duties pertaining to the Steward. Masters ''gave tickets'' and boys ''got tickets'', but they were as fictitious as invisible exports. It was a strange anomaly that the master should issue tickets, though the Steward (and subsequently the Warden) was the out-of-school disciplinary authority. No ticket, however, was valid without the visa of the Steward. Hear the 1837 Commissioners for the reason!

Boys to whom the masters have given tickets present themselves to the Steward before they go out, that he may see wehther they are clean in their persons, etc., and may ascertain whether by their conduct in the Hospital they have forfeited their claim to such an indulgence.

One more high-light from the same source:

Another improvement in the building which has been suggested and appears entitled to the favourable consideration of the Governors is the addition of warm baths, not only for the use of boys when sick, but for their occasional use when in health. Formerly two tubs and two towels constituted the washing apparatus for a Ward of fifty boys.

Possibly in response to this appeal for a nearer approach to godliness, twenty-eight baths were installed in a ''warm bath room'', with the result that, by careful organization, each boy was able to have a warm bath at least once a fortnight. The daily wash was managed under a range of taps over a trough, usually with some twenty-five boys washing, while in the same small lavatory the other twenty-five were cleaning their shoes and splashing the washers with liquid blacking.

Such then were the externals of London life. It will be seen that the outlook of the boys on life must have been extremely restricted – literally cloistered. Cabinned, cribbed, confined, amid the massive buildings, shut in by stout walls and iron railings, guarded by beadles watchful and greedy as Cerberus at the gates, they could not but feel that C.H. was their microcosm, that the outer world was an alien country which would not concern them until they left school. In his delightful *Wayside Thoughts*, D'Arcy Thompson sums up such impressions by ending his recollections of Christ's Hospital (thinly disguised as St. Edward's) with this passage:

Naked came I into St. Edward's – literally naked: for I was stripped to the skin, and reclad in my blue regimentals. Naked came I in; and what am I carrying out in my carpet-bag? Let us examine: one very great friendship and some few lesser ones; affectionate and grateful recollections of three masters and friends; some mathematics and French

stowed away neatly and compactly, and a great lot of classics rather confusedly huddled together; and bless me! in amongst the classics has tumbled a deal of alcaic sawdust, hexametrical cinders, iambic chaff, and other intellectual marine-stores. Well, never mind; if these latter are of no earthly use in the outer world, they are highly valued at the university of Camelot to which I am proceeding; so we may just as well take care of them for three more years, and then we may with safety throw them all away into the eternal dustbin.

1902 and the end of the London School is in sight. The Medical Officer of the City of London has proclaimed that ''Christ's Hospital is a pestilential area'' and decrees that ''the nuisance must be abated''. The Bishop of London comes to Christ Church to bid us farewell and God – speed; the Archbishop of Canterbury gives us good advice and his benediction in St. Paul's Cathedral; the Lord Mayor and Corporation watch us leave the liberties of the City which has given us birth, fostered us, and loved us; yet in spite of heart-burnings, even of tears, they know as we know that whatever happens to us, and wherever we be, Christ's Hospital is and will always remain the City's School.

I venture to put into print anything of another far more poignant farewell which had to happen. No one who did not know Richard Lee, Head Master and himself an Old Blue, can form the vaguest notion of what he stood for the boys. He was small, he was stout, he was pedantic; but he was dignified, and he was horrific. He could roar as gently as a sucking-dove: but woe betide the evildoer when he did. Yet he had a heart, which must have been racked with anguish when he made his way to the Hall on the 18th April, 1902, to wait for the last assembly of the boys. He said little, but impressively commended them to the grace and protection of God, the unusual tremor in his voice and the breaks in his sentences betraying the emotion under which he laboured. As they filed past him, he shook hands with each boy, adding in most cases a few kindly words of encouragement and hope for their future.

A frolic of the Grecians on the last night of term (of which, though not a Grecian, *pars magna fui*) provided the lighter side of these (literally) moving times. In those days the idea of a Grecian ''degrading himself'' to any species of fun or humour seemed too great an impossibility to contemplate; yet on this night a peculiar and unique cremony was invented, instituted and performed. Forming a long single file, each holding a lighted candle (of four to the lb.), the Grecians ''beat the bounds'' of the Hospital, kicking the walls at such well-known spots as the ''Gymmer Door'', ''Sixes Tubby Hole'', ''The Rid's Staircase'', and ''Haggery Stairs''. The round completed, they stretched across the Hall Playground and, having solemnly extinguished their candles (in the best Papal manner), they marched up and down three times, singing lustily "Auld Lang Syne". The unexpected appearance of the Warden dispersed them suddenly to their Wards.

One of Allan's younger contemporaries, J. E. W. Wallis (the brother of Barnes Wallis), in his *Rights of Memory,* an autobiography, written several years after the publication of Allan's book, provides a fitting post-script to Allan, and a valedictory for Newgate Street.

During the long holiday that followed I went up once to see the old School . . . Through the railings I could see the noble façade of the Dining Hall, still unmutilated. But the Hall Play itself was encumbered with piles of planks and scaffold-poles and all the apparatus of the destroyer. On two boards raised high above the top of the railings were two inscriptions. One gave the name of the contractors' firm

    Blount & Sandford
    Housebreakers
    55 Southampton Street
    Camberwell

The second line made my heart thump unpleasantly. Here, where so many boys had built the spiritual houses which they were to inhabit through life, here the very *Hospitium Christi,* the House of Christ, Housey in our familiar talk, was to be broken up by Mr Blount and his partner, Mr. Sandford, of Southampton Street, Camberwell! I knew nothing of either of them, and I am sure that they were very

honest and hardworking men doing the job to the complete satisfaction of the Council of Almoners. Nevertheless!

The second board bore this inscription:

GOOD, OLD BRICKS FOR SALE

The grammarian within me wondered at that comma. Why not: GOOD OLD BRICKS FOR SALE? Or if some mark of punctuation was desired after the first word, why not: GOOD! OLD BRICKS FOR SALE, to sound, as it were, a note of gloating satisfaction over our downfall? Thus pondering I went back along Newgate Street and entered the School premises by the old familiar Lodge. It was empty. No Beadle! No boys! The place was forlorn and deserted. The last of the furniture had scarcely been removed. Mr. Blount and Mr. Sandford had hardly begun their task.

I walked along the Giffs and on to the further end of the Hall Play. As I returned, a short figure dressed in black issued from the Hall Cloi and confronted me, his hands clasped behind his back.

"Well, Wallidge, did you think term had begun?" Richard Lee grinned up at me.
"No, Sir," said I, "I came to see whether life had ended."
"Life never ends," said he, "it may, it must – (and he slowly waved his hand towards the contractors' materials lying around us), "it must change its environments and its expressions; but it does not end."

Some of this topography is not quite apodeictic. Let me explain. A "Tubby Hole" was a little lobby below a staircase, used as a store and recreation room by the Tubbies, who like the Weird Sisters were three in number, and, judging by the way they swept up the grounds, had about the same deficiency of eyes. Their names were Satan (Mason), Fudge (Ryan), and Ratcatcher (Groves). "The Rid" was Mrs. Riddiford, Ward Matron of XVI (who had two smashing daughters). "The Haggery" was the abode of three repulsive looking females who washed up the crockery. The one we called "Old Mother Beer-barrel" had really been christened Amanda! — G.A.T.A.

CHAPTER FOUR

Customs Past and Present

Christ's Hospital being a Royal Foundation, it is fitting that it should be proud of its continuous connexion with royalty and that grateful acknowledgement should be made for the interest which the Royal Family has taken in us from our beginnings. The greatest of our privileges is our prescriptive right to present a Loyal Address to the Sovereign on the occasion of his state visit to the City after his Accession and we have never again been rebuffed as we were on that notorious day when Queen Mary I, as Howes relates (and as we have already commented) the citizens being:

in good hope that she would put to her helping hand and give good countenance to the good work of the Hospital. . . it came otherwise to pass, for at such time as she came out of Norfolk and was to be received into London, the Governors set up a stage without Aldgate, and placed themselves and the children upon the stage. And prepared a child of the free school to make an oration to her, but when she came near unto them she cast her eye another way and never stayed nor gave any countenance to them.

Queen Elizabeth I proved more friendly to the "blewe boys" whom her sister had "liked not of". In January 1581 she received their Address graciously at Temple Bar, her successor, James I, as graciously as he was able, at All Hallows, Barkinside. Charles II was the first in a long and unbroken line of monarchs who have accepted the Address in St. Paul's Churchyard; he on the 22nd April 1661, the day before his Coronation, when processing from the Tower to Whitehall.

The ceremony at the state visit of Queen Victoria is commemorated by a bas-relief frieze on the pedestal of the griffin at Temple Bar; the figure shown kneeling at the foot of the State coach is that of F. G. Nash, who later held one of the Hospital's benefices and who succeeded in surviving into the following reign. George V received the Address on the steps of St. Paul's as he was entering the cathedral for the Thanksgiving Service after his Coronation. His Majesty was notably generous in his response but hindsight discovers in that happy occasion a tragic symbolism. The Senior Grecian honoured with the task of presenting the Address was one of the many hundreds of Blues who, in that same decade, gave their lives for King and Country.

Three of George the Fifth's sons, the Prince of Wales, the Duke of York and the Duke of Gloucester, became in turn Presidents of Christ's Hospital. They, and the present Duke of Gloucester, our current President, have all shown an interest in the affairs of the Foundation which exceeds by far the demands of formality.

As Edward VIII abdicated before his Coronation he made no State entry into the City but his brother, King George VI, was received by us, according to the custom, on the steps of St. Paul's on 24th May 1937 and his daughter, our reigning monarch, on 9th June 1953, the year of our Quartercentenary, just before she entered St. Paul's for her Coronation Thanksgiving Service.

The arrangements were then much as they had been for several centuries. The Queen and the Duke of Edinburgh came up the steps preceded by the Lord Mayor carrying the City's Pearl Sword. On the landing outside the West Door the members of the Christ's Hospital deputation – the Treasurer, the Vice-Chairman of the Council of Almoners, the Clerk, the Headmistress, the Head Girl, the Head Master and the Senior Grecian – were presented and then, on bended knee, the Senior Grecian presented our Loyal Address and the Queen was "graciously pleased to hand to the Senior Grecian. . . the Reply to the Address".

Neither Loyal Address nor Royal Reply was read aloud but both are reproduced here as a matter of historical record.

May it please Your Majesty:

Since King Edward VI of Blessed Memory in 1553 granted His Royal Charter to the Religious, Royal and Ancient Foundation of Christ's Hospital the children of Christ's Hospital have from time to time been granted the gracious privilege of presenting their humble duty on the occasion of their Sovereign's first visit to the City of London after the Coronation.

In this the four hundredth year of our Foundation, we offer our humble and loyal greetings to Your Majesty, deeply sensible of the honour which Your Majesty has bestowed upon us by becoming our Patron and of the privilege we enjoy by virtue of the Presidency of His Royal Highness the Duke of Gloucester.

That Your Majesty may have a long, happy and prosperous Reign is the earnest prayer of the Sons and Daughters of this ancient House, who share the hope of all Your Majesty's subjects that Your Majesty and His Royal Highness the Duke of Edinburgh may be blessed with many years of health and happiness.

9th June, 1953

Queen Elizabeth II replied:

I thank you for your loyal and dutiful Address.

It is with great pleasure that I receive your loyal greetings in the year when you are celebrating the four hundredth anniversary of your Foundation. By its work through the years your ancient House has won a high reputation and as your Patron I share with you your happiness on this notable landmark in its history.

I am confident that your fine traditions will continue to inspire all who pass through your Schools to give of their best in honourable and devoted endeavour and service, as their predecessors have in the past.

May God bless the work of the Schools throughout the years that lie ahead.

Signed: Elizabeth R
9th June 1953

It was at one time the custom for the Sovereign to receive boys of The Royal Mathematical School annually either at Windsor Castle or Buckingham Palace when they exhibited examples of their work. Two pictures – invariably and appropriately drawings of ships – were personally chosen by the Sovereign for his collection and the artists were rewarded by the gift of a gold pencil-case. This custom ceased late in the nineteenth century.

Regularly twice in every year, for the Spital Sermon and on St. Matthew's Day, the Hospital is officially represented at a service in a City Church.

At one time the Spital Sermon was delivered on the same day – then Easter Tuesday – when the boys visited the Mansion House, but the ceremony ante-dates by almost two centuries the Foundation of the Hospital. In 1598 John Stow celebrated in his *Survey of London* the bicentenary of the Sermon.

Here it is to be noted that time out of mind it hath been a laudable custom that on Good Friday in the forenoon some especially learned man, by appointment of the prelates, hath preached a sermon at Paul's Cross, treating of Christ's passion: and upon the three next Easter holydays, Monday, Tuesday, and Wednesday, the like learned man, by the like appointment, have used to preach in the forenoons at the said Spital to persuade the article of Christ's resurrection. . . Touching the antiquity of this custom, I find that in the year 1398 King Richard, having procured from Rome confirmation of such statutes and ordinances as were made in the Parliament begun at Westminster and ended at Shrewsbury, he caused the same confirmation to be read and pronounced at Paul's Cross and St. Mary Spital in the sermons before all the people. In the year 1594, the pulpit being old, was taken down and a new one set up, the preacher's face turned towards the south, which was before towards the west. Also a large house (on the east side of the said pulpit) was then builded for the Governors and children of Christ's Hospital to sit in. But within the first year the same house decaying and like to have fallen, was again (with great cost) repaired at the City's charge.

Apparently the Governors or the City Fathers were not slow to realize the potentialities of this annual opportunity to plead the cause of charity, and C. H. soon appropriated it for its own use. Christ Church did not at once become the place where the sermon was preached. Sometimes it was at Paul's Cross, sometimes at St. Bride's, Fleet Street; and by degrees it has fallen now to the Lord Mayor to appoint the preacher, who is always a Bishop, presumably to ensure that he shall be an "especial learned" man.

(Three times in this century the learned prelate has been also an Old Blue.)

In the past there was no little friction between the Governors and the Lord Mayor as to the place of the function. About a century ago matters became so strained that the Lord Mayor summoned the Governors to attend at St. Bride's, while C.H. invited them to Christ Church. The sermon was preached at Christ Church!

St. Matthew's Day is the other City day for C. H. It was on St. Matthew's Day that the Governors of the Royal Hospitals used to hold their annual meetings, most likely because, as the school was ready for occupation in September, 1552, the following St. Matthew's Day fell at the end of a complete financial year. The St. Matthew's Day preacher is fond of taking up his parable from St. Matthew sitting at the receipt of custom, straining for some parallelism in the Governors' sense of civic duty and their sacrifices on behalf of their charges. Keeping to the more prosaic and practical explanation of why this day of all Saints' Days should be chosen, we find that St. Matthew's Day was very early fixed for the election of Governors, and it was naturally not long before Governors on election were shown round the school. Equally natural was it that this visit should become also an inspection, when those Scholars who were "pregnant and apt to learning" were picked out by their Masters to "show off" to the Governors by saying their little recitations. From this it was but a step to making known to a wider public how well C.H. taught and cared for its children. The little pieces became studied eloquence, the halting repetition advanced to rhetoric; the Annual Orations on St. Matthew's Day became the archetype of what is still known as the English Oration, the equivalent of the Headmaster's or Headmistress's annual report of other schools, but at Horsham delivered by the Senior Grecian and at Hertford by the Head Girl; twenty or more minutes of eloquence and immaculate detail spoken invariably without benefit of script or notes.

An old print by Rowlandson and Pugin shows the ceremony, as it was in their day. The hall is cleared of tables and forms, the visitors are seated along the sides and on tiers of benches at the end; the Lord Mayor is provided with a table at which he sits in solitary state; in the centre of the hall is a raised platform on which stand two orators, and behind the platform stands the Head Master, complete with wig and gown, ready to prompt if need be from the paper in his hand. There is also a not uncommon print of a painting by Thomas Stothard, R.A. (exhibited at the Royal Academy in 1799, and presented in 1937 to the Art Gallery at Guildhall) which is interesting on account of its "key" and as showing a full-face likeness of Coleridge's Head Master, James Boyer. This is said to be the only extant picture of Boyer, but there is a silhouette of him in the present Head Master's study, presented by his great-great-grandson.

With the years some of the panoply of St. Matthew's Day has been transferred to Speech Days, held at both Horsham and Hertford in the Summer Term. On St. Matthew's Day the Lord Mayor receives Christ's Hospital in his own City and in his own residence. On Speech Day Christ's Hospital in his own City and in his own residence. On Speech Days Christ's Hospital receives the Lord Mayor. Both occasions symbolise the reality that, though the Hospital is no longer situate in the City, it has not lost its City heart.

The Orations are now the climax to Speech Day; all else is but supporting attraction; but since the exodus to Sussex the Boys' School has added some entrancing ceremonies.

Chapel in the morning – but no sermon – is followed by a march past, as substitute for the antique bowing procession of Public Suppers. Gawping visitors gather in the Quadrangle. The Band arrives from the Music School and is marshalled in front of the Dining Hall. The Treasurer and the Head Master escort the Lord Mayor's party to a saluting-base and then, as the whole company stands in admiring and, it must be admitted, silence that is loaded with sentiment, the smallest boy in the School files out from under the Western Archway, makes his extravagantly dignified way to a point level with the Lord Mayor, turns right advances upon the Lady Mayoress, bows, and presents her a bouquet.

Whilst strong men blow their noses and weaker ladies mutter in delight, the small boy bows again, makes a military about-face and, pretending to ignore the applause, returns to anonymity. The Band strikes up and the whole School, advancing in column of houses, marches past the saluting Lord Mayor. Custom decrees that the military music shall always include "Sussex by the Sea" (which has become virtually the School's own march), and sometimes, if he has seen service, the Lord Mayor's own Regimental Quick March.

Lunch in Dining Hall ends with the Head Master (or at Hertford Headmistress) proposing the two Toasts peculiar to C.H., "Church and Queen" and the Housey Toast, then all but the Lord Mayor's party and the Governors take their place in Big School.

The Governors, each carrying what one of their number has called his Malvolio stick, his staff of office, shamble in two by two to the "March from Rinaldo" on the organ (it was until recently played by trumpeters in the organ gallery but this was abandoned when it was found impracticable to issue umbrellas to the audience) and form a guard-of-honour for the Lord Mayor.

The Lord Mayor replies to the Oraton delivered by the Senior Grecian (or Head Girl) and most Lord Mayors are ready to concede that by comparison they are indifferently eloquent.

Until the Second World War there was one other custom practised on Speech Days. During the celebrations the First Parting Grecians (or their Hertford equivalents) moved among the assembled company carrying white gloves into which all present were invited to drop silver, or preferably bank-notes, the whole collections to be divided among those boys proceeding to universities – the First Parting Grecians themselves. The custom was abandoned because it was thought to be somehow undignified; a decision that does not have the support of one who benefited.

In accordance with custom a sermon was the natural concomitant of any such function as our St. Matthew's Day celebration. The Lord Mayor, Aldermen, Sheriffs, and members of the Corporation attended at Christ Church – as long as it stood – to hear a sermon delivered by a distinguished former Scholar of the House.

Apart, however, from the annual Orations, St. Matthew's Day was, by Act of Parliament, the day on which the lists of Governors of the Royal Hospitals were handed to the Lord Mayor, and thereby received the implicit approval of the City to those who had been elected to carry out what the City considered its own duty. Up to 1902 the ceremony took place in the Court Room of Christ's Hospital after service; but, again in accordance with custom, such a ceremony was "not to be enterprised, nor taken in hand, unadvisedly, lightly, or wantonly", and the visitors must first be strenthened and refreshed. The table was spread with cut plum cake, macaroons, and ratafia biscuits, claret and port – never anything else – and, lest the visitors considered the Hospital parsimonious, half-pound packets of macaroons were provided for them to take away in their pockets. The ceremony now takes place at the back of the Church. The Clerk of Christ's Hospital makes a formal and archaic speech and hands to the Lord Mayor a list of Governors. In the past the Lord Mayor was not always well-briefed and to-day this bemusement is perpetuated. He looks with apparent helplessness to the Town Clerk, "What am I to do with this?" he asks. The Town Clerk ends the formalities by taking the documents from the Lord Mayor and by assuring His Lordship that they will be placed in safe keeping in the archives of the City.

Since the exodus to Horsham the Spital Sermon has customarily been preached on the second Wednesday after Easter and the Easter Tuesday celebrations have been moved to St. Matthew's Day.

On that day all the senior boys save the very youngest and some of the girls come up to the City. After the service, (which, since Hitler destroyed our own Christ Church, has been held in St. Sepulchre's, another church with long associations with the Hospital) girls and boys form up behind the Boys' School's superb Band and, headed by the Band's three superb drum-majors, march to the Mansion House.

When photographers at last tire of taking pictures of the Senior Grecian and the Head Girl shaking hands with the Lord Mayor, boys and girls file past to receive largesse from the Lord Mayor. Until Britain went off the gold standard Grecians and their female equivalents received a golden guinea, thereafter, until the nation adopted decimal currency, still the Lord Mayor presented to each of these lordly ones a pound and a shilling. Monitors used to receive half-a-crown, the generality a shilling – all newly-minted coins. (Little boys and girls left behind at Horsham and Hertford were at one time sent, each of them, a sixpenny-piece.) Whether the difficult computation consequent upon decimalisation fell to the City Fathers or to the Counting House is not recorded; all that can be said for certain is that so far no allowance has been made for inflation.

Money having changed hands the School moves on into the magnificent Egyptian Hall and to a munificent buffet-lunch. A short speech from the Lord Mayor, loud cheers from the refreshed "children", and the ceremony is completed.

It was to Christ's Hospital that the State itself turned, as an adjutant to the Goddess of Chance, for assistance with the public lotteries which in less puritanical times made a by-no-means insignificant contribution to the health of the Exchequer. A dozen boys were chosen by the Treasurer and sent to Coopers' Hall to draw the lucky numbers. Just as, in more recent times, nurses are selected to draw tickets for the Irish Sweep on account of their youth and charm so also were these boys pulled out from the rest because *their* obvious youth and apparent innocence made it inconceivable that they could be party to evil schemes organised by unscrupulous ticket-holders.

Honesty forces the admission that such confidence was at times ill-founded but discretion suppresses the details, and it was all long-ago. No C.H. boy has drawn a public lottery-ticket (either honestly or dishonestly) since 1826.

In earlier times one of the great features of the Easter Term was the Public Supping, said to have originated when the Governors tried "to think of a way how to prevent the rabble of people coming into the Great Hall on Sunday nights to see the children at supper, which causes great disturbance and interruption in that affair!"

In the eighteenth century the performance was stylised and then confined to the Thursdays in Lent. The number was later reduced to four, at which figure it remained till the last. The supper on these occasions was exactly the same as on every other night: there was no window-dressing in that respect; but nearly everything else was different. The Ward Matrons wore their best frocks and bonnets, the boys all gave themselves a double dose of spit and polish. Each table bore four antique wooden candlesticks decorated with flowers – their arrangement the subject of fierce competition between Wards – and also with those trophies held by the Ward at the time of the Supping. The privileged visitors were placed at the west end on tiers of benches, and some additional accommodation was provided at the sides of the Hall at that end. At the appropriate moment, to triumphal strains from the organ, a gorgeous procession entered, led by the Head Beadle wearing his ceremonial gown, carrying his old mace or staff with silver head. He was followed by the Governors carrying wands of office, Aldermen in scarlet robes, and last of all, the important personage who was to occupy the presidential armchair. After his election as President in 1854 the Duke of Cambridge attended almost annually on one of the Thursdays. Queen Victoria and the Prince Consort were occasional visitors, but in general the chair was taken by the Lord Mayor or the Treasurer. During supper the Governors would walk round the Hall, each addressing a word (and usually giving a tip) to his presentee. Those who had given cups, or were interested in the sport which they represented, would often drop a sovereign or two into the trophy to provide a "gut" – a treat – for the lucky Ward. [G.A.T. Allan remembered with delight the occasion when his Ward held the Fives Cup and the donor, Lord Roseberry, enriched it, and the Ward, with a five-pound note.] Supper over, the tables were

Above: The bas-relief of Queen Victoria at Temple Bar in 1837. (From a photograph c. 1901).

Right: St Brides, Fleet St from a print c. 1814.

Right: St Matthew's Day orations in the 18th century — from a print by Rowlandson.

Left: The silhouette of Coleridge's headmaster, James Boyer.

Right: Drawing the Lotteries in Coopers' Hall — a custom abandoned since 1826

52

St Matthew's Day — *(above left & left) Marching to the Mansion House, different generations, different hair styles but the happy continuity of a time honoured tradition.*

St Matthew's Day — *(above right & right) Receiving the Lord Mayor's Shilling. The girls in the uniform dress of 1947, R. E. Oldfield, the Treasurer and H. L. O. Flecker, the Head Master look on. The boys (below) are of a later generation but their uniform is changeless.*

Chapel, in ascending order of seniority, the Grecians at the back and the Senior Grecian last of all (as similarly their Hertford equivalents). Then as each name is called the leaver moves up the aisle to receive from the Head his crested *Bible* and, if a Grecian, also a crested *Book of Common Prayer*, and then there is read out to him to Solemn Housey Charge

> I charge you never to forget the great benefits that you have received in this place, and in time to come according to your means to do all that you can to enable others to enjoy the same advantages; and remember that you carry with you, wherever you go, the good name of Christ's Hospital. May God Almighty bless you in your ways and keep in you the knowledge of his love.

The custom of presenting Bibles to school-leavers is not yet a century old but it has distant antecedents in our history. In 1652 Christopher Meredith provided in his will for as many "small Bibles plain-bound and clasped" as could be bought for £4. A few years later, in 1661, Richard Young was more ambitious, more generous and more egotistical. He gave £25 annually for producing three books written by himself, 2000 of each to be delivered to the City Chamberlain for distribution to apprentices and Freemen of the City, the residue to the Treasurer for the Hospital's children. In 1701, Charles Adams came closer to modern practise. He ordained that, on leaving, every child be given one or more of three theological works, *The Whole Duty of Man, Holy Living and Dying* and the first part of Scott's *Christian Life*. (Why only the first part neither original author nor subsequent editor has troubled to discover. No more, it might be suspected did many of the beneficiaries.) In 1751 William Smith added to this awesome and improving list *The Great Importance of a Religious Life Considered* and somehow reduced the solemnity of his bequest by insisting that the books be bound in calf-skin.

From the beginning of Christ's Hospital time the Foundation has benefited from testatory benefactions of all kinds. Many were accompanied by conditions which now seem archaic but which were in their day deliberately utilitarian and even of these some survive to this day, and the wishes of their originators are still scrupulously observed. Many were merged when the new Scheme was instituted.

Though the boys and girls might think otherwise, it no longer seems necessary to honour bequests for the provision of roasted meats or legs of pork but the many – and early – benefactions specifically related to the employment of masters to teach particular subjects or to provide funds for exhibitions or apprenticeships would, even to-day, be welcomed by the Council of Almoners.

Of this kind was the benefaction of Robert Dow, received in 1609. His first thought as he wrote his will was to augment the salary of the music master

to teach the art of music and prickesong, &c., to ten or twelve of the children of Christ's Hospital, and to teach all his singing children the whole catechism appointed and set forth in the Book of Common Prayer, to teach them to write, and make them able to sing in the Choir of Christ Church, for which purpose he and his successors should not fail to bring the children every Sunday and every holyday and their vigils to the said Church.

After leaving 6s. 8d. "for gloves for the said children" Dow reverts to the music master, who is to have £4 a year

to teach three or four of the singing children to play upon an instrument, as the virginals or viol, and that he should not only attend during prayers in the church, but should be there after the sermon both morning and evening, in order to play on the organ a psalm which the congregation should sing.

Other, and to us stranger, bequests came from such as Peter Symonds (who also founded a school in Winchester patterned after C.H. and still flourishing). From him came 30s. to be divided on Good Friday among "three score at least" of Christ's Hospital children, a further 3s. 4d. to buy them raisins and all of 1s. 4d. for the beadle who accompanied them to All Saints, Lombard Street for the distribution.

Robert Hilson was interested in the children's clothing. In 1582 he left an annuity of £10. 14s. 8d. towards the cost of eqipping all the boys with black caps.

Dame Dorothy Edwards was similarly intrigued by the possibility of enlivening the uniform but her will, proved in 1596, entitles her to an honoured place as one of the earlier predecessors of what later – much later – came to be called a Donation Governor (though that honour can only be acquired and exercised in the life-time of the benefactor). Dame Dorothy left £10 "to the intent that six poor children should be maintained and kept in Christ's Hospital with all the necessities to them belonging, only to be distinguished from the other children of this House in the colour of their caps or in some other note of difference".

Fifteen years later William Stoddard followed in the sumptuary line. He left sufficient funds to enable the Governors to comply with his instruction that "ten poor children received into Christ's Hospital might wear green caps and green facing to their coats, whereby they might be discerned and known from among the rest of the children". (He arranged also for an augmentation of the Steward's salary and still, when G.A.T. Allan was himself Steward he received annually the sum of 10s. from Stoddard's bequest.)

Perhaps the most extraordinary of all these early eccentric benefactions directed especially at improving or enriching the boys' clothing was that originated in 1669 by Edward Arris who left £6 a year:

to be laid out as follows every Easter, *imprimu*, 240 boys, each of them to have a pair of white gloves, and every one of them to wear a paper with these words written on it, *videlicet*, in great letters, "He is Risen", and this is to be done upon Easter Sunday, Monday, Tuesday and Wednesday, and the papers visibly to be seen.

Arris's wishes were followed faithfully each Easter until the middle of the nineteenth century. In his lively *Recollections of a Bluecoat Boy* W. P. Scargill, who was at C.H. from 1794-1802, records still the foppish embellishments:

The boys on that occasion wore their best clothes, and had a piece of paper with the words "He is Risen" pinned on the left side of the coat. Many of them used to provide themselves with nosegays, or with single roses. . . The boys of the writing school wore red feathers in their caps.

The obsession of so many of these early benefactors with ensuring that their charity be memorialised by appropriate variations in the uniform is now no longer compulsive upon the Governors and, indeed, almost the last relics of such instincts are the shoulder-badges of the Royal Mathematical School (which, incidentally, had in their time a most practical use for those who had worn them in their school-days for they served, in adult years, as prophylactic against the attentions of the press-gang) and the similar shoulder badges of the Oliver Whitby and Royal Air Force Foundations.

Similarly, the interest shown by so many of these early supporters of Christ's Hospital's charity in breaching the uniformity of the uniform is now (as it has been for 250 years) antithetical to C.H. philosophy. For us, as for our predecessors since the early eighteenth century, Housey dress is much more than observance of an antique custom; because all boys wear uniforms that can be differentiated one from the other only by the *cognoscenti*, all are visibly made equal heirs to the Christ's Hospital tradition. The uniform is our most potent sociological instrument.

To the outsider it may seem paradoxical that, even so, the variations in the uniform are themselves evidence to a severe class-structure but, in truth, these are the outward and visible signs of privilege conferred by Christ's Hospital and within Christ's Hospital; they carry no implication of parental status, of comparative wealth or social background.

Some of these variations are so esoteric as to deny easy identification even by an informed observer – for example, the manner in which a boy wears his girdle to proclaim his seniority. The broadie girdle itself with its silver buckle is more easily discernible but the most easily distinguishable is also the most distinguished. The noble uniform of the Grecians proclaims them as the school's nobility. Whereas all those of humbler degree have but one large silver button and six small on their coat-fronts, Grecians display fourteen large silver buttons and also velvet cuffs on coats of superior cloth.

If in those early days bequests designed to further the spiritual and physical well-being of the Scholars – and to improve their appearance – were at least as common as gifts to improve their formal education, there were also some (then as through the centuries) intended to direct the minds of the children – and perhaps also the Governors – to their temporal duties. In 1731 Samuel Davenport presented to the Hospital a portrait of Queen Anne with five guineas to buy "the Annals or History of the said Queen". It could be that the money was diverted from its proper use and certainly no copy of the book could be found in our archives by G.A.T. Allan, but the picture hangs to this day in the Dining Hall at Hertford.

Later benefactions have been many, generous and generally less inhibited by the testator's directions. Of their number a goodly proportion have come from Old Blues of both sexes, inspired, even before it was written, by the spirit of the Charge to do all "according to your means. . . to enable others to enjoy the same advantages". Richard Thornton, for example, "the Duke of Danzig", a merchant adventurer who died in 1865 possessed of a fortune of several millions left part of his estate to his old school and, much more recently, (as will be seen later in this book) the great inventor, Barnes Wallis, whilst still very much alive, turned over to the Hospital for the establishment of the Royal Air Force Foundation, all the money he received for his war-time inventions.

It was Wallis, too, when Treasurer, who insisted on perpetuating an antique custom available to the Hospital, the privilege conferred upon the Worshipful the Treasurer of walking on the right hand of the Lord Mayor in the precincts of the City ("save only when the Sovereign is present").

This is but one of many customs that are privy to the Governors and generally unknown even by the majority of Blues and Old Blues. Of these most dramatic if perhaps also the least significant and the least utilitarian is the last survivor of many similar ceremonies which were at one time practised religiously. It is consequent upon the will of one James St. Amand, who died in 1754. That will (with lawyer's repetitions edited out) reads as follows:

In the name of God, Amen. I, James St. Amand, of the parish of St. George the Martyr, Queen's Square, in the county of Middlesex, Esquire, being of sound and disposing mind, memory, and understanding (thanks be to Almighty God) and considering the great uncertainty of Life, do make this my last will and testament in manner and form following (that is to say) First and principally I humbly recommend my soul into the hands of God my Creator, in hopes of mercy through the merits and mediation of my ever blessed Redeemer, and my body to the earth, to be buried in a private but decent manner at the discretion of my executors; and I desire to be buried in the Cloisters of Christ's Hospital in the City of London, with this inscription; Here lyes a Benefactor, Let no one move his Bones; and nothing more, not even the initial letters of my names.

Then follow minute details as to the disposal of his books, prints, Mss., and papers – to be sent to the Bodleian Library and Lincoln College – ''the boxes and trunks so packed up shall be put up in clean straw and covered over with coarse cloth which is to be sewed up so as to keep the straw together'' and ''sent to Oxford in a waggon to be hired for that purpose only, and not by water''.

Item, I give unto Christ's Hospital the Original Picture of my grandfather, John St. Amand, Esquire, drawn in miniature and set in gold, on condition that the Treasurer do give my executors a receipt and a promise in writing that he will upon no account whatsoever sell or alienate the said picture or suffer the same to be sold or alienated by any person or persons whatsoever.

Provision is then made for the residue of St. Amand's estate to pass to the Hospital and for the investment of the proceeds in 3% Consols which shall never:

on any account or pretence whatsoever be sold or changed for other securities, but that they shall remain untouched till they are paid off; the income to be applied either to increase the number of children or for their apprenticeship.

And my will and mind is that the Picture of my grandfather, John St. Amand, Esquire (which is valuable in itself as being an excellent Piece but still more so to me as being the Picture of an Ancestor to whose memory I justly pay the highest respect and veneration) shall be for ever kept in the Treasury of the Hospital with the same regard as if my grandfather and not myself was the Benefactor to it, and that it never shall be in the power of any person whatsoever to sell or otherwise to alienate it. And my will is that the Treasurer shall produce and shew the Picture at every first general Court held by the Governors after the first day of January in every year; and that such part of this my will as relates to the preserving it, and also to the disposal of the income intended for the Hospital, shall be audibly and publickly read at the same time in open Court.

The remainder of the will outlines some hideous penal clauses which will be invoked if the Vice-Chancellor of the University of Oxford should demand and be refused a sight of the portrait.

Each year at their January meeting the Clerk reads considerable portions of this will to the Court of Governors. The portrait is then produced – a charming miniature in a gold frame and let into the lid of a massive iron box – and is passed round, whilst the more devout Governors bow their heads in awe – and the more impertinent calculate what the legacy would have been worth had it not been restricted to those poor-yield investments, (now legitimately 2½% Consols worth in capital terms £26) and whilst the more venal wonder what price they could get for the exquisite miniature, if only they could subvert Oxford's Vice-Chancellor.

There is a pretty legend that the face in the portrait is that of the Old Pretender and for more than a century that possibility tempted the curious to commit a breach of faith. The authorities held firm but even they had some hope that the legend would become history when the secret drawer in the escritoire in the Clerk's office was opened (in all probability the very desk at which the eccentric elaborate will was drafted). Their aspirations were frustrated; there was no documentary evidence either to prove or to disprove the tale. And now we know that we cannot pretend to this particular Royal connection. Scrupulous scholarship has identified the miniaturist as by John Hoskins and, alas, Hoskins could not have painted the *soi-disant* King James the Third.

We leave it then that this other James, St. Amand, whose gifts to Christ's Hospital were several, rich and royal, may serve as representative of our many benefactors. For them all we continue to honour his wishes and his memory.

''No man knoweth of his sepulchre.''

CHAPTER FIVE

Antiquities and Treasures

There can be few with soul so dead that they do not thrill at the thought of treasures which the Hospital has accumulated in 430 years. Although the Governors quite properly, like Cordelia, think of their children as their most precious jewels, they are justly proud of their temporal possessions. The temptation to sell treasures has come frequently and the need by no means rarely, but almost always the Governors have resisted temptation and have found other ways to meet immediate needs.

However, because the Hospital's archives are of enormous interest to historians and the Office not possessed either of the professional competence to preserve and collate documents or of proper facilities for research, in 1968 it was decided to deposit the bulk of documentary material in the Guildhall Library.

Encouraged by the Council, the late G.A.T. Allan began work on the mammoth task of preparing for publication the Admissions Registers.

The first Register begins on 10th April 1563 with the names of 331 children "now remaining" but Allan was able to add many names of children admitted after 1556 by reference to the Minute Books of the Court which opened in 1556.

From 1563 to the present day the record is complete. Every child's name has been entered in huge volumes and with it, except in the very earliest days, also his or her age at entry, the date of admission and discharge, the father's name, occupation and place of residence, and the apprenticeship or other employment or place of further education.

Volume One of *Christ's Hospital Admissions* was published in 1937. It listed 3631 names but took the record only to 1599. Alas, there has never been a second volume.

Nevertheless, that first book revealed a fascinating picture of English life in the last decades of the sixteenth century. Several children were "born at Calice", others were listed as children of fathers "sent into Flanders" or "slain in Her Majesty's service". There were those orphaned by the disaster to the waterworks at Bridge House and some, children of "Egyptians" and of parents with homely names such as Morgan and Large, who were admitted because a parent, the only guardian, had committed suicide. We can read of one, the child of a mother who killed herself in the Tiltyard at Greenwich, who was admitted through the intervention of Mistress Skidmore, waiting-woman to Her Majesty the Queen. Still more children had one or both parents still alive but incarcerated in the Counter, the Fleet, Bridewell or Ludgate prisons.

An heritage of this kind brings no blush to the cheek of an Old Blue historian of Christ's Hospital. (Almost four centuries later a great headmaster boasted that he presided over the only public school which did not trouble to hide the fact that it had in its numbers "the son of an unsuccessful burglar and the son of a dead bishop".) Much more shaming is the entry against Alys Chaundler, apprenticed from the Hospital at the age of 13 and "received in again for that she would not behave herself justly".

This, nonetheless, like many other entries, demonstrates that already thus early in its history the Hospital was concerned for the after-care of its children. Ellin Parker was "received again from John Williams who with unreasonable correction misused her"; Erasmus Harding "for that he was very ill used by them that took him"; Margaret Norden "for that Agnes Marcie of Romford who had taken her as her own child ran away and left her unprovided for"; Dorothea Brooker "for that the mother is frantic and hath six children more and not able to keep them"; and Jane St. Thomas who "was put upon liking and with one month after bound by pence to Christopher Moseley and Katherine his wife and continued with them in service until the 16th February, 1592, upon which day the said Johan upon information of their neighbours of the grievances and ill usage towards her was by the Matron of Christ's Hospital fetched from them and brought into the nursery of the said Hospital where she died the 24th February, 1592, and according to custom the crowner and a guest sat of the magistrates''.

Faith Hodges was "delivered to nurse" to Lucy Jones, who, dying, gave "and disposed her goods amounting to £2,15s.9d. to the said Faith Hodges''; an example of kindly generosity similar to that of John Kelly, draper, who gave to Isake Jones 40s. "conditionally that he should go to Church with Dorothy Kelly his wife and there in the church to receive the same''; and a rather more elaborate method of assisting a child was adopted by the purchase of a terminable annuity:

> In respect of the £50 per contra received there is to be paid to Mrs. Angel or her assigns for ten years from Michaelmas 1574 towards the education and bringing up of Daniel Parry, 40s. by the year to be paid quarterly . . . with promise that the children of this House shall be at her burial being warned thereunto so far forth as the same be in this city or suburbs of the same.

Differences of opinion between parents and officials were not unknown even in earliest days. More than once we read that the mother took away the child by force out of the sick ward; but there is a curious instance of a parent insisting on taking away a child which the officials were quite certain was not her own. Frances Faith was "discharged the House by Gerard Sumons, one of Her Majesty's Governors in the Tower, and Jone Langley of Lincoln, who supposed that this child is the child of Jone Langley sent into this House in the marolty of Sir John Langley, Knight, but the child which he sent in, which is the child indeed, is dead: notwithstanding they persuaded them this to be their child''. The child who died, named Sara Shorte, has this record:

> This child was sent in by Sir John Langley, and was the child of one Jone Langley of Lincoln, who the 16 of May 1588, took out of this House Frances Faith, thinking that to be her child.

Originally applications for admission were made as requests from the parish which would otherwise have been responsible for the care of the individual child, and were supported by a bill or bond undertaking to discharge the Hospital of the child when so required. It is unlikely that this indemnity was ever claimed for the Hospital arranged apprenticeships or other employment for all its children.

At a later date this mode of applying for places was abandoned and in its stead came the Presentations. Parents provided birth certificates for the child, copies of their own marriage-certificates and details of their circumstances attested by churchwardens and three householders. This was transformed into a Presentation by the addition of a statement signed by a Governor:

> I present N. or M., son of A.D. and C.D. his wife, whom I conscientiously believe to be a proper object for admission into Christ's Hospital, the full names of the child and of his parents being by me inserted at full length.

With but a few *lacunae* all Presentations given since 1674 have been preserved and these are frequently the object of genealogical and other historical research. They reveal some interesting links which might otherwise go unobserved, and of them all one of the most fascinating (or should it be notorious?) is the Presentation given to the son of Robert Burns and Jean Armour. For them there was no possibility that they could provide the statutory marriage certificate but, charitably, the Hospital was satisfied with a certified extract from the records of the kirk session of Mauchline:

> Robert Burns, tenant in Mossgeel, and Jean Armour in Mauchline, came before the session upon the fifth day of August in 1788 and acknowledged that they were irregularly married some years ago. The session rebuked both parties for this irregularity and took them solemnly bound to adhere to one another as husband and wife all the days of their life.

These "irregularities" of which the session complained are now a commonplace and the Hospital is content with a statutory declaration as to the truth of all statements that are made by parents but it asks questions about their financial state much more searching than was once the case. Even so the form of the Presentation is much as it was three hundred years ago. Christ's Hospital does not readily break with tradition.

Book-keeping systems have altered, of course, and now no-one in the Office (or anywhere else) has either the time or the skill to spend half-a-day on the decoration of initial letters or on that exquisite calligraphy which made the Hospital's account-books into works of art.

From their beginning in 1556 the Minutes of Courts and Committees form a complete inner history of the Foundation. In them is recorded every transaction concerning the many estates and trusts, the appointments of all Masters, Mistresses and Officers, every detail of authorised expenditure, *et hoc genus omne*. Each page reveals some item of more than passing interest, all demonstrate with what meticulous care and loyalty the Governors have consistently continued their self-imposed task in the best interest of the children and the Schools.

As examples (and no more) a few items taken at intervals of approximately 50 years.

1564 It is agreed that there shall be paid to Jasper Vandaler, surgeon, for cutting and healing of William Lewis, by consent of this Court, in consideration of the poverty of his parents not being able to pay the same, for that otherwise the same child should have perished for want of curing of the said disease of the stone. [The amount of the surgeon's fee is not stated.]

1615 Whereas the vicarage of Ugley is now void by the death of Gorge Darlowe the last vicar therein, in whose room and place there is one to be presented, and for that the said vicar Darlowe was a man of turbulent disposition, the Governors advised what course they might take for to prevent the like hereafter, which they thought might be done by taking a bond of him that shall be presented of a good sum for the surrendering up of the same at all times when it shall take advice of some man learned in the law concerning the same. The Governors, bethinking themselves whom they shall present to the said Vicarage of Ugley, have thought fit to present James Hiat, late one of the children of this House, who hath been brought up at the University of Cambridge at the charges of this House.

1702 Mr. Treasurer intimating to this Committee that he having take notice that the children of this House at this time of year are rung up out of their beds at six o'clock in the morning and to school at seven, and thereby are exposed to the cold and dark mornings, and when at school cannot see to do anything till near eight o'clock, this Committee hereupon taking this matter into their serious consideration, did order and determine that it shall be henceforward observed as a rule that from All Saints to Candlemas Day the bell instead of ringing at six shall not be rung till seven in the morning to call the children up and at eight to call them to school.

1755 [Report of a journey to Hertford and Ware]. We set out with a coach and four horses on Tuesday, the 29th April, from Moorgate Coffee House about six o'clock in the morning and reached Ware about ten o'clock, and on examining the childen in their reading and writing found them very defective in both, which appears to be owing to the negligence of the master, who has often been reproved for his neglect; therefore think he should not longer be continued, as it will be of great prejudice to the children's education; but leave it to the Committee to act therein as they shall think fit.

1804 The Committee, at the suggestion of the Treasurer, having considered the propriety of a course of lectures calculated to improve the morals of the boys of this House being given upon the evenings of Sundays in the Great Hall of this Hospital, in consequence thereof submitted the following proposition: That the Committee are of opinion that if the Scriptures were explained to the children in the Hall on Sundays in a discourse adapted to their age and situation by one of their own Masters, it would have the effect of impressing their minds with a due sense of religion and greatly improve their morals and behaviour.

At Easter, in the first centuries, all the children were brought in from their ''nurses'' and this was the time when their disposition was either renewed or revised. This then was the moment when the Governors could best show to the public the results of their careful attention. And, because this time when a majority of the children were gathered together coincided with the Spital Sermon, the Governors made full use of the heaven-sent opportunity to replenish the coffers of the Foundation. Every preacher of a Spital Sermon was privately encouraged to exhort his congregation to deeds of charity, and the Governors added on their own account some useful propaganda in the form of a broadsheet setting out the numbers cared for in all the Royal Hospitals.

In the early seventeenth-century – as might be expected of that age – they added another persuasive practise, commissioning each year a Christ's Hospital Easter Anthem. All are rich in sentiment, most, according to the tastes of 1983, poor in literary or musical quality. The earliest extant example dates from 1610.

Because the Foundation owns or has owned estates all over the country the archives contain many title-deeds, some of them of great antiquity. There are at least 16 specimens of the Great Seal of England, the earliest on a grant by Henry III in 1265 to Roger de Taylup, his valet, of a house in the London parish of St. Pancras which belonged formerly to William Gratefige, citizen of London and one of the King's enemies. Next in seniority is that of Edward I, on his licence, granted in 1279, to hold in mortmain from the King-on-chief the priory and convent of Berden and also 18 acres of land and the church of that Essex parish. Other Great Seals appear on exemplifications of bills, answers, replications, leases and depositions of witnesses in Chancery suits. And there is one Great Seal on a document even more interesting than most by reason of the historical associations conjured-up by the names it contains. It is affixed to a deed dated 1679 conveying the feoffment for a fine of £350 and the surrender of an existing lease. That lease is signed by, among others, Charles the Second's Queen, Catherine of Braganza; and Henry Hyde, 2nd Earl of Clarendon; Philip Stanhope, 2nd Earl of Chesterfield; and Denzil, 1st Baron Holles.

It is in the nature of things that these documentary treasures are rarely visible and, if for a different reason, the same must be said of the Foundation's rich collection of silver (of which more later). Christ's Hospital's pictures, however, are hung proudly, at the Office in London, at Horsham and, for the moment, at Hertford. Together they make no mean record of the great events in the Hospital's history, of its children and its worthies.

In all probability the oldest painting in the Hospital's possession is the portrait of Sir Richard Dobbs, Lord Mayor of London in 1551-2, with its six lines of caption

Christ's Hospital erected was, a passing deed of pity,
What time Sir Richard Dobbs was Mayor of this most famous city;
Who careful was in government and furthered much the same,
Also a benefacter good, and joyed to see it frame;
Whose portraiture here his friends have set, to put each wight in mind
To imitate his virtuous deeds as Good hath us assigned.

This eulogium supports Ridley's famous panegyric quoted by Stow:

O Dobbs, Dobbs, Alderman and Knight, thou in thy year did win my heart for evermore, for that honourable act, that most blessed work of God, of the erection and setting up of Christ's holy Hospitals and truly religious Houses, which by thee and through thee were begun: for thou, like a man of God, when the matter was moved for Christ's poor silly members to be holpen from extreme misery, hunger, and famine; thy heart, I say, was moved with pity, and, as Christ's high honourable officer in that cause, thou calledst together thy brethren the Aldermen of the City, before whom thou brakest the matter for the poor.

In former times it was believed that the Hospital owned three Holbeins. Then, some hireling-scholar unearthed Holbein's will – and now there are none. Even so, the two portraits of the Founder King are among the Foundation's most prized possessions, as much for the delicacy of their painting as out of reverence for their subject (just as the carved statue of King Edward is honoured even if it is not, as some believe, by Grinling Gibbons) and the portraits are without doubt "school of Holbein". The third so-called Holbein is almost certainly a seventeenth century pastiche but painted at a time close enough to the event it commemorates, the granting of the Royal Charter, to justify the belief that it is based on some earlier records of Blues of both sexes in Christ's Hospital uniforms.

The Hospital has observed faithfully the wishes of the early eighteenth century benefactor who left three portraits of members of his family, the Dyers, with the request that they hang always on one wall and many still believe that the Hospital still shows similar respect to the terms of a bequest made later in that century by an Alderman and Member of Parliament for the City of London, Sir Brook Watson, for there is in the Court Room corridor at Horsham an excellent copy of the extraordinary and famous picture, *Brook Watson and the Shark* by John Singleton Copley, which he bequeathed to "the Royal Hospitall of Christ". The original was, in fact, sold some years ago to America – and for this act the Hospital need make no apology for

Copley was the greatest American artist of his generation and Brook Watson's connection with Christ's Hospital was tenuous. He was not, as some assert, himself a Blue.

All Christ's Hospital's pictures are precious to the Hospital if they have intimate associations; not all match artistic quality to their undeniable historical interest but the artist who painted the exquisite portrait of Young Susannah Holmes in C.H. uniform, which hangs now in the Dining Hall at Hertford, merits honour alongside the Hospital's Lely and its Kneller.

Of all Christ's Hospital's pictures the one that is inevitably noticed by all visitors to Horsham and the one that is best-remembered by all Old Blues, is also the largest, and some say the largest in the Kingdom. Celebrating the foundation of the Royal Mathematical School by Charles II, it occupies almost one whole wall of the Dining Hall at Horsham – and the Dining Hall is huge..

The origins of this monumental work are recorded in the Minute Book for 1684:

Whereas His gracious Majesty is not only the royal Founder but a bountiful benefacter to the Royal Mathematical School in Christ's Hospital, and the Court having resolved to draw such a design of the Mathematical Foundation as may transmit to posterity the honour due to His Majesty and the Hospital's gratitude and piety to his memory by painting, and whereas Seignior Vario, historian painter, hath several times been conferred with about the same, and drawn a design which hath been approved, but nothing further as yet done therein, now, that this good work may forthwith be put in hand and finished, the Court desired certain members to go to Esqr. Pepys and to request his company to Seignior Vario, and to let him know that the Court do make it their earnest request to him that he will with all convenient speed go in hand with the same design and finish the same, the Court having left the whole management thereof to him, as also to place the same in such part of the Great Hall as he shall think fit, and if the picture of Edward the Sixth is in his way, to let him know that the Court have resolved to remove it to some other place.

A fortnight later Signor Vario himself appeared before the Court and accompanied the members to the Great Hall, where he pointed out the place he would like the picture to occupy. The position chosen involved the blocking up of one window at the end of the building and the enlarging of two others, as well as the removal of Edward VI:

to all which the Court did readily assent, and desired withal to know of him what satisfaction he expected for doing of it well. He said he would do it so well that if any artist that should see it did not say it was worth one thousand pounds he would give the poor

of this Hospital one hundred pounds. The Committee prayed to him to express plainly what he expected. At last he said £300, viz. £100 in hand, another £100 when he had finished a third part of the work, and the other £100 when he had finished the whole, which he would endeavour to do by May next.

Alas for his good intentions! Nearly four years later – three years and a half after he had proposed to make some alteration to the design "in regards His Majesty King Charles the Second of blessed memory is lately deceased" – the Court desires a letter to be written to Vario,

> letting him know that if he do not forthwith finish the picture which he hath had in his hands ever since October, 1684, and hath already received £200 money in part, they must be compelled to complain to His Majesty of his ill usage.

The picture was at last finished; the inconvenience

Left: The front of Big School, Horsham. The statues of Sir John Moore and Charles II by Grinling Gibbons came from Wren's building in London.

Below: The Charles Lamb Medal.

Left: Francis Page's painting of the young Queen Victoria now in the Dining Hall at Horsham.

occasioned by the death of Charles II calmly erased by painting-in as the central figure not the Founder of the Royal Mathematical School but his brother, James II. Charles himself Verrio memorialised by an inserted medallion-portrait. In London the Verrio covered three walls of Dining Hall and by 1902 it was virtually invisible under a coating of City grime. When it was taken down for cleaning and removal to Horsham it was discovered that one section was thick with mildew and that the back-lining had disintegrated almost to powder. The magnitude and complexity of the task of restoration of a canvas which measures some 87 feet by 16 feet, had to be constructed to produce a new lining made of pure flax, and the complexity of the problem of rehanging is exemplified by the fact that the frame has 40 supports, each eight inches long, made of wrought iron and cemented into the wall.

The impertinent substitution of James for Charles does not erase altogether Verrio's claim to integrity in portraiture. All others of the many adults in the group were taken from life. Samuel Pepys stands there, close to the King (and he, at least, might have welcomed this artificial but appropriate position of proximity to one who shared his love for the Royal Navy). We wait still for some cunning authority to establish the identity of all others in the group.

And we wait still for some cunning detective to unearth the sketch which Verrio made before he began his work, and for some generous benefactor to install it where properly it should be. Twice in the last 50 years this sketch has appeared in a sales-room; twice Christ's Hospital made an offer; and twice it was outbid. Its present location is known only to its owner, his acquaintance – and, perhaps, to Sotheby's.

Throughout the centuries, by purchase and by gift, Christ's Hospital has added to its treasury of pictures. There are portraits of both Coleridge and Lamb, a handsome picture of a handsome young Queen Victoria by Francis Page, fine drawings by an Old Blue, Philip Youngman Carter (drawn originally for the *Christ's Hospital Book*) of a great headmaster, William Hamilton Fyfe, a great schoolmaster, A. C. W. Edwards, and a great Old Blue poet, Edmund Blunden. Recently there has been added to the collection, as memorial to another great schoolmaster, David Roberts, an interesting painting by one of the most eminent Old Blue painters, Keith Vaughn. Headmasters and Treasurers, most of them glaring austerely from the canvas, hang in the Horsham Dining Hall; their magnificent service to the Foundation suitably memorialised by the dignity of their position but seldom by the quality of the painting.

There is, however, in the Chapel at Horsham, a series of twentieth century paintings which stand comparison with the finest that the Hospital has acquired in all its four-and-a-half centuries.

In advancing this laudatory opinion the author of the revised edition of this book dares impertinent disagreement with his distinguished predecessor for, both in print and in conversation, G. A. T. Allan made no effort to conceal his distaste for the 16 paintings by Sir Frank Brangwyn. Even Allan could not despise the vastness of Brangwyn's project – all but two of the sixteen measure 14 feet by 8 feet, and the two are only slightly smaller. Nor would Allan have denied that there was boldness – rare in those who manage institutions – in the decision to turn to one of the most advanced, original and controversial artists to produce the focal decoration for the new Chapel. What Allan did argue was that boldness is a virtue that does not necessarily – and in this case did not – produce great art.

It is with this verdict that his successor ventures dissent for in his opinion every one of the pictures is close to being a masterpiece, full of life and interest, and the manner in which, painting over a period of 10 years, from 1913 to 1923, Brangwyn managed to combine all in one harmonious scheme turns the walls of the Chapel into a supreme demonstration of early twentieth century art.

The pictures tell the history of the Christian Church from the first Whit Sunday to the twentieth century. Some, like Allan, favoured none; most who know them well have their particular favourites; for this author the last in chronological order is unforgettable; by presenting the paradoxes of shabbiness and brilliance, of poverty and hope, Brangwyn created a miraculously important picture that could well stand by itself as one of his finest works. Yet it is by considering this single picture in the totality of Brangwyn's great design that the quality of his achievement must be measured. Compare it, for example, with another picture in the series – the St. Ambrose picture. The two deal with similar subjects, with choirs singing, but in the St. Ambrose painting all is ordered, set in clear pattern, and all the singers concentrate upon the Saint. In the Street Scene, as if to symbolise the despair common to this century, there is no defined line, figures huddle together as if to seek in contiguity defence against chaos; but their eyes look out beyond the harmonium-player, beyond the street, to an uncomprehended and yet certainly anticipated salvation.

Brangwyn's technique, and notably his use of the medium, tempera, is dexterous. There are at least 150 heads in the series, and all are distinct, for the many who have sat, day after day and year after year, before these pictures it is not so much technique, nor detail, nor yet the narrative logic of the series which makes these 16 pictures memorable, but rather the brilliance and lightness of the colours. This is not religion dim but religion optimistic and cheerful.

In common with many another ancient foundation Christ's Hospital has an exceptionally fine collection of plate.

The earliest piece is a rare late-mediaevel drinking horn (*circa* 1490) mounted in silver-gilt and encircled by a decorated band engraved 'In God is al'. (The engraver conceded to God an 'all' limited to one l!) A pounced inscription proclaims it as the gift in 1602 of Thomas Banks though there is in the Hospital's Account Book an entry which shows that the Foundation owned a drinking horn as early as 1567.

Unlike most of the pieces in the collection this horn is unmarked. For the rest, though many are clearly hall-marked and therefore can be dated, it is not always possible to identify the maker of any item before 1696 – the year when the early records of the Goldsmiths' Company were lost in a fire.

A silver-gilt gourd cup, the gift in 1602 of Mr. John Bancks (presumably, despite the variant spelling, a member of the same family as the donor of the drinking horn) was hall-marked in 1594. The gourd cup is clearly of German design and affords an interesting comparison with a silver-gilt lobed cup made in Nuremberg some sixty years later by the master-goldsmith Reinhold Niel, but the influence of Newgate Street is apparent in the silver seventeenth century statuette of a boy which has replaced the original finial; his dress resembles closely that worn by the actor Robert Armin when he played the role of John in the Hospital, '"Innocent and early Inmate of Christ's Hospital,"' in 1609.

One of the most important pieces in the collection is a silver-gilt, three-tier 'Bell' salt (1607). This, the largest-known of its kind is yet another gift of the Bancks (or Banks) family.

The Bancks armorials appear, together with the crest of the Mercers' Company, on a set of three octagonal silver-gilt wine cups of surpassing elegance. John Bancks was Warden of the Mercers' in the very year the cups were made (1615). The Mercers' crest – the Virgin Mary couped at the shoulders – appears again as finial on a set of twelve unusual maidenhead spoons, hall-marked 1630, the year when John Bancks was Master of the Company and the year of his death. These John Bancks commissioned from Robert Jygges.

Twelve rare slip-end spoons the Governors actually purchased themselves. Ten were made by William Cary in 1640; the other two (as replacements for spoons lost or stolen?) by Lawrence Coles some fifty years later.

The Hospital's wine cups are beautiful in their simplicity. One, the gift of Thomas Cleave, is dated 1617, and a set of three Bancks cups bear the hall-mark for 1630.

A fine silver-gilt chalice (1662) with a gilt cover was within living-memory still in use in the Horsham Chapel.

In 1640 Rowland Willson presented two handsome tankards, hall-marked a year earlier; a third tankard (1667) was the gift of Thomas Barns. A charming sweetmeat dish of 1654 by Arthur Manwaring makes an excellent contrast with the severe lines of the tankards.

'Out of love and affection' John Johnson gave to the Hospital a superb and rare pair of fluted Doric Column candlesticks (1680) – maker's mark TD in monogram.

The Christ's Hospital Mace, which is carried somewhat casually at the head of the procession of Governors on Speech Days, has been surprisingly overlooked in earlier published accounts of C.H. treasures. Yet it is among the most important of the Hospital's possessions. It was made in 1704 and the original design, unfortunately unsigned, was discovered only recently in the Department of Prints and Drawings at the Victoria and Albert Museum.

In the collection, and of the pieces that survive, there is after the Mace a gap of almost half-a-century. In 1756 James St. Amand, a generous benefactor of C.H. (and he of the eccentric will which gave to the Governors Hoskins' miniature and their dutiful annual rite) presented several pieces, the most interesting a silver-gilt salver and porringer (1686 and 1687) by Robert Smythier, a pair of candlesticks (1697) by Anthony Nelme and a set of three fine 'light-house' castors (1699) also by Nelme.

A century and a little more earlier ewers and basins had become sideboard pieces. The C.H. silver helmet ewer of 1638 does not match the silver-gilt basin of the next year but both bear the armorials of the Haberdashers of which Company the donor, Thomas Cleave, was a liveryman.

Another silver-gilt ewer of a much later date (1810) is the work of Paul Storr. Its design is based on a Greek wine-jug but, unfortunately, later embossing, profuse and incongruous, has almost obliterated its neo-classical lines.

The nineteenth century brought rich additions to the collection. In 1826 Dr. A. W. Trollope, who as a schoolboy at C.H. had been a contemporary of Coleridge and Lamb, gave a campana shaped cup (1826), maker Benjamin Smith, to mark his retirement as Upper Grammar Master.

1840 brought the only rococo piece, a salver made almost a hundred years earlier, in 1743, by Robert Abercromby, as well as a neo-classical silver-gilt cup and cover of 1775, the work of John Denziloe.

In 1841 Thomas Weeding presented a silver-gilt alms dish bearing the maker's mark of J. E. Terry and Co and in the next year his gift was matched by John Alliston.

An Old Blue, the former Rector of St. Giles Without Cripplegate bequeathed two salvers presented to him by his parishioners, both by William Ker Reid (1832 and 1834).

When in 1845 Queen Victoria and Prince Albert attended a Public Supping the occasion was commemorated by Thomas Wilby who, well-prepared for the event, had commissioned from E. Barnard and Sons a silver-gilt cup and cover (1844). From the cover a statuette of the Founder King gazes down at the cup-handles, fashioned in the form of C.H. boys.

There are other and fine pieces in the collection,

some of more recent date, and several association-items in the possession, not of the Hospital itself but of Common Room and the Amicable Society of Blues, but it could be appropriate to end this necessarily cursory account of C.H. silver with a reference to one item which, though it carries the strongest of C.H. associations and has been a cherished possession of some privileged Old Blues, is not owned by the Hospital or by any Housey organisation.

When, in 1875, the Governors thought to celebrate the centenary of the birth of one of the greatest sons of this House, Charles Lamb, they decided to institute an annual medal-competition for the best English essay by a boy. Inspired maybe by the high quality of the silver in their hands they turned to one of the finest medal-designers of the time, A. B. Wyon, and he reponded with a design of rare elegance and, for that age, of rare simplicity.

Once a year for more than 60 years a delighted and generally amazed Grecian carried home this handsome silver medal as reward for an essay written, originally pseudonymously on a topic unseen until he entered the examination-room, and judged outside the School, often by a distinguished author.

The Medal, but not the Prize, was discontinued in the austere years of the Second World War. The incumbent Head Master hopes to revive it. Sentiment must urge that his ambition be satisfied but, as he looks smugly at the Charles Lamb Medal that is his, the author of these lines who is by now almost the only surviving owner by right of competition, cannot resist the nasty wish that he be allowed to remain just one cub in a pride of 65 eminent literary lions, among his predecessors Sir Richard Lodge, Sir Cyril Burt, Edmund Blunden; almost his only successor Keith Douglas.

It is, indeed, as wrote another in that pride, Middleton Murry, 'A beautiful thing, one of Wyon's completely satisfying designs', on one side a superb profile of Elia and on the other an engraving of the C.H. crest.

And, hefting the weighty silver in his hands, that same author takes on his newer role as Almoner and rationalises his selfishness by considering the state of C.H. finances.

CHAPTER SIX

The Scheme and the Exodus

Though for most of its history Christ's Hospital had justified its royal lineage and though its Governors had in almost every generation maintained its high traditions and charitable purpose by scrupulous administration, it could not escape entirely the consequences of early nineteenth century reforming zeal. The Industrial Revolution, the enlarged franchise and, among the population at large, a growing sense that no preserve could any longer be considered entirely private, encouraged politicians to launch a series of public inquiries. For Christ's Hospital this tendency reached culmination in 1837 with the appointment of a commission to investigate charities.

That part of the Commissioners' work which concerned the Hospital was published in 1840.

The Report took up more than 300 printed pages and, if it achieved little else, it is as thorough a history of the Hospital, of its administration, as any previously produced and also a detailed account of the Hospital as it was when the Commissioners were at work. There are contained in it tables of the number of children educated in C.H., and of the number at various times in its past. All the Masters and others are named, with their salaries. There is a rent-roll of the Hospital's properties and a remarkably complete list of all benefactions ever received, each one annotated with the terms of the trust involved.

Some 30 pages of the Report cover the long history of Governorships and contained within them there is the fullest account available from any source of antique disputes between the Hospital and the City Corporation over the Corporation's claim to the right of appointing Governors. That this claim had been accepted as supererogatory even by the Corporation as early as 1700 and that, after one more attempt to assert supreme authority, the issue had been settled in favour of the Governors by an Act of Parliament passed in 1782 which left the City only the formality of the St. Matthew's Day confirmation of elections does not appear to have deterred the Commissioners from spending much time and much paper on an obsolete issue.

Of more immediate relevance and so of greater eventual significance was the attention paid to the continuing dispute between Governors in general and the inner circle, the "Committee Governors" who were accused of taking all decisions to themselves, of providing for the children of the Hospital education that was unsatisfactory, and of denying to the Governors at large access to minute-books and accounts.

Before ever the Commissioners sat one Governor, a Mr. Tarbutt, had enshrined these complaints in a petition to Parliament and had asked for an inquiry. Parliament refused his request and the Committee Governors had their own way of dealing with Mr. Tarbutt. A sub-committee of the Court conducted its own investigation and commented that his petition had "assured as true, statements which were unknown to the Court; which, if true, deserved to be corrected, and, if untrue, deserved the severest reprobation". Mr. Tarbutt could not justify his allegations. He was, therefore, "excluded from the Hospital" and, though he attempted to avoid his consequent dismissal from a Governorship by offering in writing an apology for his conduct and a promise not to offend again, the Court refused to accept it.

Initially the 1837 Commissioners were not satisfied but, having looked they reported:

It seems also to have been surmised that the Committee have consulted their individual private interests in dispensing the Hospital's revenues; that they have voted money to members of their own body; also that some of them, or their partners, were employed directly or indirectly in supplying articles to, or performing work for, the Hospital. But of these allegations, the two former were at once satisfactorily answered; and, as to the latter, it appears that of the articles for the Hospital consumption the account-books are the only one which is purchased from a Governor.

So far as Christ's Hospital was concerned nothing

came of this Inquiry except the voluminous Report but two decades later Government turned its attention from charities to the Endowed Schools and it was the Reports of the Commissioners appointed for this purpose in 1858, 1861 and 1867 which led to the Endowed Schools Act of 1869 and thus the Scheme for Christ's Hospital, prepared by the Charity Commission.

The Act empowered the Commission to make provision for such schemes

> as may be conducive to the advancement of the education of boys and girls, to alter and add to any existing trust and to make new trusts, directions and provisions which affect such endowment and the education promoted thereby.

It also allowed the reform of governing bodies.

Thus much was general and applied to all endowed schools but the Report of the 1864 Commission included some firm comments, and one seemingly sensational recommendation, which were to carry great weight with the Charity Commissioners and which would have remarkable consequences for the future of C.H.

"We have thought it advisable", wrote the Commissioners, "to report specially on a few Schools of unusual magnitude and importance" and to this end they had inspected "eight of the Largest Endowments", Christ's Hospital first among the eight.

> We have written freely, venturing to point out what we ourselves believe would be the best arrangements for their regulation. Nor do we deny that the whole of our recommendations have a practical object, and we should wish them to receive immediate consideration from those in authority. Mr. Fearon [one of the Commissioners to whom Christ's Hospital was allotted] has found much.

He calls for amendment in the methods and practice of the school's teaching; much that is unsatisfactory in its results. But the most practical suggestion with which he concludes is that the school should be almost wholly removed from its present site, and revolutionized in character, being transformed into five large boarding and day schools, within a large area round London – is one which in substance others have made before him, and which does not, in fact, depend on the success or failure of the present system of instruction in the school.

> It would be perfectly possible, and it ought not to be a matter of much time or difficulty, to remedy every one of the defects of which Mr. Fearon speaks. The question would still remain, Is it the best possible application of a net income of £40,000 or £50,000 to have a large middle-class boarding school in the heart of London?

Their answer to their own questions was a clear negative. They were not prepared to recommend that the funds of the Hospital be used to provide large day schools in London, and they gave their reasons in terms so sympathetic that, as they relate to C.H. in particular, they have been repeated over and over again by many authors – (including the authors of this book), and, as they relate to education in general might well be rehearsed daily before the legislators and dogmatists of the latter part of the next century:

> In the first place, admission to Christ's Hospital has never been confined to London, and the school cannot be considered as the exclusive property of the metropolis. The Londoners may fairly claim a share, and we shall presently recommend the assignment to them of a very substantial share in this splendid endowment. But we cannot consider that a school which has hitherto been open to the whole of England, ought now to be practically confined to a single section of Your Majesty's subjects, even though that section consists of the inhabitants of the capital City.

> To this it may be added that some consideration seems to be justly due to the past history of so remarkable a school, and to the attachment which it has inspired in the hearts of many of its scholars. Christ's Hospital is a thing without parallel in the country, and *sui generis*. It is a grand relic of the mediaeval spirit; a monument of the profuse munificence of that spirit, and of that constant stream of individual beneficence which is so often found to flow around institutions of that character. It has kept up its main features, its traditions, its antique ceremonies, almost unchanged for a period of upwards of three centuries. It has a long and goodly list of worthies. It is quite as strong as Eton or Winchester in the affection of those who have been brought up in the school. And, whatever educational faults there may be in it, that affection is at least well earned by the admirable care and unstinted liberality bestowed on the nurture of the children (extending to an unlimited supply, as may be required, of the smallest articles of extra clothing); the result of which is shown in their singular enjoyment of good health, of which there is irrefragable evidence, and which we think must be more due to that peculiar care than to any other cause.

> Further, it may be observed, the one good thing that results from the present unsystematic state of education in this country is great variety of type. . . There is something consonant to our character in allowing all kinds of excellence a fair field to show themselves; and in this way much true energy, that would be repressed and perhaps killed in a more uniform system, gets fair play. The most stringent measures for improving the teaching in Christ's

Hospital would be quite consistent with retaining all that is really characteristic in the Institution.

The Commissioners then made proposals: abolish the Hertford school and use the money thus saved to establish day schools in London (this in addition to the boarding-schools on a new rural site), changes in educational practices, reform of the Governing Body. Out would go Donation Governorships and instead of Presentations all scholars would be selected from the Board schools of England and Wales by competitive examinations taken at 13 years of age. They proposed also the abolition of what the Head Master of the time called "the state of acephalous anarchy" which gave him no authority over the boys outside the school-room.

Perhaps the most important of all, they asked for the removal of "the striking injustice by which the claim of girls to participate is admitted, but the number to whom the advantages are extended is deliberately reduced to a minimum – eighteen girls against 1,192 boys".

Many of these proposals were impracticable and, though the Endowed Schools Act was passed in 1869, again nothing was immediately enforced upon Christ's Hospital. But the seed was sown which germinated for several decades and which blossomed eventually in the fields of West Horsham. And from the Taunton Report came the inspiration which made C.H. into a great school for girls.

Nine years later the Hospital was again subjected to Governmental scrutiny. The immediate cause was the suicide, on 4th May 1877 of a 12 years old Blue, William Gibbs. The outcry that followed forced the Home Secretary to set up a Commission of Inquiry to investigate "as well into the circumstances under which such suicide took place as into the discipline and management of the said school".

The Commissioners were a formidable group; the Rt. Hon. Spencer Walpole, MP as Chairman, the Rt. Hon. Russell Gurney, MP and Recorder of the City of London, Rt. Hon W. E. Forster, MP, architect of the greatest educational reforms of the century, the Very Rev. H. G. Liddell, the father of Alice, and Dean of Christ Church, and John Walter, MP of *The Times;* and they worked swifly and diligently. Their first meeting was held at the School on 9th July, they met nine times inthe next two weeks, and had their Report ready for the Home Secretary on 10th August.

Perhaps surprisingly, the Commissioners found that in the affair of Gibbs' suicide they could attach no fault to the Hospital authorities or to the monitors but on the more general issue of administration and discipline their criticism was vigorous and their recommendations shrewd.

Many of Christ's Hospital's peculiar difficulties, they commented, stemmed from the ambiguous status of the Head Master and henceforth, they suggested, he must be Head overall (with the Warden as subordinate). To him must be given the entire right to appoint and dismiss masters and to these masters allotted duties of ward supervision – and Grecians at last brought into the disciplinary process, as monitors in place of senior boys (not Grecians) who had previously exercised such functions. The intimate responsibility of the Treasurer should cease and his office be transformed into something only a little more grand than that filled by the Chairman of Governors of any other school.

Most potent of all their recommendations was the re-iteration of the proposal that the school must move from the City. It was by now a hoary proposal; even the Governors had considered it in 1870, and had rejected it only by a narrow margin. But one voice was always raised against it and he, the President, the Duke of Cambridge, could out-shout anyone.

Even the Commissioners were hesitant:

We should not enter on this subject were it not that some of our most capable witnesses consider that such removal bears strongly upon the matters into which we are directed to enquire. It has been pressed upon us by eminent authorities to whom we especially refer, Mr. Bell and Dr. Haig-Brown [both Old Blues, Headmasters respectively of Marlborough and Charterhouse, and Bell formerly Head Master of C.H.], that this removal is absolutely necessary in order to enable the Head Master, with his staff of assistant Masters, to exercise control over the boys which is so advantageously exercised in all other large schools. . . We feel a great unwillingness to aid in destroying the ancient traditions and venerable memories of the place. But these associations may be too dearly purchased, and for a thorough reform in the management and discipline of the school, we think that the removal from London is indispensable.

The exodus was now virtually certain and when, in 1881, Charity Commissioners took a hand and published their first draft Scheme for the administration of Christ's Hospital, they too insisted on removal in terms that were irrefutable. Only slightly amended they appeared again in the Scheme that was admitted 10 years later. "The Hospital Schools shall be maintained within a convenient distance of London."

It was not this fiat which aroused the fighting spirit of the Governors. Indeed, many welcomed it as an excuse to get their own way against H.R.H. the President. They objected to the instruction that Donation Governors be abolished and, after a brief enforced retreat, won that battle, but in truth they resented above all the peremptoriness and, as they saw it, the Commissioners' bewildered incomprehension in the face of all evidence about the traditions and purposes of C.H.

For nine years the Governors fought against the Scheme. At that moment when the draft was published, Christ's Hospital resisted objections. The Charity Commissioners, they averred, had no authority to use the Endowed Schools Act as basis for altering Christ's Hospital for the Foundation was much more than an educational institution.

Back came the Commissioners. In order that this objection might be fully considered the Hospital must submit a detailed statement giving a precise account of every endowment, donation or legacy for which exception was claimed, indicating its origin and the present form of investment. An Assistant Commissioner was appointed to pursue inquiries with the Office.

For four years this work proceeded. Two years later the Charity Commissioners produced a second draft Scheme.

This time the Education Committee accepted the Scheme, but not the Governors as a whole. Instead they appealed to the Privy Council to reject the Scheme, on the old grounds that it was not drawn in conformity with the provisions of the Act and could not so be derised because it purported to deal with the general properties and resources of the Hospital as if they were exclusively educational endowments, and with special endowments, such as those connected with the Royal Mathematical School, with advowsons and rights of preferent to livings which were outwith the prerogatives of the Charity Commissioners. Further, argued the Governors, the Charity Commissioners had no authority to direct the use of benefactions received fifty years before the passage of the Act, or with endowments received since the Act received the Royal Assent. And the Governors pleaded to have the Scheme ruled erroneous in its construction of the "Conscience Clause" for it was not the intention of the Act to require of any Governing Body that it exempt those in its charge from the duty to attend prayers or religious worship.

A formidable array of Counsel appeared before the Lord Chancellor ruled that all the causes for appeal save one be rejected. The Commissioners were right in treating the general endowments of the Hospital as broadly educational within the meaning of the Act, and that all endowments spent on improving or maintaining property could not be removed from the Scheme. In this, however, the Scheme was erroneous: the Charity Commissioners could not present endowments received within 50 years before the Act or since its passage, and they had no authority to make regulations about religious education.

Nothing more was to be said and it could be because the Lord Chancellor emphasised a view (not shared by all the Charity Commissioners) that the Scheme paid regard that was not illusory but substantial, to the rights of Donation Governors, nothing more was said even by the most obstinate members of the Council.

The Scheme as finally drawn – with the objectionable religious condition withdrawn – received Queen Victoria's Royal Assent and came into force on 1st January 1891.

Inter alia it directed that:

as soon as conveniently may be after the date of the Scheme, the Council of Almoners shall provide for the School, upon convenient sites, buildings suitable, in the case of the Boys' School for 700 boarders, in the case of the Girls' School for 350 boarders, in the case of the Preparatory School for 120 boarders.

The emphatic and definitive nature of these prescriptions was inescapable and all was made even more peremptory by the Conditions that were added. The schools as re-constructed were "to be maintained within a convenient distance from the City of London" and those buildings hitherto used for the Boys' School could be maintained for the purposes set out under the Scheme until other suitable accommodation was found – but no longer.

The threat was close to being explicit. Make haste – or else! But the wording was far from explicit. What was "a convenient distance"? The debate – what came to be called "The Christs's Hospital Controversy" – raged in the Press, among Old Blues everywhere, and most vigorously on the Council where this and the excitement of exploring for suitable sites put to flight all feelings of resentment for the rebuff the Almoners had received.

However, one individual from outside the Council, Sir Henry Peek, became the most vocal protagonist. He was in no doubt about the conditions that must be observed in choosing a site. It must be:

in easy range from London so that the home and social life of the children may be continued by the periodic visits of parents. . . It need not be pointed out how vitally and enlightening a feature in education is the maintenance of and cultivation of social and family intercourse.

This was a view of one aspect of boarding-school life which was not generally acceptable to the Victorians nor yet to their successors for half-a-century, though to-day when reading Sir Henry's statement of principle one might take him for an advanced thinker, were it not that his true motives are now clear. He knew the exact location where his precept could be made manifest. There it was, and available, in Wimbledon, and here were other good reasons for selecting it:

The railway journey would occupy less than twenty minutes. (Mr. Fawcett, the late

71

Below: The Rev George Charles Bell,
Headmaster 1868-76.

Right: The Rev Richard Lee, Headmaster 1876-
1901.

Postmaster-General, was often seen walking both ways). . . With regard to the supply of provisions, vans and carts from the best markets begin unloading before 9.00 a.m. . . As the Scheme provides a royal re-foundation, it is important that the site should be within easy reach of Her Majesty and the Princesses, who, it is understood, take a special interest in the operation of the Scheme, which provides permanently for the training of 750 [sic] girls.

All very convincing and the more so because the one hundred acre site at Wimbledon could be bought at ''the same price per acre as that which the Mercer's Company paid for low-lying back land at Hammersmith where the new St. Paul's School has been erected''. Convincing? Yes, especially as the prospective vendor was Sir Henry Peek.

This ingenious piece of special pleading was summarily dismissed by the Council and after-knowledge must lead all beneficiaries of their disdain for a notable example of chicanery to bless them also for their foresight. Fifty years later, St. Paul's, though a day-school, was forced to seek a more commodious site.

The Council had plans more ambitious. In May, 1892, the Chairman of an Old Blues dinner, himself a member of the Governing Body, admitted that he had been to view two sites, one in Hertfordshire, one in Sussex, both over a thousand acres; and an official statement was published a month later that the Council, after considering over a hundred different properties, and personally inspecting many of them, had decided to purchase the estate of the Aylesbury Dairy Company, near Horsham, for a site for the new boarding schools.

Hands were held up in horror at the enormity of the idea.

The endeavour to take, as it were, a pre-eminent position as a public school by the costly and useless possession of a site of 1000 acres is entirely unjustifiable on every ground. . . An area of a half or a third of the extent secured is shown by the experience of our great public schools to be quite adequate for effective use, even having regard to a wide margin of extension in the range of the institution.

And again:

Destroy the metropolitan character of the foundation on account of its distance from London.

It would inflict hardships on the relations of the children:

A cruel matter for the working classes generally were they called upon to give up half a day, and spend far more shillings that can easily be afforded, every time a child is visited.

Such were the jeremiads fed to the newspapers by (mostly) anonymous writers. Some of the objections were immediately stifled by the announcement that the London, Brighton and South Coast Railway had arranged to provide a new station close to the school and to issue cheap return tickets to visitors at a half-crown fare; but others quickly took their place. The water-supply was unsatisfactory; there was no drainage; if the Aylesbury Dairy Company could not farm their cows at a profit, could it be a good site for boys?

Other voices stressed the effect of the Scheme on the finances of the Hospital, the total drying-up of one of the principal sources of revenue – the funds obtained from Governors – and the need of a large capital outlay in the near future. ''Such is the first great result of the Scheme'', said *The Times*, early in 1894:

It has created a financial crisis which must bring consternation into the mind of everyone who wishes well – and who does not? – to Christ's Hospital, and it has alienated, and it would seem alienated permanently, those who in the past showed themselves among the number of its warmest supporters.

and continuing its gloomy prognostications the same paper went on to say a day or two later:

Immediate measures are necessary to prevent the extinction of one of the noblest foundations which royal charity ever established in this country.

Meanwhile, on account of a serious outbreak of scarlet fever, the London school was closed from October, 1893, till the middle of the following year. G.A.T. Allan was one of those who received an unexpected nine months' holiday.

I recall the occasion with mixed feelings, but I must agree that no estimate can be formed of the hardship to individual boys and parents, nor of the effects of the dispersion on the work and efficiency of the school.

But the outcry still went gaily on. Complaints came not only from outsiders, but even from within. A meeting was called at the Mansion House, where the Duke of Cambridge – the fiery President who held office for fifty years – gave vent to most dismal forebodings.

I am one of those who are perfectly prepared to go with the spirit of the age in which we live, but I confess that I am also one of those who do not love change for change's sake. To upset an old and long-standing institution of principles perfectly unknown to any of those who have hitherto conducted such an institution is a very dangerous experiment to try. . . There was a decided principle laid down and nothing in it was to be modified. The consequence is that we must accept the inevitable, and must do the best under this new principle, and it is for you, not for me, to say whether the principle has been successful. To tell you the honest truth, as President, without attacking any one, which I do not desire to do, I cannot for the life of me see how we are not to end in absolute ruin. I do not see where any modification is to come from, unless some thing is changed and directed into another groove. We are called upon to leave London. I confess that I always thought it a great mistake to leave London. I will tell you why I thought so. First, we had the most magnificent premises; in the next place, our boys were healthier than the boys of any other public school in the country; and in the third place, and most important of all I think, in the interests of this charity – the boys were seen by this great community of London. That community wished them well and were always ready to help the boys, and the boys, I am happy to say, always turned out with credit to themselves and honour to the institution. Therefore, I say, why on earth change all this?

The Mansion House meeting had a good press. The papers, which only a short time previously had been avid in their comments about the administration of the Hospital and loud in their demand for a public inquiry, now turned upon the Schools a loving eye and unanimously insisted that there must be a public inquiry to establish how it had come about that this noble institution was to be exiled from London. The *Daily Telegraph*, for example:

Ruin is an extremely unpleasant word to be compelled to use in connexion with any magnificent and historical institution such as this has been for many years; and if an unfortunate attempt to live up to the times, or rather, perhaps, a love of change for its own sake, has brought us within appreciable distance of a catastrophe, the community at large has a perfect right to know how this has come about, and whom to hold responsible for the issue.

So it went on, but there were some, better qualified than any journalist and less artfully involved than Sir Henry Peek, who were not prepared to accept the popular view that the Scheme and the move to Horsham spelt the end of Christ's Hospital's great tradition. On the very day when one newspaper reported Sir Henry's bland – and, from his vantage point, perversely optimistic – opinion that the planting

of the School at Horsham would never become an accomplished fact, G. C. Bell raised his loyal, authoritative voice in the columns of *The Times:*

I am sanguine to hope and believe that, if Christ's Hospital is developed on a new site according to the provisions of the Scheme, drawing into its class-rooms the pick of the elementary schools of London, and of the Endowed Schools of the Kingdom, its future reputation will be such that Blues will find a better welcome than ever in the public services and in professional and commercial life.

Sir Henry, for one, refused to be silenced. He bombarded the Press with letters and offered interviews to any journalist who might be prepared to take up the cause he favoured, and at last Bell was goaded into revealing to the world what that cause really was – and in that process proved himself true heir to Cassandra. Again in *The Times* he wrote:

Even if the owner would make a free gift of the Wimbledon estate to Christ's Hospital, it could not be used as a site for the new boarding schools. Wimbledon is a suburb of London, included in the suburban directory; it has a population of at least 14,000, rapidly growing; in a few years, or a few decades, it will have been absorbed by the appalling growth of London. The new boarding schools of Christ's Hospital must be placed on a site absolutely free from such risk of absorption into London.

Sir Henry and his supporters were now reduced to blustering, and bluster they did. Even *The Times*, in its editorial policy, usually so moderate and perpicacious about the Hospital, fired one last desperate shot at those who had settled for the move:

By the proposed migration from London so much of the old character of the schools must be destroyed that it would perhaps be an anachronism to preserve the rest; and we must reconcile ourselves to see the distinctive characteristics of Christ's Hospital effaced, if not soon, at least in the near future.

But the Council had decided. Throughout the Controversy, when the atmosphere was highly-charged, a majority among the Almoners had ridden out the difficulties in a manner remarkable alike for its determination and for its wisdom. In the face of an opposition that must have crushed weaker or more narrow-minded men they had shown fixity of purpose. The verdict of posterity is unanimous: there were also prudent and far-sighted men to whom all succeeding generations owe a great debt. The ''distinctive characteristics'' of Christ's Hospital have not been effaced and even now, when times are difficult, the Hospital is still a long, long way from ruin.

The acceptance, however, of the verdict that the School must leave Newgate Street (which was, after all, in tune with the long-held conviction of many Governors) did not carry with it easy acceptance of all that the scheme might involve. The Governors could still fight.

There were, for example, those endowments which the Scheme could not touch – those received within 50 years before and since the passage of the Act. For these the Governors were Trustees and the Lord Chancellor had ruled that, even of these endowments, such as had been destined for educational purposes must be used for those purposes and those alone. But he had not insisted that they must of necessity be dedicated to the furtherance of the Scheme. When the Charity Commissioners tried to lay their hands on these excepted endowments the Governors took up arms once more and this time, in a suit in Chancery, they won the day. In consequence, had they so wished, the Council could have established a rival Christ's Hospital and we might have had the situation, which indeed arose at some other endowed schools, of the Governors carrying on two entirely disparate schools, perhaps even two with the same name, both descended from the same parent stock, and yet each conducted according to a very different educational and administrative formula. Instead of adopting this alternative the Council chose to exercise its limited advantage to substantial effect. Far-sighted and possessed of the cunning of the serpent, they offered the excepted endowments as bargaining-counter. These endowments would be paid over to the Council of Almoners for use in the implementation of the Scheme provided Donation Governors received in return most of the rights of presentation of which they had been deprived by the Scheme of the Charity Commissioners. The deal was sanctioned by the Court of the Chancery and, despite gloomy forebodings, there has never since been any shortage of individuals or institutions willing and eager to take up Donation Governorships.

Planning for the move was scrupulous but rapid. In the light of events destined to take place almost a century later it is interesting to note that for a while – a very brief while – it was contemplated that the girls, too, would be moved to Horsham, though none involved so much as mentioned the shameful word co-education. The estate in Sussex was so spacious that there would be room for an extensive *cordon sanitaire* between the Girls' School, up near Sharpenhurst at its farthest south-western extremity, and the Boys' School.

But the girls were left at Hertford and the Council of Almoners selected half-a-dozen leading architects, considered their proposals, and chose the plans submitted by Aston Webb and Ingress Bell.

It was the turn of the Charity Commissioners to consider the drawings and Christ's Hospital owes to them a great debt for this (as for many subsequent favours) as they removed much of the ornamentation and "artistic embellishment" which the distinguished Victorian architects had thought essential.

By Founders' Day (23rd October) 1896, sufficient progress had been made for the foundation-stone to be laid, with full masonic rites, by the Prince of Wales on behalf of Queen Victoria. Special trains carried the whole School, boys and girls, staff and all the guests to West Horsham, where detrainment took place at a siding erected for the occasion. Marquees had been erected for the ceremony and for lunch, given to all, but these temporary structures were all that was visible in the wind-swept waste of sticky clay. But none who attended ever forgot the bleakness and bitter cold of that day and at the time there were many who were tempted to agree with the Hospital's consultant engineer. This Horsham site, he had said, could not in any circumstances be made suitable for a large school.

CHAPTER SEVEN

Horsham

When first this book was published the exodus to Horsham was a recollection still vivid in the minds of middle-aged men. Some who had passed all their school-days in Newgate Street were not yet far beyond their fiftieth birthday, many who, in 1902, had made the move from the City to rural Sussex were, in 1937, only in their mid-forties. The last of that generation of masters who, with Upcott as their Head, had opened the new epoch had only just retired. Now, almost a half-century on, there are left only one or two very old Old Blues who remember Newgate Street and all of the staff who succeeded to Upcott's young men have themselves retired. Nevertheless, even for those Old Blues and young Blues to whom the events of 1902 seem as distant as the signing of the original Charter or the establishment of the Royal Mathematical School, the move holds its place as one of the seismic adventures in C.H. history, its circumstances and its consequences as proof, if proof be needed, that the Hospital is always ready for change and, as C.H. comes close to another revolution, a powerful support to the confident assertion that, whatsoever amendments may be wrought in the structure of the Hospital, its spirit remains immutable.

When Moses stood on Pisgah's height [wrote G.A.T. Allan in 1937] his view of the landscape was a harmony of milk and honey; to the early climber of Sharpenhurst hill the prospect of the proposed land was a discord of natural green and artificial red, the arresting brilliant red of new bricks.

Already when in 1937 the original version of the book was published, Allan remarked that 'time had laid its kindly mellowing hand' on the Horsham site. To-day C.H. has settled into harmony with its surroundings, the Sussex Weald has become the School's natural background and a latter-day observer (either from Sharpenhurst or, better still, from the top of the Water Tower) feels no shame for a scar inflicted on a gentle landscape but rather a sense of gratitude for the vision of his predecessors which settled this huge complex so comfortably in green fields midway between the North and South Downs, and of admiration for the generosity of their design which rejected all meagreness of concept or aspiration and which conferred upon successor generations magnificent and virtually unrestricted possibilities for expansion.

The exodus was much more than a move from London to West Horsham, from the inevitably restrictive setting in the heart of the City to the freedom and expansiveness of bucolic Sussex; with it came changes, some subtle, some obvious, but all substantial in the life and organisation of the School. It follows, therefore, that the contribution made to the continuing success of C.H. by those – masters, administrators, estate staff and boys – who were Horsham pioneers merits particular attention.

The School assembled in its new home for the first time on 29th May, 1902. The organisation – one of the details of life for which Christ's Hospital is, or should be noted – was as nearly perfect as it could be. The school had arrived in a carefully graduated series of intervals: the Steward and kitchen hands first, Matrons and domestics next, then Masters, then at last the boys. But there was much finding of ways to Houses, class-rooms, and playing-fields, acquaintances to be made; time-tables to study; and fresh notions to be learnt.

If for no more than for his choice of staff – and some, but not all, would say for much more – Upcott ranks among the great Head Masters. Of the forty-odd masters (the adjective applies to their number not to their character) who opened Horsham, half came with the School from Newgate Street and half were newcomers. Upcott did not have entire discretion in the selection of survivors (though it does appear to have been in part his fault that Collingwood Banks, an Old Blue, a fine musician and composer of the *Votum*, was dismissed into obscurity) but his was the unique task of finding new men, keen and adventurous, who would nevertheless meld their efforts with the guardians of Newgate Street methods and traditions.

In this arduous process his achievement was superb, and the result abundantly successful. He picked few lambs but his young tigers lay down with his predecessor's aging lions and, on those rare occasions when there was friction in the den, Upcott bore it – or bore down upon it – with alacrity if not always with equanimity.

Glory be to him and to his pioneers. Their's was no simple role but they carried it superbly. And so too did those who were exiled from Newgate Street, though some of what was now demanded of them was shocking and all novel.

In London there had been no house-mastering. At 4.15p.m. on each working-day off went the teaching-staff, to return again at 9.15 the next morning. They concerned themselves not at all with the life of the boys outside the class-room and their own private lives meant nothing to the boys. Perhaps they had wives and families; if so, the boys neither knew nor cared. Humans they might be; if so, the boys neither knew nor cared. But at Horsham they lived their whole lives subject to ever-curious inspection by adolescents and they were responsible for every boy for every hour of his day, for his recreations, his spiritual well-being, his physical state and also (as they had always been) for his academic progress. These men, many of them already for a life-time Cockneys, had to make themselves into rustics, to amend their habits from those of suburban journeymen (what would now be called commuters) into the modes of resident full-timers. And these were the very men – much more even than the newcomers – who had to sustain the sense of continuity, to uphold the best traditions of C.H., to change the School while keeping it the same as it always had been, these the men – as the schoolmen would say – who held the responsibility for altering the accidents without affecting the essence.

The boys, no less, of that sensational epoch were subject to metamorphosis in this passage from chrysalis to *imago*. Walking the streets of London their greatest excitement had been a meeting with a "Bob Gent" who pressed a shilling into an eager palm with the murmured benediction 'in memory of Charles Lamb', their greatest interest shop-window gazing. In Sussex there were new delights, wild flowers, streams, woods and all the bustle of a rich agricultural countryside. The new Christ's Hospital, wrote Blunden,

> is fortunate in its neighbourhood. It lies in the lowland yet with near variety of wood and hill, its further prospects of heights and blue horizons.

Here the country-bred boy – the Coleridges in each school generation – who in London had been out of place and an anachronism, at last had the better of his sharp, town-bred contemporaries – the Charles Lambs who have always made the majority at Housie ("These are thy pleasures, O London, with thy many sins. For this may Keswick and her giant brood go hang!") But soon, by its immediate magic and with the aid of a determined staff, Sussex became part of the heritage of every Housey boy. ("The chiming name of Chanctonbury was ever with us, and the ring often beckoned us southwards".) And yet, for all the gloomy soothsayings, the City of London remained, as surely as it was ever an integral part of the C.H. ethos.

Christ's Hospital, Horsham as it is to-day is much altered from the School that was first occupied on that summer day in 1902. Developments in the curriculum, changes in social patterns, both within C.H. and in society at large, benefactions and even ephemeral shifts in fashion: all have been responsible for new buildings or for alterations to those constructed according to the original plan. Since 1902 C.H. has added a Manual School (now re-named with latter-day refinement, the Craft and Design School), a New Science School (bigger even than the first, which as might be expected of the school which pioneered Science teaching, was itself the largest and best in the country), a second library, a headquarters for the Scouts, a Grecians Club (with its own bar!), several masters' houses, a range of squash-courts and, most recently, a magnificent Arts Centre. Many of the Houses have been dramatically improved. The old Isolation Sanatorium has been converted into flats for the Infirmary nursing staff, the Tuck Shop has been enlarged – and altered three times, there has been built an extension to the Pavilion, a new block of class and assembly rooms (intended originally for the Preparatory School), a new study and additional offices for the Head Master, and the Geography School has been made into a Court Room which doubles as an extension to the Dining Hall. The challenge to the omnipotence of the two major sports, cricket in the summer and Rugby Football in the winter, is now made palpable by the proliferation of tennis courts, Association Football and hockey pitches and a cinder running-track.

Even so, were one of the pioneer Horsham Blues to return to the 1200 acres site he would find Christ's Hospital, Horsham still recognisable, its emphatic configuration virtually unaltered.

Let that lively ghost (or a curious visitor) come then, entering by the Main Gates (moved from Newgate Street) on the road from Horsham.

The Avenue runs roughly east to west, curving slightly north at its extremities. All the eight Blocks front the Avenue on the north side; facing them are the masters' houses and 'the Palace', the Head Master's house.

Past four Blocks and through the Eastern Archway: the physical and spiritual heart of the School, the Quadrangle, at its centre the statue of the Founder King and on its four sides, to the north Dining Hall, to the south Big School, to the west, Chapel and to the east, the old Science School. Along the Quad side of

Chapel and Science School run the Cloisters, off to the south-east corner, the Arts School and to the north-east the Libraries. Beyond the Libraries there is another quadrangle, with one side flanked by the Libraries, another by a classroom block, and to the east, the New Science School. The fourth, southern, side is as yet open to the Quarter-Mile and Big Side.

Administrators propose but boys dispose. In 1932 the Council decreed that the new quadrangle be named The Garden in affectionate recollection of a Newgate Street playground. Their fiat and the stone tablet in which it was enshrined arrived just one week after the Prince of Wales (later the Duke of Windsor) had landed his little red plane in a field just outside the Ring Fence (that distant landing-place chosen by him, it was said, from fear of the wrath of the head groundsman should he have committed the sacrilege of touching-down on a cricket-pitch) and had been driven in the Head Master's Delage to open the New Science School. 50 years later the quadrangle is still known by the name given to it in those seven days: the New Quad.

Class-rooms flank Big School, behind it stands the Arts Centre which incorporates the old Music School. The Infirmary is at the extreme east and behind Leigh Hunt (the old Preparatory School) the Grecians Club, the Craft and Design School, some fives and squash-courts and the Scouts Headquarters across Lamb Asphalt; behind the other Houses at the Eastern end of the Avenue, the Tuck Shop, more fives and squash-courts and the shooting range across Coleridge Asphalt behind the other Blocks at the west end.

The Centre Path to the north through the playing-fields of Little Side leads first to the Post Office and then on to the Swimming Bath, Gymnasium and Armoury, to the Laundry and School Farm and so on to Christ's Hospital Railway Station.

There was a time, and that not so long ago, when the Station was one of Christ's Hospital's jewels, a fine example of late Victorian railway architecture, with six platforms and much traffic. To this station from Victoria the Christ's Hospital Special brought the bulk of the School at the beginning of each term and among the most vivid of school-day memories which remain with older Old Blues is marching to the station through the dark of a winter morning on the first day of the Christmas holidays. To-day most parents even of C.H. boys own cars. This and general cuts in railway-services have reduced the significance of the Station to Christ's Hospital and to the system as a whole. The Station is now only a miserable halt.

Big Side, to the south beyond the Quarter-Mile and circled by the path known as the Mile, contains the Pavilion, the School's superb cricket-ground, which is said to be the envy of the Sussex County Club and the home-pitches of Housey Rugby teams. Beyond it, on the far, southern, side of the Mile is another small range of buildings, the Science Farm, which have lost through time and changed circumstances some of the importance which once they had in the life of the School.

Even in the past boys blessed with academic excellence seldom ventured into the Science Farm or its precincts once they had failed in their juvenile efforts to work an allotment. An Agricultural Grecian would have been an inconceivable contradiction in terms and even an Agricultural Deputy Grecian was a rarity and "going on the Farm", though occasionally the demonstration of a vocation, was generally regarded as the fate reserved for boys who could not be brought to modest scholarly achievement even by the most persistent and patient of masters. And "on the Farm" many approached adult success which has amazed the supercilious among their contemporaries.

There are around the site (which regrettably even C.H. has come to call a campus) other buildings that should be noted but, lest this description descend to listing, only one that will be remarked, and that the oldest and the only building within the estate which pre-dates the designs of the architect, Aston Webb. Stammerham lies outside the Ring Fence at the south-eastern extremity, a lovely, clap-boarded eighteenth century house. It was used originally by C.H. as residence for the Medical Officer; hence the name given to the lake it faces, the Doctor's Lake. A new house has been built for the Medical Officer and Stammerham has been converted into flats for masters, but this was once the home of Shelley's mother and thus – as also in the name of the copse to the west of the Ring Fence – C.H. holds its association with the greatest of Sussex poets, the patron and friend of its own Leigh Hunt.

There is one other feature of the Horsham buildings which is not noticed by the casual tourist, which has no aesthetic virtue or historical association but which is nevertheless shown-off with unhesitant pride by every boy who escorts a visitor round the site. The Tube – an underground passage – runs the whole length of the Avenue and has also extensions under all the buildings to the south and a longer passage-way under Little Side to the generating station. It is said that Aston Webb conceived this as a duct for electricity-, alarm- and telephone-cables and gave it width so that the maintenance-staff might have easy access. Certainly he had no thought that it would be used by the boys and had designed for them, for use when it rained, a cloister along the back of the houses. This cloister was excised by the Charity Commissioners as an unwarranted luxury, and it soon became customary for boys in more distant Houses to avoid the consequences of bad weather by way of the Tube. In the Thirties, side-spaces were added for use as drying-rooms.

There was at one time an illicit Tube Exploration Society and it must have been an active member who found his way under Chapel and thrust a lighted-candle through a grating in the aisle just as the School launched into the hymn 'Lead. Kindly light'.

This much for a cursory tour but, before embarking

upon a closer inspection of some aspects of Horsham life and its surroundings, it is appropriate that certain hitherto unconsidered trifles should be picked up for in such most often is proof of the continuity of C.H. tradition and demonstration of the manner by which it has been sustained even after the move from London.

Immediately in front of the Blocks, and running the whole length of the Avenue, there runs a path. Access to this, the Grecians' Path, is denied to all boys who do not have "their buttons". (The coincidence of terminology with the Royal Horse Artillery is particularly pleasing to one who has belonged to both élites.) There was a time (and it may still be so) when Grecians, (like Fellows of Oxford and Cambridge colleges) were the only boys privileged to walk across the grass in the Quad and also the only boys permitted to use the centre-doors into the Blocks. The legend persisted well into the thirties that this latter prerogative was originally denied even to Grecians and that, in the early days at Horsham, one such (and a supplementary legend had it that this one was none other than Cyril Burt) on being rebuked by his Housemaster for his breach of the rule, replied haughtily, "But I saw Mr. Smith passing that way and he is a mere usher.")

Whether this tale be myth or history it carries an implication of status that is genuine for there is about Grecians an *hauteur,* a sense and appearance of distinction from the commonalty that, though it is less remarked now that there are so many of them, is even now too potent to permit simplistic explanation by equating them with the Sixth Form of other schools.

The distinctive elegance of their uniforms – coats of "superior blue Kersey, soft breeches, fourteen large silver buttons, and velvet cuffs" – has already been noted. So too has been the comparatively recent acquisition of a Grecians' Club. But the uniform is but an outward expression of an inward reality and the Club little more than recognition, convenient to modern social notions, of an apartness that has always existed. Long before the Club opened, whereas it was for the rest of the School uncommon and, if by *lex non scripta,* generally forbidden to make close friendship beyond the sodality of one's own House, Grecians mixed freely with other Grecians – but not often with anyone else. First Parting Grecians (those leaving at the end of the year for the universities) lunched each day with the Head Master on the Dais in Hall (the High Table of Oxbridge colleges) and for other meals sat together, also on the Dais, eating food different from that given to the majority but similar to that served in the Senior Common Room. Even, they had cups and saucers instead of the "kiff-bowls" of the rest of the School and their tea or coffee came to them in pots, with sugar and milk served separately, whereas for the other boys, 'kiff', a nauseating concoction of tea, coffee or cocoa pre-mixed with milk and sugar, was poured into "kiff-bowls" from cans.

As the Grecians are peers of the realm so is the Senior Grecian Prime Minister and Lord Chancellor in one person, the *censor morum* and the Head Master's right hand. To this exposition of his stature the voice of experience must add the comment that, on those rare occasions when the differences arise between the two any sensible betting-man would know where to place his odds.

The emphatic superiority of Grecians may have been reduced somewhat in recent years but there is validity still in the Charles Lamb's comment, included in a letter to George Dyer, written only two years before Elia's death and 40 years after he left school.

I keep my rank in fancy still . . . I can never forget I was a deputy Grecian! And writing to you or to Coleridge, besides affection, I feel a reverential deference as to Grecians. I keep my soaring way above the Great Erasmians, yet far beneath the other.

And so, by way of a parenthesis that is not in truth an *excursus,* back to the nice trivialities of the guided tour.

The statue of Edward VI that, from the centre of the Quad, watches benevolently over the bustle of Housey life and over so many of its formal occasions, is supported by four figures of C.H. boys, four of the Hospital's very greatest, Coleridge, Middleton, Maine and Lamb (again, no Leigh Hunt!) dressed in the uniform that was their's before they came to greatness. The ignorant outsider who sculpted the figures gave to Lamb fourteen large buttons. This solecism the Council (some Almoners former Grecians and therefore indignant, others less glorious in their school-days but still respectful) hastened to have corrected.

There is yet another statue of the Founder, brought from London and in recent years handsomely dressed in gold paint. The boy king looks out above the Arts Centre across Big Side to the distant South Downs but there is no truth in the story that the monarch who established Protestantism in England has his back turned deliberately upon his 'dede of pittie' as a symbolic gesture of rejection, similar to that of Rousseau in Geneva; as token of his repugnance for the High Anglicanism which in the last decades has sometimes invaded the Christ's Hospital Chapel and as particular denial from this anti-papistual young scholar of the dubious and assuredly popish claim that the casket deposited in the smaller chapel at the eastern end of the Avenue contained the bones of his predecessor monarch, St. Edward the Martyr.

In the south wall of Dining Hall is set the Foundation Stone laid by the Prince of Wales (later King Edward VII) on behalf of Queen Victoria, and on either side the First World War Memorial with its tragically long list of names of Blues who died in that hideous war. (The names of those who died in the Second War, happily fewer but nonetheless a deep scar on the memory of their contemporaries, are listed in a Book of Honour.)

If that representative Blue of 1902 vintage were to join our tour for a closer inspection he would find the major buildings largely unaltered from that day when first he saw them.

The Dining Hall, which occupies the whole north side of the Quad was said to be, at the time of its construction, the largest building in Britain unsupported by internal pillars. For the first half-century or more it was commodious enough to seat at meal-time all 834 boys and, on the Dais, staff and distinguished visitors. Then, either because C.H. food is so substantial or, more likely, because boys everywhere have outgrown their precursors, it was found necessary to overflow into the Court Room, but the most obvious change visible to the tourist Old Blue from 1902 (or even from 1967) is that the long tables, one to each House, have gone and in their place are small tables, grouped as if in some gigantic roadside café.

Verrio's huge painting still dominates Hall, and there is also, as there was in the beginning (and, before the beginning, in Newgate Street) the portrait of a young and mettlesome Queen Victoria, seemingly unable or unwilling to restrain her spirited charger, and another, inevitably more sedate, of her Consort standing by the side of an inevitably well-disciplined horse. Time has added several portraits or twentieth century Treasurers and Head Masters and in the process has added very little of artistic distinction, but here in Dining Hall there is another gem, a delicious small portrait of Edward VI.

Sadly neither the original author of this book nor his *post-mortem* collaborator has been able to establish the provenance of the finest of all the artefacts in Dining Hall, the exquisitely-carved dark oak pulpit. It is by some attributed to the master of all English wood-carvers, Grinling Gibbons, but authorities on his work insist that he never worked in hard woods. Others claim that it is not English at all but the product of a foreign craftsman. Undoubtedly it has been Christ's Hospital property for several centuries but whether it came to the Foundation from a City church or as a prime bequest none can now tell.

Yet, also certainly, for many, many years before and after every meal, the School having been silenced by a knock from the Hall Warden's gavel, a Grecian mounts the steps of the pulpit and reads Bishop Compton's Graces. The Grace before Meat.

Give us thankful hearts, O Lord God, for the Table which Thou has spread for us. Bless Thy good Creatures to our use, and us to Thy service, for Jesus Christ His sake.

and the Grace after Meat, with its elocutionary minefield:

Blessed Lord, we yield Thee hearty praise and thanksgiving for our Founder and Benefactors, by whose Charitable Benevolence Thou hast refreshed our bodies at this time. So season and refresh our Souls with Thy Heavenly Spirit that we may live to Thy Honour and Glory. Protect Thy Church, the Queen, and all the Royal Family. And preserve us in peace and truth through Christ our Saviour.

The refreshment of bodies is organised from the kitchen immediately behind the Hall. C.H. has never favoured the house dining-system practised in many other schools; all meals for staff and boys are prepared in the modern kitchens and to them, in considerable bulk, come all the stores necessary. There are, as is common to all institutions many complaints about monotonous menus and inadequate provision but the unbiased opinion of outside observers rates C.H. catering very high indeed and in the biased view of those who survived the sternly-rationed regimes of the two Wars C.H. menus to-day are positively Lucullan.

Also behind Dining Hall there is a centre of activity that is to C.H. unique: the Wardrobe. The Hospital provides for all its children without charge all items of uniform save one and indeed all clothing except games-clothes. The one exception is the silver buckle attached to the ''broadie' girdle which is issued to each boy, as replacement for the neophyte's narrow girdle, to signify his elevation from the Lower to the Middle School. This buckle he buys for himself and it is the sole memento of his uniform which he takes with him when he leaves C.H.

The Water Tower rising high above the kitchen is in truth just what its name proclaims it to be for it carries two water-tanks, each holding 80,000 gallons which ordinarily are directly supplied from well-pumps but which can also be filled from a reservoir on Sharpenhurst, the hill to the south-west of the School site. But the Water Tower has become a South of England landmark and, more yet, the symbolic centre of C.H. To its flagstaff is hoisted on great occasions the Royal standard, the City of London blazon or Christ's Hospital's own flag.

The Chapel, like Dining Hall, is in architectural terms much as it was in 1902 though a new organ was installed in 1930 and superbly renovated in 1980. It follows the pattern of many such structures designed for school use but is unusual among ecclesiastical buildings in that the sanctuary and altar is at the south end. Long and narrow with pews running in raised order down the two longer sides and a gallery at the north end, the seating arrangements are strictly hierarchical, the most junior boys at the front nearest the aisle and the seniors at the back, nearest Heaven.

Extraordinarily the Head Master is the ordinary and the C.H. Chapel has one other claim to uniqueness; it is said to be the only church in the Kingdom which has Henry VIII in stained-glass.

The embellishments to the Chapel were not all *in situ* when first the School came here to worship.

The most noticeable, and some would say the most notable, of all, the Brangwyn cartoons on the longitudinal walls were not hung until 1923. From the day when they were commissioned and most vehemently since they were unveiled these pictures have been the cause of much debate. The author of this edition has described them in what he takes to be their proper place, among the treasures of the Hospital, as fit companions for the other great paintings which the Hospital has acquired over the centuries. His predecessor held to a contrary opinion and because respect for G.A.T. Allan is no less genuine than admiration for Frank Brangwyn and for those who had the courage to employ a controversial artist to illuminate the Chapel and to produce contemporary evidence for Christ's Hospital's continuing loyalty to the Christian faith, Allan's wry but decidedly antithetical opinion must be quoted, without amendment.

Of these I prefer to say little, for all who see them receive a different impression, either of raptured enthusiasm or of hostile dislike. Unskilled as I am in the niceties of appreciation of modern 'art', any opinion of mine is worthless, but I cannot but feel that such wonderfully imaginative drawings would look better in some building designed for less sacred use. To my mind they produce no religious atmosphere, rather the reverse; and I think it is a pity to provide boys with grotesque pictures, to be studied during divine service, amongst which may be found apparent caricatures of masters and others waiting to be 'spotted'. They have to be seen to be believed.

Many of the furnishings of the Chapel – including the Brangwyns and the reredos – were purchased with money provided from an Old Blue Thanksoffering Fund. Old Blue Governors commissioned Aston Webb, the architect of the new School, to design a chalice and a patten, and gave replicas also to Hertford. Another chalice, and a ciborium decorated in lapis lazuli, were the gifts of the then Treasurer, and yet another chalice, dating from 1662, was presented by the Vicar and Churchwardens of Christ Church, Newgate Street to commemorate the ancient link between their church and the Hospital.

The western side of the Chapel was planned with flying buttresses, which were disallowed by the Charity Commissioners as adding needlessly to the cost. The Head Master's garden is therefore by that much larger than it would otherwise have been, but from an aesthetic point of view the loss is great. The statue of the Good Shepherd over the main door was given by Dr. Upcott shortly before his retirement. Inside the Chapel are mural tablets to the memory of Governors, Masters, and Officers only. Some places are provided in the ante-chapel for tablets to the memory of boys who have died whilst still at school,

and there too are placed some of the memorial tablets brought from London.

The Cloister which runs along the Eastern wall of the Chapel towards class-rooms and the Head Master's study is also embellished with mural tablets. One honours with lapidary extravagance the founding of a scholarship by public subscription in recognition of some early investigative journalism by *The Times* in "the detection and exposure of the most remarkable and extensively fraudulent conspiracy ever brought to light in the mercantile world". The memorial to Sir Henry Maine enshrines a suitably Victorian moral: "Success and glory are the children of hard work and God's favour"; that to Richard Thornton is blunt and prosaic: "he amassed a large fortune and gratefully remembered, in the disposal of his wealth, the home which had sheltered him when he was young".

It would be sinful to omit from notice the series of group photographs of First Parting Grecians which hang ordinarily in the lobby outside the Head Master's Study. (Indeed, these might well be included in the chapter on treasures.) The collection goes back to the earliest days of photography and since then, year after year, the lordly ones have been recorded. The yellowing photographs from the middle years of the nineteenth century show languid heroes, moustached and long of hair. (The occasional recurrence of long hair is in itself a contribution to social history.) The curious and expert can pick out the great when they were young and greater than ever again in their lives: Middleton Murry, saturnine already and seemingly even then prepared for his association with D. H. Lawrence and Katherine Mansfield; Blunden, unmistakably 'Bunny'; Cyril Burt, even then prepared to change the face of English education; Ross Hook, a mitre even then seemingly sketched in above his head. There is Donald Hopson, handsome at the centre of the photograph for 1934, his eyes as steady as they must have been when, years later as Chargé d'Affaires in Peking, he defied the Red Guard invaders of the British Embassy.

Big School, surmounted by the clock which every quarter-hour strikes melancholy recognition of the march to eterntiy, and bearing in front the old statues of Charles II and Sir John Moore, is used for assemblies and great functions, such as Speech Days and Prize-givings, and since the walls have been covered with acoustic tiling it is a good hall for such use. It has a pleasing ceiling of pitchpine, and it houses the oldest of C.H. organs, to which George II is said to have been a subscriber. The case still bears the marks of London pocket-knives.

In 1937 the panelling of Big School was stripped; the woodwork is now visible in its pristine glory.

If in Dining Hall, Chapel and Big School the pilgrim from 1902 would find little that, by unfamiliarity, would shatter his ghostly equanimity, and if during his spectral peregrination of the heart of the campus – the Avenue and the Quad – he would see nothing

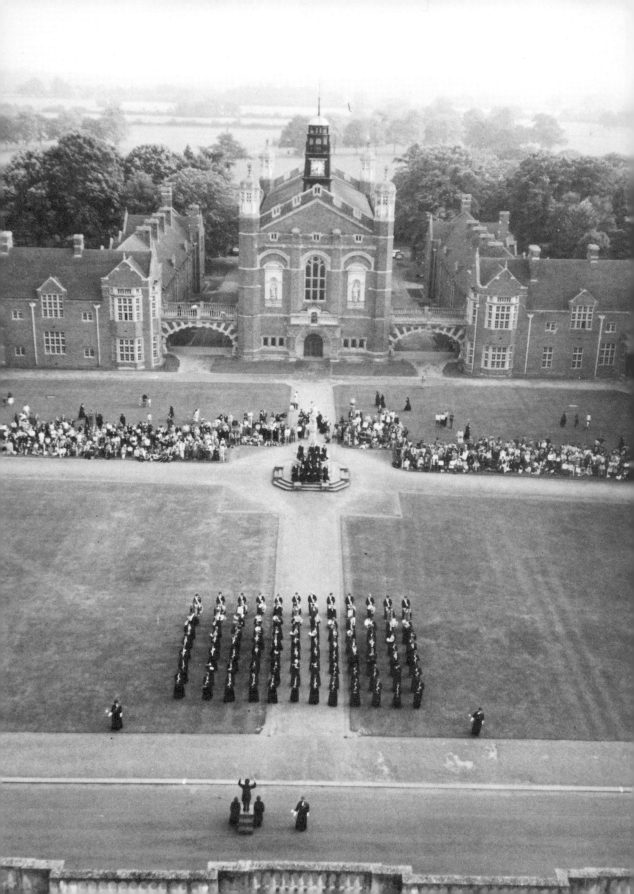

Left: View from the Water Tower — Founder's Day 1982.

Below: The Eastern Archway, 1982.

Below: The Eastern Archway, 1982.

Bottom:. The Quadrangle from the Eastern Archway, the Chapel on the west side with the Cloisters beneath, 1982.

Left: The statue of the Founder King, 1982.

Below: The Dining Room from the south side, 1982.

Right: The Arts Centre, from Big Side, 1983.

Below right: The Arts Centre, 1982.

Above: The Founder King, gilded in his niche with his back to Big School, 1983.

Left: The Dining Hall — the Dais, 1983.

The Dining Hall — two other views from the 'pulpit', 1983.

Left: The Chapel, Brangwyn's cartoons are on the longitudinal walls, 1983.

Right: Lamb House.

Right: One of Brangwyn's controversial cartoons, 'Let the people praise Thee, O God . . .'.

Left: Leaving the classroom behind Big School, 1982.

Right: The Chapel from the Quarter Mile.

substantial to amend his impression that C.H. is as it was in his mortal experience, let him but enter a Senior House and immediately he would know himself to be a stranger.

Even the term 'Senior House' would for him –as for G. A. T. Allan himself and for many Old Blues still very much alive – need exegesis.

As they were originally devised seven of the eight Blocks were laid out to an identical plan. Even the eighth, the most easterly, which was for the first half of this century the Preparatory School, was not in external form notably different from the rest though because it was built to house the smallest and youngest boys, none of them much beyond their eleventh year (and most of them entered into C.H. on Governors' Presentations) who were thought to need more immediate adult and feminine care than did their seniors the Preparatory Block was extended on either side into a residence for a married Housemaster. (Why it was that similar married quarters were added to a few Senior Blocks is a matter on which one reared without such an annexe can speculate – but only in private!)

Again because of the tininess of its inhabitants the Preparatory Block was internally organised to hold 20 more boys than the 102 settled in other Blocks.

Each Block was built to the form of a capital H; each of the two upright strokes representing one House and the cross-stroke the administrative facilities.

The Houses in each Block share an eponym (the name of a famous Old Blue) and in nomenclature differentiate from each other only by the addition of an A to the name of the left-hand House, a B to the right-hand, as for example Lamb A and Lamb B, but apart from the fact that they share also a matron, they are in all respects separate entities, each with its own Housemaster and (now) House Tutors, its own House Captain and monitors, its own House-Teams, and no less rivals with each other than they are separately and constitutionally in competition with all other Houses. Within the common fabric of Housey customs each House has its own traditions, its own prejudices and its own introverted loyalties.

Despite this emphasis upon House identity the basic organisation of life did not vary from House to House for many decades after the move to Horsham.

The patterns were set by the organisation of space within the buildings. There were (there are still, though some have been much adapted) three principal rooms.

On the ground floor: a day-room, where all but two of the boys in the House worked, played and idled (the day-rooms lined with a range of lockers, one for each boy) and at the Avenue end two tiny studies for the House Captain and his Second Monitor. Behind the day room, changing-rooms and further back still that essential facility known locally and inelegantly as the bogs.

On the first floor: the Senior Dormitory, and just one cubicle, for the House Captain; and on the second

floor: the Junior Dormitory and again one cubicle, for the Second Monitor.

All this may seem much as it would be in many a boarding-school. The beds, however, are to Christ's Hospital, unique. The iron bedsteads look much like beds elsewhere and the similarity is even more pronounced now that the antique custom of scrupulous bed-making has been abandoned (the covering blanket meticulously lined and covered, the shape of the pillow – at C.H. the "bolster" – accentuated by a blow from a pole) and with it the inspection by a monitor, as severe as anything inflicted by a sergeant-major upon new recruits. But, lift up the horse-hair mattress and there revealed is what may well be the last survival from the truly spartan days in Newgate Street; no springs but instead wooden-slats. It could be no more than another example of that rare loyalty which possesses Old Blues or even no better than the customary cry of the elderly "you should have seen how tough we were when I was young", but it is certainly not uncommon to hear Old Blues who have long-since succumbed to sybaritism boasting that in all their later lives they have never slept so comfortably as they did at C.H.

The only other furnishings in the dormitories were a table for the supervising monitors and, by the side of each bed, an iron box with a wooden lid known as a settle in which each boy kept spare clothes, and on which, at the order of the monitor, he was made to stand out if he offended against some regulation.

This then was the manner of domestic life within every House until 1964 when the nine year-old entry was abolished and so also the Preparatory School.

At the same time it was decided to separate the younger boys from the older. Prep A and Prep B became Leigh Hunt A and B (Shelley's Leontius recognised at last) and both were made into Junior Houses taking boys up to the age of 14. So also were the two Maines and the two Barnes.

All this was in administrative terms seismic but the change did not greatly affect the physical appearance of the Junior Houses. Such transformation was confined to the Senior Houses.

It was, perhaps, one of the greatest disadvantages of the old system that it denied to all but the privileged two in each House any opportunity for privacy, though it must be admitted that not all Housey boys noticed their deprivation. Now extra studies were constructed in the space formerly occupied by changing-rooms, new changing-rooms were built and a quiet room constructed at the back of the House. To add at least an illusion of privacy for those boys still not elevated to a study the day-room was divided by a series of partitions – a half-wall round individual tables. For these for the first time in its history (and it is hoped the last) C.H. lifted a name from another school: "toyces" from Winchester.

Many things are at C.H. immutable. Still, if after a fashion that previous generations would find casual, the boys make their own beds and clean their own shoes and still each boy below monitorial status has a 'trade' – a services to the community – to perform ordered to a strict hierarchy; the most menial and objectionable – 'skivvage', the cleaning of dirty plates, to the most junior; the most dignified, the task of supervising other trades, to the trades-monitors, those immediately below the monitors. But changes there have been and some so subtle that they would not be remarked even by an Old Blue unless he quizzed one of his successors.

Housey slang, Christ's Hospital's arcane language, has been slipping into obsolescence these last 80 years and is now close to being obsolete. Who now, even among Old Blues, would recognise a brother-crug as a fellow Blue? And are there many now in the School who customarily use the word crug in its other sense – the sense that was commonplace even 30 years ago – as meaning bread. Kiff for coffee, tea or cocoa slipped from general usage when the School abandoned kiff-bowls (managed according to C.H. etiquette with one hand) and took to genteel tea-cups. Spadge (to walk in the gait once peculiar to Grecians, or, by some eccentric process of association, to be friendly with a boy from another House) was already 50 years ago, a word bandied only in the Preparatory School. Flab (butter), gag (meat); all have vanished.

Titch (to beat) went with corporal punishment and swobs (what other schools call fags) with the abolition of swobbing.

The disappearance of these two words, swob and titch are indeed symptomatic of two of the amendments of C.H. life which many Old Blues would regard as the most substantial differences between the C.H. of their day and the School as it is to-day.

Only those who initiated the abolition of swobbing can explain their motives. A less-informed and more prejudiced observer may suspect that the disappearance of the practice – in its day seldom resented by underlings and never by their seniors – may explain why it is that to-day even Grecians may be detected with dirty shoes – something which, in the past, would have brought sorrow to their swobs as indeed to any other miscreant who had somehow escaped the daily shoe-inspection.

Corporal punishment is something else. In Newgate Street days and at Horsham well into this century C.H. was infamous even among generally brutal public-schools for the severity of its discipline. Even in the headmastership of Fyfe, who proclaimed himself "not given to corporeal correction" beating did not cease altogether but to-day not even masters resort to corporal punishment and the somewhat ambiguous right once given to monitors (legalistically ambiguous but not actively so to those who suffered) has been extinguished entirely. Beating is still within the prerogatives of the Head Master – and there have been some in this century who have set themselves up as rivals to Jimmy Boyer, Head Master to Coleridge,

Lamb and Leigh Hunt and, with Keate of Eton and Busby of Westminster, the most famous of all flogging headmasters – but it is doubtful that the present Head Master has ever exercised his right, or his right arm, and certain that the Council no longer favours this mode of punishing offenders.

Changes in the academic ethics have been sensational though their imposition has often been gradual. The effect of these changes is most obviously remarked at the upper end of the School. For several centuries Grecians were just what the title implied: boys considered qualified to study Greek. Already before the move from Newgate Street there had been added a few Mathematics Grecians. C.H. pioneering of Science teaching produced in the early days at Horsham the first Science Grecians (Barnes Wallis, the greatest of all C.H. scientists was picked for the honour, but refused it.) By the 'twenties History (according to the author of Housie's own detective-story, "the primrose path by which the brilliant but idle boy gets to the University") was whispering a challenge to the age-old supremacy of Classics, and by the 'thirties the whisper had become a shout. There was, by then, already an occasional Modern Language, Art or Music Grecian and even some Engineering Grecians. English came later. To-day Classical Grecians are rarities.

Throughout the School the curriculum has been enlarged and enriched. Russian is now almost as popular as French, more popular than German. And now the School has its own computer.

Even more significant than this development of the curriculum has been the virtual elimination of the old, and formerly severe, superannuation system by which, before the Second War, it was demanded of every boy that by a specified age he reach a prescribed academic level or else be asked to leave. This system prevailed even before, at last, and some would say unfortunately, C.H. succumbed to the fashion of taking public examinations but after this surrender and in the climate which has fashioned employment prospects in the last decades it has been found to be no longer feasible and no longer charitable to decant into the great world outside the Ring Fence 15 or 16 year-olds who have no paper-qualifications to present to putative employers, and harsh beyond the possibilities of consent from the Council to dismiss them to the dole-queue.

The consequent tendency to extend the school-life of the average Housey boy has been given further impetus by the substantial enlargement of opportunities in higher education. It was formerly the case that, with a very few exceptions (notably candidates for commission in the Forces and some destined for Medical Schools) no C.H. boy stayed on much after his seventeenth birthday unless he was considered to be capable of winning a university place by competitive examination. To-day, when there are more than 40 universities in Britain and many other institutions of higher education, the chance of a place is open to many more boys – but not often before they are 18.

The consequent advantage for C.H. boys is obvious; but less so the potential disadvantage to the Foundation. In the past C.H. profited hugely from the benevolence of Old Blues who, having left school at 15 or 16, made careers and fortunes, most often in the City. It is at least possible that in the future C.H. will add handsomely to its already rich record of distinguished teachers and famous administrators. Such may fill the pantheon – and perhaps the Kingdom of Heaven – but not the coffers of the Hospital.

It is beyond possibility that even the most curious and determined visitor will comprehend the variety of C.H. life and beyond the competence of the most assiduous reporter to set to print an account that is much more than an anthology of impressions and that, because it must be selective, reveals also as much – and perhaps more – about the selector's prejudices than it tells about C.H.

There are to-day at Horsham open to every boy activities outside the class-room in such profusion that it may well be questioned if ever again even the most fortunate Old Blue will have access to such richness – or ever again be faced with a problem of choice on this scale.

Every boy takes part in some sporting activities and so many are the sports available that he would be an unusual youth who did not find one to his tastes, and he a physical misfit or something of a rarity if he did not discover one which he could master. But, though Christ's Hospital teams have triumphed on many fields and though sporting competitions between Houses are fought (and sometimes no other word is apt) with determination and vociferous support from partisan onlookers, it is the especial pride of Blues that C.H. has never suffered from the disease, devastatingly rampant in many other schools, which sets scholars against athletes, aesthetes against 'bloods'. There is at Housie as much pride in our poets as in our county cricketers, and our poets have sometimes been our best athletes. The bustling front-row of the Christ's Hospital First XV is not infrequently made up of three burly 'muddied oafs' who, once the game is over and mud and blood washed away, change into the dignified uniforms of Grecians.

Pleasure in athletic competence is, of course, intense; School-colours and House-colours are coveted and worn with a satisfied air; but ineptitude is not considered shameful. For many years there were regular matches between House Worst XV's and the matches were as titanic, if the participants far less skilful, as games for the House Cup or between C.H. and its rival schools.

The Natural History Society – once among the most prestigious of all C.H. extra-curricular organisations and assuredly the only society in any school which could boast a poem written in its honour by a poet who had already won the Hawthornden Prize – has lapsed but there is scarcely a sensible activity (and few that are futile) that does not have within C.H. its formal association of enthusiasts. Debating, shooting, literary endeavour, scouting, canoeing: these are but a few among the many. The Verrio Guides show visitors round the School. C.H. has been represented, with success, in the School Show-jumping championship and in yachting-competitions. There is also a mountaineering club, but whether these be sports or pastimes or hardships it is not for this chronicler to decide.

There is also a private telephone-system, built, maintained and manned by boys. Assuredly to the relief of the Service establishment – and undoubtedly approved by a whole generation that, having suffered throughout its school-days from Friday afternoons encased in scratchy khaki and tight puttees without learning from their hardship anything of tactics or strategy, then went on to fight and win a war – military training is no longer compulsory. Perhaps for that very reason the A.C.F. and A.T.C. flourish. So also does the principal alternative to pre-Service training, the Duke of Edinburgh Award.

By way of these multifarious activities, to two, Drama and Music, that overflow the boundary-lines between curricular and extra-curricular, and, by way of these two, one can revert to the tour of inspection to take in the most recent addition to the list of major buildings, the Arts Centre.

It is no longer possible to establish when first C.H. boys took to theatrical performance. Almost from the beginning the stylised nature of many C.H. public functions demanded of all Blues some histrionic capacity, and later – but for a few – this requirement was made emphatic by the call to read Grace in Hall and (later still) to read the Lesson in Chapel each morning and prayers and a Lesson at Duty each evening in the day-room. There were, already in the eighteenth century, occasions when boys performed plays. A Grecians' Dramatic Society was established in the last decades in Newgate Street and has its vestigial representative in the play offered to the whole community by the Leaving Grecians at the end of each Summer Term, but with the move to Horsham Thespis came to full voice. Every Easter Term day-rooms were transformed into theatres, the long tables grouped together at the study-end to make a stage, lighting-systems created, curtains fixed. House-masters were magicked into directors (unless there was in the House some budding Stanislavsky), matrons became wardrobe-mistresses, masters' wives were dragooned to serve as make-up artists and, in these happily make-shift circumstances, boys of the House – sometimes to their horror, found themselves emulating Gordon Harker, Owen Nares or, sometimes to their own amazement, Sybil Thorndike or Phyllis Calvert.

House-plays continue to this day but have now been transferred to the more 'professional', if no more amiable, setting of the theatre in the Arts Centre.

These essentially voluntary performances apart, Drama and even Dance are now intrinsic to the curriculum. The School has its full-time Director of Drama (which makes one wonder why it is that there has been such a noticeable decline in the general standards of elocution and why it has been found necessary to install an amplifying-system in Chapel!)

The musical tradition of Christ's Hospital is older and generally more distinguished than is the dramatic. As has been remarked several early benefactors – and notably William Parker and Robert Dow – gave money for the specific purpose of training boys to play instruments, including even the organ, and their intentions have been followed in every generation as they are still to-day when a remarkable number are made into proficient – and a few into exquisite – instrumentalists. The orchestra is good; the Band *non-pareil.* Commentators in every century have remarked – as still they do to this day – on the magnificence of the Chapel Choir. But for many years now the greatest glory of C.H. music has been, not so much the glory of its greatest exponents, but the all-pervasive importance of music in Housey life and thus in the significant part that music plays in the life of many Old Blues who have no overt musical competence. And that is the first, the truest and the most useful purpose of music in a school.

It was ever thus, if to a lesser degree than it is to-day. Lamb, who attempted to con the world into thinking him unmusical, recalled:

the hymns and anthems, and well-tuned organ; the doleful tone of the burial anthem chanted in the solemn cloisters . . . and the carol . . . which when a young boy, I have so often lain awake from seven till ten, when it was sung by the older boys, and monitors, and have listened to it, in their rude chanting, till I have been transported in fancy to the fields of Bethlehem and the song which was sung at that season by angels' voices to the shepherds.

It was, indeed, ever thus; and Old Blues of each generation will claim that their fervour for music they owe to the Director of Music who ruled in their own school-days. It is, therefore, in no way extraordinary that a survivor from the 'thirties sets all to the credit of C. S. Lang. Himself no mean composer in the Stanford mould, he made Chapel services glorious even for those who had "no ear", but his greatest contribution to C.H. musical life and to the musical education of the boys sprang from his zest for exposing them to outside, and professional, expertise. The programme that he organised, of concerts, recitals and visits, was rich indeed; the jewel in his crown annual visits by the London Symphony Orchestra.

On these occasions the School was given a free day. In the morning the Orchestra rehearsed in Big School. Attendance by boys was voluntary, and most of the School volunteered. Lang conducted himself, magnificently informal, jacket-less, in pale blue shirt and red braces. As at Robert Mayer's Children's Concerts each section of the Orchestra demonstrated its own peculiar skills, often with nicely impertinent frivolities. In the lunch-break we played asphalt-cricket (our own variant of MCC custom, played with a tennis-ball and shorn-down bat) against teams from the LSO. (The most memorable sporting-achievement of the author of this section is: the Leader of the LSO caught-and-bowled; bat to cigarette, to wall, to hand; first ball!) In the afternoon, the Concert, and there on the Big School platform our friends from asphalt making magic, and from them the much-interrupted and erratic labours of the morning, its punctuation of exasperation or frivolity, given wholeness and transformed into superb artistic achievement.

This was musical indoctrination at its liveliest and best; and for many its potency has lasted a life-time.

The annual visits of the LSO were not resumed after the War but, if nothing quite so sensational took their place, the totality of musical experience to which the School was exposed did not decline.

Then, in 1971, it was decided that C.H. needed a focus for its attention to the performing arts, more suited to encourage its age-old enthusiasm than Big School, more adaptable and in every sense more "professional".

As ever the call went out to Old Blues and to friends; as ever Old Blues and friends responded generously.

The result was the Arts Centre, a handsome complex which incorporates the Old Music School and which contains practice-rooms, a Band Room, some elegant class-rooms, a fine octagonal library and a theatre, superbly adaptable to all manner of theatrical forms and said to be the best small theatre in England.

The primary purpose of the Arts Centre was to add to the amenities and educational opportunities accessible to the boys but there was also another motive powerful in the minds of the Council and the Head Master. It is one of the advantages of the Horsham site that it is self-contained, spacious and private. This quality, though in so many ways beneficial, carries with it also an unfortunate concomitant, an exacerbation of the isolation from the everyday, the sense of monastic seclusion, that is inevitable in all boarding-schools. It was hoped that the Arts Centre would bring to C.H. not only professional artists but also, as audience and in large numbers, men and women from Southern England who hitherto had known C.H. only as a view of the Water Tower glimpsed from a car.

This aspiration has been amply fulfilled. The Arts Centre has become in a very real sense the theatre and concert-hall for a considerable proportion of the population of Sussex and Surrey, and no wonder when the Royal Shakespeare Company, the Contemporary Dance Theatre, the Kent Opera and many other eminent groups and many a soloist look upon it as country-home.

And there lies the rub. The benefit to the boys – the major concern of Council and Head Master is potentially beyond doubt but there has been, from the very first days of the Arts Centre, a danger that a programme devised to attract experienced audiences might not stimulate the less sophisticated among the boys. There were, too, question-marks set and obvious to those in authority, that puzzled the communal conscience. How far could C.H. go in acting as benefactor to a constituency not its own? And was it right to use substantial funds even for the benefit of those of its charges whose artistic tastes were already so advanced that they would come regularly, eagerly and voluntarily to theatrical or musical performances that would bring in also a large, cultivated and paying adult audience.

After some years of experience it was clear that these hesitations were well-founded. At times boys were crowded-out by the School's enthusiastic neighbours; at other times intimidated by the esoteric nature of the offering.

The intellectual dilemma thus presented to the Council was given practical edge by the harsh facts made obvious by the Arts Centre balance-sheet. It is no new experience for an impressario to discover that it costs a great deal to maintain a complex such as the C.H. Arts Centre and to sustain within it a continuous programme of high-quality professional performances but the bitter economic circumstances of the last few years have brought many managements of organisations, similar to that at C.H. (save only that the furtherance of the arts and of entertainment is their sole concern) to the sad conclusion that centres of this kind cannot survive unless they are held to life by substantial transfusions of money from the State.

The drain on the Hospital's resources could no longer be permitted. A compromise was planned; a compromise that many on the Council considered as more appropriate to its purposes and in educational terms preferable. Visits from professional companies and soloists were not discontinued but their number was reduced. The general public was still encouraged to look upon the Arts Centre as its own. But more time in the Centre was given to teaching and more to performances organised within the School community.

The implementation of these plans is still in progress and it is as yet too early to judge its educational, social and financial effects, but the omens are auspicious and it is at least possible to predict that, without significant sacrifice in its role as focus for the artistic interests of a larger society, the Arts Centre will become, what it was always intended to be, a magnificent addition to the cultural life of the boys (and soon, the girls also) of Christ's Hospital.

There is the logic of regular event in moving from consideration of the Arts Centre to the Dinner Parade for it is from the Band Room in the Centre that, on every day in term except Sundays (and when there is rain) the Band marches out to its station in the Quad but, even were it not so, no account of Christ's Hospital, Horsham would be complete did it not include reference to this routine if nonetheless unique and dramatic ceremony and, whether he comes in person or by the essentially limited route of printed-page, no visitor has seen Christ's Hospital who has not watched Dinner Parade.

The form is not so very different from that (already described) which the Parade takes on Speech Day except that there is no Lord Mayor to salute and that the Houses form up at both ends of the Avenue. The Band arrives, ninety strong and headed by its three drum-majors. (This must be the only band in the world that boasts in its list of former drum-majors a general and a Prince of the Church!) The Band plays, better now than ever it did in the past. Each headed by a boy carrying the House flag, the Houses march, alas, with less panache and less discipline than once they did. In front of the eastern door the Houses from the East End of the Avenue turn right, in front of the western door those from the West End turn left. House Captains shout an order and the House files into Dining Hall. (That order demonstrates yet another aspect of C.H. which is, in all probability, *sui generis*. Christ's Hospital must be by now the one place in the world where columns march in fours and "form two-deep".)

It has been said, and even by G. A. T. Allan, that Dinner Parade was devised as a convenient method of getting 830 boys through two narrow doors speedily and without jostle, but there is good evidence to substantiate the claim that the daily Parade was well-established long ago in Newgate Street.

However mundane its origins and intentions Dinner Parade remains a prime example of Christ's Hospital's capacity for pageantry, and, even more than that, of its genius for transforming a practical exercise into a symbol of community and continuity.

CHAPTER EIGHT

On Heroes

The substance of a great educational institution cannot be established by rehearsing the names and accomplishments of those of its products who, in the adult world beyond the school, have contrived achievements so extraordinary that their names are held to posterity. The glory of Christ's Hospital has been sustained throughout the centuries as much by hosts of men and women, once scholars of the House, who have no memorial, for these too "were merciful men, whose righteousness hath not been forgotten, with their seed shall continually remain a good inheritance".

It is, nonetheless, both natural and proper that Christ's Hospital's sons and daughters hold in proud remembrance those of their predecessors who were "leaders of the people" for these make up the identifiable part of that inheritance with which all are endowed on entering the School, these the ancestors whose gifts and triumphs are the models which inspire in later generations the will to emulate. "No sadder reproof can be given by man of his littleness", wrote Carlyle "than disbelief in great men."

It is not a reproof that can be urged against C.H. Blues are, most of them, intensely loyal to the Foundation – their critics might say obsessively so – and as Carlyle went on to suggest, loyalty is "an effluence of hero-worship, submissive admiration for the truly great".

Any attempt to set down a roll-call of heroes is befuddled at the outset by the intractability of establishing an arithmetic of greatness. Should, one, for example, proclaim in the record those who were well-known in their day but whose names are now no longer household-words even in the households of devout and learned antiquarians? If so, C.H. could allow into its pantheon many sly shades of rural deans, many portly ghosts of city merchants, and many crabbed spectres of learned professors.

But we have another, and more practical difficulty. Particularly for the early days it is not always easy, and it is sometimes impossible, to identify those whom we might have authority to call our worthies. Some admission registers for those earliest years have been long-since lost and, perversely, for later years the records are so full that only the most diligent and omniscient investigator can cull from the archives, with certainty, all those names which can truly be considered as notable. (For the days before school magazines, before newspapers, before recollection of school-fellows became fashionable, and before the publication of reliable biographical reference-books, it is chance when it can be discovered if A.N. Other was at Christ's Hospital or at Eton, and for those same centuries, and especially for a school such as Christ's Hospital, so many of whose alumni made their careers overseas, the chance is happy indeed if one identifies the school-day background of some person distinguished in far places.)

There is, too, another problem in this sort which is close to being unique to us. When compared to other great schools C.H. is remarkably miserly in conceding the honour of membership to its community. In this respect Eton, Winchester, and many other great schools, admit to their honoured ranks without question both those who have been "on the Foundation" and all others who have been reared in the institution. (Oppidans are as Collegers without doubt Etonians.) Until this century, with one notable exception, Christ's Hospital has denied recognition to non-Foundationers. To-day all of our Non-Foundationers are children of masters, mistresses or other officers, but from the beginnings of C.H. until 1869 many, even of the gentry, paid to have their children within Christ's Hospital and alongside fully-fledged Blues. Such as these we have rigorously excluded from our roll of honours. A little more generosity – or a little more greed – and we could claim Warren Hastings (and, some would say, also Samuel Richardson) as Old Blues. (Hastings did become a Governor, proof either to his affection for the House or to the scale of the peculations of which he stood accused.)

That one exception to this otherwise implacable self-denying ordinance is truly sensational. The Elizabethan poet, George Peele, is honoured above all but seven other Blues for his name was picked as eponym for one of the residential blocks when the Boys' School moved to Horsham. Peele was undoubtedly educated in the Grammar School and the Hospital met part of his expenses at Oxford but he was never in the legalistic sense "a scholar of this House". He was, however, son of the Clerk and as such in this century would undoubtedly be considered truly an Old Blue and so it is that, even by our severe doctrine, his honour stands against all criticism – if only *ex post facto*.

That choice of names for the Horsham blocks was in other respects eccentric. Coleridge, one of the few truly great English poets and metaphysicians, and also among the most devoted of Old Blues, would have selected himself before any Congregation of Rites and so also his friend of a life-time, Charles Lamb, finest of English essayists and another unshakeably loyal son of the House. But when the blocks were first named (and for 60 years thereafter) recognition was denied to the third glory of the Golden Generation, Leigh Hunt, a friend to them both, another dedicated Old Blue, the most perspicacious editor in English literary history, author of a fine *Autobiography* that includes chapters on C.H. which match anything in the same *genre* by Coleridge or Lamb, and himself no mean poet and a considerable essayist. His exclusion did no credit to the Council of Almoners and less to Queen Victoria or to the Hospital's vehement President, the Duke of Cambridge, who are said to have contrived it because Leigh Hunt had libelled their ancestor, the easily-libelled Prince Regent. (So also had Charles Lamb but, in his case happily, knowledge of literary history was among the Royals less obvious than family prejudice.)

That a block was named for Sir Edward Thornton, an obscure diplomat, could be forgiven to an age which did not expect to find an ambassador among the products of a school whose sons were by definition born to families not blessed with the wealth or status that then habitually guarded entrance to the Diplomatic Service. It is unforgivable to us of a C.H. generation that has seen six of its contemporaries as British ambassadors (the most distinguished, even of that distinguished crew, Sir Donald Hopson, H.M. Ambassador to Venezuela and to Argentina) and another representing the Commonwealth of Australia, but for a reason which should have been apparent even to our predecessors 80 years ago, the sanctification of Edward Thornton has always been a blasphemy. Long-since Leigh Hunt himself expressed for us our distaste when he wrote of Thornton:

We have had an ambassador among us, but as he, I understand is ashamed of us, we are hereby more ashamed of him, and accordingly omit him.

Better that we pretend that the block is named for that other Thornton, Richard (no relation to this unnatural Old Blue) for he, the "Duke of Danzig", not only amassed a fortune of several million pounds by his own diligence and ingenuity but was also consistently devoted to the House and was one of its most generous benefactors.

Similarly, if less dishonourably, a block was named for the "wrong" Barnes, for Joshua and not for Thomas. Joshua Barnes was a seventeenth century divine, a scholar of enormous erudition (he had written five books before ever he left school) and eccentric manner. He became eventually Regius Professor of Greek at Cambridge but if we were to consider a University Chair sufficient cause for the highest honour open to us we would have to build three or four hundred blocks. Thomas Barnes, on the other hand, was the greatest of our many great journalists, for 25 years in the early nineteenth century Editor of *The Times* and the man who put thunder into the voice of "the Thunderer".

Thomas Middleton, "a scholar and gentleman in his teens" (and another friend of Coleridge and Lamb) was (if only just) a more respectable choice. Middleton was the first Bishop of Calcutta. His statue is in St. Paul's Cathedral:

in all the pomp of wig and lawn. He stands blessing two nude and tiny Indians, male and female, and by the unlearned is frequently mistaken for the Almighty creating Adam and Eve.

Perhaps any Old Blue whose effigy can be thought to be a facsimile of the portrait of the Deity deserves from us at least the respect of a block named for him.

The last of the seven original *eponymi* was eminently reputable and reputably eminent. Sir Henry Sumner Maine, the distinguished Victorian jurist and scholar, holds still some of the fame he gathered in his life-time; his *Ancient Law* remains a classic – in its kind.

Old Blues given to that kind of amusement from time-to-time play a game of the class of choosing an All-Time, All-Country's Test Team. Its purpose: to consider the selection if the task of naming the blocks were to be begun all over again, the only prohibition: (that same consideration weighed upon our predecessors) no name to be considered qualified whose bearer is alive or recently dead.

The list, again like the selection of those mythical Test teams, varies according to the prejudices of the selector but in these ecumenical days one name would almost certainly join the three of the existing eight, Coleridge, Lamb and Leigh Hunt (for Hunt received his due sixty years late), who would win universal support. Edmund Campion is among those of whom there is no certain record in our registers (but that is no surprise for the years of his boyhood are the very years for which the archive is fragmented). His brother's name we have, but that is no surety. Much more substantial as evidence is the unanimity of the tale current among near-contemporaries that Campion was a boy at Christ's Hospital; even fellow-Jesuits vouch for it and they would have grudged such hallowed association to a stubbornly heretical foundation unless it was so well-known to their countrymen as to be beyond ignoring or denial. But the ultimate seal of authenticity was granted only recently and from no less an authority than the Supreme Pontiff himself. In 1970 the Pope invited two English schoolboys to Rome to witness the ceremonies that marked the canonization of Edmund Campion. One was the Head Boy of Jesuit Stonyhurst, the other the Senior Grecian of Christ's Hospital.

Few, if any other, Protestant schools in Britain can boast a saint among their alumni. If we could but give to St. Edmund Campion a block to himself it would be a tribute in our eyes scarcely less momentous than canonization and thus we could turn the tables both on Catholic Mary who spurned him and on Protestant Gloriana who burned him, and even without that lively conclusion to an ancient debate, we take pride in Campion, Old Blue and stalwart Englishman, one who at the very last, and without fear, proclaimed:

Whereas I have . . . adventured myself into this noble Realm, my deare Countrie, for the Glorie of God and the benefit of souls, I thought it like enough that, in his busie, watchful and suspicious worlde I should either sooner or later be intercepted and stopped of my course.

And it is particularly pleasing to us, proud as we are of our rich literary tradition, that our saint is the patron-saint of booksellers.

With four of the eight places reserved for immortals the author of this chapter leaves to others the task of finding four distinguished mortals to fill the remaining vacancies. Professional prejudice must have persuaded him to give one place to Campion's predecessor at C.H., the greatest of all our many great historians, William Camden, "the nourice of antiquitie and lanterne into late succeeding age", but he recognises that the similarity in the names of Campion and Camden might lead to touch-line confusion. As demonstration of lack of prejudice of any kind he might be tempted to nominate Warren Hastings or perhaps even Susannah Holmes but there were slurs upon Hastings' reputation more sinister than his brief career as a Blue and Susannah Holmes has no reputation left to her other than the loveliness of her Hertford portrait.

It is perverse proof of the ambiguity of religious loyalties in our first half-century (but assuredly no argument for placing him in the top eight) that another of our earliest worthies was a recusant. David Baker went from C.H. to Oxford; there he was "sadly gay" but, having been suddenly converted, he became in time Spiritual Director of the English Benedictine nuns. For us he has another distinction: as the author of an autobiography which contains the first recollections of Christ's Hospital.

Much has been made already in these pages of our especial affinity with literary art and the profession of journalism. The greatest of our writers, Camden, Peele, Coleridge, Lamb and Leigh Hunt, are great by standards untouched by parochial piety. So also, from more recent generations, are Edmund Blunden, one of the finest poets of the First World War and Keith Douglas, now generally acknowledged as the finest poetic voice of the Second War. So, arguably, is Middleton Murry: at very least he stands firm in memory as the author of one of the noblest tributes ever paid to C.H. (in his autobiography *Between Two Worlds*) and in the more selective and less generous annals of English literature as one of this century's most perspicacious critics.

It could be that we should take no glory from the appearance of one of our number among the targets for Pope's poisoned arrows in *The Dunciad:*

How, with less reading than makes felons 'scape,
Less human genius than God gives an ape
Small thanks to France, and none to Rome or Greece
A vast, vamp'd future, old, reviv'd, new piece
'Twixt Plautus, Fletcher, Shakespeare, and Corneille,
Can make a Cibber, Tibbald or Ozell

Even so our James Ozell wins some credit as the first English translator of Racine. A Blue from a century later has a no less distinctive claim upon fame than Ozell's. Thomas Surr (who in his non-literary career led where many Old Blues have followed, into the service of the Bank of England) in his most successful novel is said to have caricatured so successfully Georgina, Duchess of Devonshire that the shock of self-recognition brought on her death. After Surr came W.P. Scargill, whom Leigh Hunt dismissed as "a Unitarian minister, author of some tracts on Peace and War etc.", but then Scargill was a Tory, Hunt in his day a notorious Radical, and in truth Scargill won some reputation as a novelist and wrote also recollections of his school-days which are a worthy footnote to Hunt's own. H.S. Leigh's fame as a writer of light verse might have been greater had he not been a contemporary of Gilbert and Calverley.

Still very much alive when Hunt, Coleridge, Lamb and Scargill were school-boys, and, though considerably their senior, still very much alive when Coleridge and Lamb died, is one Old Blue who, though he produced many scholarly works of his own, and not a little verse, is best-remembered for the warmth of affection he aroused in other, and greater, writers, including above all his fellow-Blue authors. George Dyer, Lamb's *amicus redivivus*, passed his days "in an unbroken dream of learning and goodness'', and was "famed and loved for his marvellous forgetfulness''. It was said of him that "his loyalty to Christ's Hospital never faltered in a long life''.

Edmund Blunden complained once that, though the literary glories of C.H. are many, we have produced few novelists. Omit Richardson, as (despite Leigh Hunt's certainty) it appears we must, and the comment must be accepted but the gap is fast being filled. One of our current Members of Parliament has transposed the capacity for fiction essential in that profession to the writing of a successful novel. An Old Blue better-known perhaps (if he is known at all) as historian and biographer, has also published several short stories. A much younger contemporary who came to Old Bluedom by way of an exchange with an American school, is not only now one of England's young poets – and the most-respected of all editors of modern poetry; he has also produced what was judged by some critics to be the best novel of 1980.

One name from among contemporaries has come, like that of Keith Douglas, too soon to the possibility of identification in these pages and with that name, Arthur Thompson, known to millions of readers as Francis Clifford, we have a novelist of great quality, one who, with such as Graham Greene, Eric Ambler and John Le Carré, has raised the thriller to first-class citizenship in the republic of letters.

The colour, diversity and unique traditions of C.H. would seem ideal for a novel about school life. Rich though we are in reminiscence C.H. has produced no school-story since the eighteenth century and even then, though some claim for "An Orphanatrophian" priority in this *genre*, his *The Fortunate Bluecoat Boy* (published in 1770) is much more the record of the post-schoolday and extra-marital adventures of "Mr. Benjamin Templeman; Formerly a Scholar in Christ's Hospital" than it is an account of life in Newgate Street.

There have been, however, two novels which, though the setting is thinly-disguised, are obvious to any Blue as Christ's Hospital books. The first, *The Public School Murder* was by R.C. Woodthorp, once a Horsham master. The second, a romance, is *Sweet is the Breath of Morn* and the author's pseudonym, Mary Hamilton, is to any Blue of the William Hamilton Fyfe era as easily penetrated as is the identity of many of its characters.

One more novel, most certainly not by an Old Blue, deserves mention for the proper respect shown by its author to the grandest of all C.H. offices. Tom Cantey, the pauper in Mark Twain's *Prince and the Pauper* is, at the end of the tale, rewarded for his loyal and judicious impersonation of Prince Edward (Edward VI) by being elevated for the rest of his days to the rank of The Worshipful the Treasurer of Christ's Hospital.

A short step from literature, the craft of editor has Thomas Barnes as Old Blue father-figure. Of Barnes

Leigh Hunt his school contemporary and close-friend, wrote, "no man (if he had cared for it) could have been more certain of attaining celebrity for wit and literature" and Lamb compared him favourably with Fielding.

Barnes has had his many successors. Since the days when he was the most powerful newspaper editor in Britain and Hunt himself the editor of two of the most influential magazines, Old Blues have occupied editorial chairs of newspapers, magazines and specialist journals in Britain and elsewhere. English-language journalism in South East Asia could hardly have survived without us. H.K. Beauchamp edited the *Madras Mail*, J. M. Maclean the *Bombay Gazette*, and H. C. Lipsett the *Civil and Military Gazette* (more famous, perhaps, as employer of Rudyard Kipling). In this century C.H. has provided editors to the *Atheneum* (later incorporated in the *New Statesman*), *Penguin Parade*, the *Radio Times*, the poetry magazine *PM*, surprisingly to *The Field* and, most surprising of all, to *The Tatler*. R. H. Gretton, a most distinguished journalist, was London Editor of the *Manchester Guardian* and, as editor of the *Yorkshire Post*, Linton Andrews gave national, and at times, international, authority to a provincial newspaper.

The number is uncountable of Old Blues who in recent years have earned their living by pen and typewriter. As example to the totality, sufficient to report that, since first *The Times* confessed to the names of its contributors, the truly Top People have found on several mornings the whole of the paper's leader-page taken up with the writings of fellow Old Blues.

Or, if additional evidence be required: a more distant but still vivid recollection of that night in 1952 when, under the chairmanship of one of the Hospital's greatest headmasters, Sir William Hamilton Fyfe (himself no inconsiderable writer), 65 of what Fyfe called his 'inky Blues' sat together in the Reform Club to dine and to discuss the production of *The Christ's Hospital Book* as contribution from what all 66 present regarded as Christ's Hospital's premier profession to the celebration of 400 years of Christ's Hospital history.

The Hospital's especial affinity for the arts of communication has led Blues also into the suburbs and colonies of literature, into publishing and into the most recent (and, some would say, the most powerful) of the media, broadcasting.

The Green of Longman, Green was a Blue, so also, from the later days in Newgate Street, was Bertram Christian, one of the first Presidents of the Publishers Association, and, since the Second War, there have been Blues powerful in the counsels of the Oxford University Press, Methuen, Nisbet, Bell, Christophers, Penguin, Maxwell Cavendish, Hamish Hamilton and Carcanet.

There was a time, and that no so long past, when

three of the BBC's seven Senior Announcers came from C.H. and to-day it is said that there are no less than 100 Old Blues, of both sexes, working in radio and television – at their head until recently the Director-General of the BBC.

In recent years, too, there has been a considerable Old Blue presence in advertising (a distant colony of literature?). Three (at least) of Britain's largest agencies have had Old Blues as managing-director.

An afterthought, lest it be suspected that Blues possessed of literary talent all enter the service either of the Muses or of Mammon: the hymn "Lord of the Dance", which is, all over the English-speaking world, the most populat of all hymns written in the last decades, was written by an Old Blue.

In the arts other than literature the achievement of Old Blues has been, until the twentieth century, far less substantial.

Despite those early benefactions designed to enhance particularly the musical education of C.H. boys, despite the long (and still unquestionable) excellence of choral singing within the school, and notwithstanding the remarkable ability of two eighteenth century Music Masters, John Barrett and Robert Hudson, the school's professional contribution to the score of English music was negligible (and hardly warranted the flattering inclusion of a hymn called "Christ's Hospital" in Ravenscroft's *Psalter*), though its exalted status may be explained by the fact that Thomas Ravenscroft was himself Music Master at C.H. In its first century C.H. produced one Falstaffian musical luminary (the word is used advisedly) Thomas Brewer. Brewer entered the school in 1614 at the age of three, there learnt the viol, and became in time the most eminant performer of his generation – and a composer of quality – but among his contemporaries he was even more famous for "his proneness to good Fellowshippe". Thereby he:

> attained a very Rich and Rubicund Nose. Being reproved by a Friend for his too frequent use of strong drinkes and Sack as being very Pernicious to that Distemper and Inflammation of the Nose – Nay, Faith, sayes he, if it will not endure Sack, its no Nose for me.

After Brewer and for three centuries, some cried up Haydn, some Mozart but few heard memorable notes from an Old Blue. S.S. Wesley, distinguished son of a famous family, we could claim as one of us if only we were less dismissive of non-Foundationers. The Victorian Collingwood Banks we remember as truly a Blue wherever we sing our *Votum*, but few others remember him at any time. Then (but only in the last 50 years or so) Housie found its voice, and it was sweet.

John Hunt was the first British pianist to appear in Soviet Russia. Frank Philips (even better-known as a BBC announcer) sang solo parts in the Albert Hall

Hiawatha (written by one whose name, Coleridge-Taylor, makes him an almost-Blue). Wilfred Brown was one of the finest tenors of the 1960's but by then Christ's Hospital music had already produced its richest blossom. "Constant Lambert", writes the leading Old Blue musicologist of this generation,

> was virtually the creator of English ballet. He was, among musicians, a writer of high distinction. . . His greatest benefit has been his understanding of the need for lightness of heart.

Lambert won fame also as a conductor. Since Lambert's day there has come out of C.H. another conductor (anonymous in these pages but not easily disguised) whom many regard as the best of all British conductors and not a few as the finest conductor of Mozart anywhere in the world. And so it is that the conductor of the Royal Ballet, of Covent Garden and the 'Proms' ("one in three and three in one") claims that he learnt his musicianship in the Housey Band.

Yet another living Old Blue has been largely responsible for the pre-eminence of the BBC as a patron of "serious" music.

These are happy and notable breaks with what was for centuries seemingly a dismal story but they do not tell all. These are the peaks of creativity but the plateau is high. There is among Old Blues generally a love of music that could well be more significant to the excellence of their education than any grand performance. Perhaps it was always there and it is beyond doubt true that even Charles Lamb, the Old Blue who above all others, denied that he was sophisticated in musical appreciation, by the terms of that very denial and in a myriad of other allusions, proved himself rarely qualified with a knowledge of music.

Again it must be quoted:

> Some cry up Haydn, some Mozart,
> Just as the whim bites; for my part,
> I do not care a farthing candle
> For either of them, or for Handel. . .

And, in our own times, two of our most caustic journalists (and one of them a Member of Parliament!) have, like Elia, broken with their generally provocative custom to write learned books on "several eminent composers".

Just as, in the light of the excellence of musical training within the school, it is disappointing that so few Old Blues have become musicians of note, so also it is sad that, despite the long history of the Drawing School few Old Blues – again until this century – have made much impact in the visual arts. Undoubtedly the prime skills cossetted by the Drawing School were accuracy and neatness and so the most distinguished products calligraphic and cartographic. The refinement of Christ's Hospital calligraphy survived long after the dissolution of the Drawing School and, encouraged as one likes to think by the award each year of a prize for handwriting, even into this century. Blunden manuscripts are collectors' items almost as much for their superb penmanship as for the exquisite quality of his poetry and it is pleasant to recall that, in his turn, one of the greatest of Christ's Hospitals' athletes, F. M. McRae, rugby footballer of international class, England squash-player and Somerset cricketer, whose heroic death when Surgeon on an Arctic convoy earned him a place in Lord Moran's book *On Courage,* was a winner of the Gold Pen. Since the eighteenth century C.H. has not sent out map-makers but from that century, Irving and Thompson stand among the finest.

Of artists in more aesthetic manner we hold in affectionate recollection especially Henry Meyer, and he above all for his happy portraits of his three school-fellows, Coleridge, Lamb and Leigh Hunt but, in claiming as Christ's Hospital's greatest artist and architect Augustin Pugin, the author of this revision takes issue with his distinguished predecessor. Allan dismissed Pugin as one of those "not quite Old Blues" who had benefited from C.H. teaching but not from the Foundation. However, Pugin himself always insisted that he was "schooled in Christ's Hospital" and his pride in that heritage seems to justify our pride in him. Pugin was one of the fathers of the Gothic Revival – and, some would say, also of Functionalism – a prodigy who had designed furniture for Windsor Castle and stage-settings for the London theatre before he was twenty years old, who came in time to assist Charles Barry in designing the new Houses of Parliament (not only the facade but also many of the furnishings – even the ink-stands and hat-racks – were by Pugin). An immaculate draughtsman, alas, he was "rarely allowed to show in stone and wood the sparkling lavishness he could achieve on paper".

In this century C.H. has had its artists, Maurice de Sausmarcz, Keith Vaughan and Philip Youngman Carter among them. Carter was one of the most versatile men of his time, and a dedicated Old Blue. He edited *The Tatler* and a magazine for others, like him, devoted to good living, *The Compleat Imbiber.* He was, for a while, dramatic critic for the *Evening News.* He wrote some of the best reminiscences of Horsham school-days, and also travel-books, some detective-novels but is probably best-known to millions all over the world who do not know his name, as the model for the detective-hero, Albert Campion, in the books by his more famous wife, Margery Allingham. It may well be, however, that he will come to be remembered for his paintings and drawings and already with us his fame is secured by the three strong portraits of C.H. celebrities – Blunden, Fyfe and A. C. W. Edwards – which he drew especially for *The Christ's Hospital Book.* The originals of all three now hang at Horsham.

As with music so also with painting, fear of the invidious holds back the names of the living but there is at least one Old Blue painter in the list of great artists of a generation now nearer the end than the beginning of their careers and two distinguished portrait-painters.

The professional theatre has been – once more until recent times – largely ignored by Old Blues. There is only one Old Blue actor in the *Dictionary of National Biography* and he, William Powell (not, alas, William Poel) might as well not be there for all that anyone knows of him. Edward Terriss founded a theatrical dynasty, Henry Bedford was an actor-manager in the Irving manner, A. W. Baskomb is remembered, by many of an age that must imply that they will soon be few, for his performance as Marine Ogg in *The Middle Watch* and Geoffrey Tandy (brother of a more famous theatrical sister and of one of our ambassadors) for his Cyrano de Bergerac. (His career was cut short by illness.)

Fame is, for all but a few, short-lived, and histrionic reputations notoriously ephemeral. There was a time – and that not so long ago – when all over the world the hearts of young women missed a beat at the very mention of the name Michael Wilding. To-day he is best-remembered for the wives he married, yet it cannot be questioned by any who saw him in the plays of Wilde or Rattigan that Wilding was a better actor than his more popular performances with Anna Neagle ever suggested, and in terms of the statistics of applause Wilding's status as the best-loved Old Blue actor of all times cannot be denied. (And, had he not moved, almost by accident, into the theatre, as a water-colourist he might have added more than a little to the gallery of Christ's Hospital artists.)

Now that we have, at Horsham, a theatre of our own more lavish than that owned by any other British school and, in London, an Old Blue impressario who with his successes out-matches even the backers of *The Mousetrap,* we may look to improve our theatrical record.

But where are the Hertford actresses? And where, for that matter, C.H girls turned writer, musician or painter?

Whereas Housie's contribution to music, and to the dramatic and visual arts has been in the past meagre, and in no way comparable to the magnificence of C.H. gifts in literature, the achievements of Old Blues in the art and science of healing has been superb – and inexplicable.

There were Old Blue doctors already in the sixteenth century but the first of our truly great medical men, James Jurin, was a Grecian in 1702. From Trinity College, Cambridge, he moved to Leyden and thence, as Master, to the Royal Grammar School, Newcastle-upon-Tyne. At Cambridge again in 1716 he took his medical degree, became a Fellow of the College of Physicians three years later, Secretary of the Royal Society in 1721, an F.R.S. in 1725 and President of the College of Physicians in 1750, the year of his death. We have the authority of none other than Voltaire for acclaiming him as 'the famous Jurin'.

In the history of medicine he is honoured still among the pioneers of inoculation and as one of the first to relate the wisdom of mathematics to the study of physiology.

No Old Blue has succeeded Jurin as President of the Royal College of Physicians, though we have had our President of the British Medical Association (C. G. Wheelhouse), but the scalpel suits us better. Three Old Blues have been President of the Royal College of Surgeons and Christ's Hospital is the only school which, in this century, has educated two P.R.C.S. (Lords Moynihan and Brock).

This plethora of distinguished surgeons (and there have been several Vice-Presidents of the Royal College as support to the grandeur of the three Presidents) should not dim the fame of one at least of Christ's Hospital's most influential sons – and he a physician.

Edmund Parkes had won for himself, already in youth, a place in C.H. history which had little connection with the history of medicine but which, even had be done nothing for the rest of his days, should have secured for him a mention in any annals of Christ's Hospital, for he was one of the first Old Blues – and probably the very first – to recognise that Oxford and Cambridge no longer represented the totality of English university education. He was, indeed, one of the earliest graduates of University College, London.

The way that Parkes led was followed by many Blues and in the 1930's a few, even more eccentric or even more obstinate than the rest, discovered that universities exist far beyond the boundaries of Britain and moved to take their degrees in Australia, North America and South Africa. The huge expansion of universities after the Second War and heightened opportunities abroad have now made it a commonplace to find among the list of honours gained by leaving Blues places at Manchester or Sydney, Warwick or North Carolina, but it must be admitted that, even a century-and-a-half after Parkes left for the University of London, the C.H. authorities (the teaching-staff if not the Foundation as such) are still reluctant to accept that the modes of tertiary education began to change in the first half of the nineteenth century and are now altered beyond recognition. Still an antique prejudice lingers on. Still in this as in little else C.H. follows too readily the conventions of the public schools. Still an award or a place at any other university anywhere is somehow regarded at less creditable than entrance to Oxbridge.

If there be fault in this none of it can be laid at the feet of the man who first trod the path. By his subsequent activities Parkes proved himself to be one of Christ's Hospital's most ditinguished products and in his chosen career, as in his choice of university, a notable pioneer.

A brief tour, as an Army surgeon in India, gave him his grounding in tropical medicine and, whilst still overseas and not yet thirty years old, he wrote two papers which the greatest of his disciplines and most enthusiastic of his many enthusiastic students, Sir William Jenner, later described as among the most remarkable in medical literature.

Elected Special Professor of Clinical Medicine at his old college in his thirtieth year, Parkes set about a successful revolution in medical education. There was still another pioneering career before him: as the true founder of military medicine.

The fame and notoriety of Florence Nightingale has dimmed the lamp carried by Parkes but it was he who designed the hospital at Scutari which, for all Miss Nightingale's strictures, was to that date the finest ever built for the express purpose of caring for the British Army at war. Parkes' zeal on the subject of hygiene in the field was recognised by Florence Nightingale's friend, Sidney Herbert, who, when Secretary of State for War, persuaded him to leave University College and to go to the new Army Medical School as its first Professor of Hygiene.

None before Parkes had ever considered the relevance of hygiene to military success and to the well-being of men under arms. The lessons that he taught were too often ignored but even so his teaching endured and was, in its own way, as significant a contribution to future victories as was the genius of any general. More so, perhaps, because it influenced not only the British but all European armies. When he died the Professor of Military Medicine at Vienna wrote of him:

All the armies of the Continent should at parade lower their standards craped. . . because the friend and benefactor of every soldier, Edmund Parkes, is no more.

Blues were, in the past, inescapably handicapped if they sought to make a career in those professions which customarily required a private income as support to talent. Colborne (of whom more later) did manage to scramble his way up every step in the military ladder from ensign to Field-marshal without buying one promotion, and, from time-to-time, an Old Blue found his way into Parliament, but it was not until after the Second War that any entered the Cabinet. Then, however, the invasion was on a grand scale; no insignificant office, but the Secretary of State for Foreign Affairs, no less – and the incumbent, eventually our fourth peer.

The Bar, too, and for the same reason, until very recent times, was generally barred to us but William Moses, who left C.H. in 1639 with an exhibition at Pembroke Hall, Cambridge, overcame a late start, and the opposition of both Cromwell and Charles II and, having been thrown out of his office as Master of Pembroke, took to the law with such alacrity that he became a serjeant-at-law, counsel for the East India Company and for Christ's Hospital, and died 'a rich batchelor'. He stands among C.H. worthies not only as probably our greatest lawyer but also as one of our

Not quite a hero — not quite a Blue? — Warren Hastings.

Charles Lamb.

Leigh Hunt.

(Ætat 36)

Samuel Taylor Coleridge.

noblest benefactors. By his will, his considerable fortune was divided between his old college and his old school.

Only in the last few years has a Blue been elevated to the Bench in England but overseas, where in the past it was easier to practise without benefit of private means – as lawyers and civil servants – Old Blue lawyers had greater success. There was a Chief Justice in the Sudan (Sir Humphrey Bell) and in the Leeward Islands (Sir Henry Ludlaw) as Advocate-General, and several Judges in India, an Attorney-General in Trinidad, and Crown Prosecutors in Australia, Canada and Egypt.

But, after Moses, probably the most notable of all Old Blue lawyers (as also, in a sense, one of Christ's Hospital's most eminent politicians) came to his greatest glory not as a loyal servant of the Crown but as a distinguished rebel.

Gabriel Jones was born in Virginia (and that too must make him rare among Old Blues – though no longer unique). When his father died his mother

Above: Richard Thornton — 'that other Thornton' — 'the Duke of Danzig'.

Left: Joshua Barnes — 'the other Barnes'.

Edmund Blunden.

Constant Lambert.

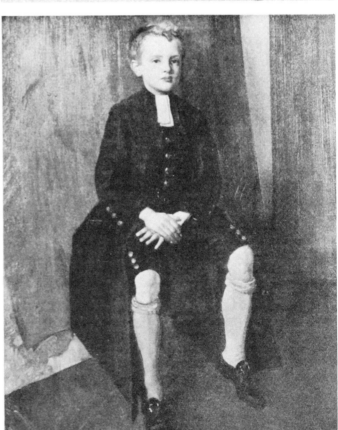

brought him back to England and he came to C.H. in 1732. Seven years later he began a legal career in London but soon returned to his native Colony where he became an attorney, close friend to George Washington (whose election to the House of Burgesses he engineered), executor to Lord Fairfax, a King's Attorney, himself a Member of the House of Burgesses, of the Continental Congress and of the Convention which adopted for Virginia the Constitution of the United States.

The Civil Service at large was always a refuge for Old Blues but it is doubtful if any in more distant generations could have forecast that the time would come – as it did in the period immediately after the Second War – when six Ministries would have at their head men who had been educated in Christ's Hospital.

There can be no connection, but it was at that same time, that according to one of them, Barnes Wallis, there were more Fellows of the Royal Society from Christ's Hospital than from any other school except Eton. Wallis, who should have known, insisted that it was a direct consequence of Christ's Hospital's pioneering of scientific education, and particularly of the heuristic method, that so many Old Blues came to originality in scientific exericse.

Wallis himself (a recent addition to the list of those who can be named, for he died in 1979 at the age of 93) was not by any means the first from C.H. who made his name in engineering and analogous professions. One such – and one who, for reasons that are inexplicable, has been consistently ignored by C.H. historians – created and gave his name to a firm that took its place among the most celebrated of all British industrial empires. On leaving C.H. Arthur Dorman went for a short time to Paris and then, in 1866, he was apprenticed to a Stockton iron-master. Less than 10 years later he, with his friend Arthur Long, founded the steel-making firm of Dorman, Long. It was Dorman himself who added bridge-building to the firm's interests and so it is that Old Blues have an especial right to look with pride on Sydney Harbour Bridge, opened in 1932, just after the death of Sir Arthur Dorman.

But it is not only the prejudice natural to his biographer that sets Wallis as first among those who have magicked promptings received in boyhood into the vast and magnificent practicalities of technology and, in this century, first also in the list of the benefactors of the Foundation.

Wallis entered Christ's Hospital in 1900 and left in 1904. He belongs, therefore, to that generation which knew both Newgate Street and Horsham and, in later life, as Donation Governor, representative Almoner of the Royal Society, and as Treasurer, he dedicated much of his phenomenal energy to ensuring that, whilst Christ's Hospital would remain forever a leader in British education, it must never lose its rare sense of continuity.

His career began humbly, as an apprentice working on the last battleship built on the Thames, but from 1913, when he moved to designing rigid airships, almost until his death, he set his dancing imagination to the service of aeronautical engineering. His contribution to aviation was stupendous. *R80*, the most satisfying of his many exquisite designs; *R100*, Britain's only successful challenger to German airship supremacy; geodetic construction; *Wellesley*, which held the long-distance record for 9 years; *Wellington*, the much-loved and virtually indestructible "Wimpey" of Bomber Command; the sensational weapons, the 'bouncing-bomb' which destroyed the Ruhr Dams, Tallboy and Grand Slam; swing-swing; and that fantastic dream of his last year, the so-called "square-plane": all these came from a mind that needed only the inspiration of a question to find an answer. Indeed, with the exception of the jet-engine, almost every major advance in aeronautical engineering in this, the century of aviation, owed something to his ingenuity. But not aeronautical engineering alone: he contributed also to the development of nuclear submarines and radio telescopy, gave time and genius to the design of vehicles for the disabled, was a propagandist for better education in the sciences – and invented a steam-proof shaving-mirror.

Save only in the unnaturally enlivened years of the Second War, Wallis was sadly frustrated by circumstances. He worked in a field where the costs of originality and experiment are phenomenal and the rewards often speculative and always long-delayed, and in a period when Britain could no longer afford the vast expense of exploiting his brilliance. His early career rhymed with the brief ebullient youth of the British aircraft-industry. There was for that industry no prosperous middle-age and already before he was old, it had come to impoverished senility and virtually to death. But neither the tragic background to his labours nor the sad paradox that he, a devout Christian, was permitted fulfilment only when he was creating weapons of destruction, deterred Wallis, and it was his ultimate consolation that from the most honoured but most brutal of all his many achievements he gathered the inspiration and the money to enlarge the gentle four-hundred-year-old charity of Christ's Hospital – as tribute to the men who had gone 'in jeopardy of their lives' to carry to the enemy his weapons of destruction.

The Royal Air Force Foundation (known sometimes – colloquially but accurately – as the Barnes Wallis Foundation) was established by Wallis with money granted to him – reluctantly – by the Royal Commission on Awards to Inventors in recognition of his war-time inventions. The Foundation was modelled, deliberately by Wallis, on the Royal Mathematical School. No child should be selected by competitive examinations. Instead, wrote Wallis:

I earnestly desire selection to be based upon the

service record of the father, as being a man who has shown himself, in the words of Cecil Rhodes, to be a man of truth, courage, devotion to duty and sympathy for and protection of the weak. . .

As the Royal Mathematical School three hundred years earlier, so now the Royal Air Force Foundationers Trust had as prime purpose the 'benefit of His Majesty's Dominions'.

The gratification Wallis derived from his personal 'dede of pittie' was much augmented when, in response to his suggestion, the Royal Air Force Benevolent Fund added £10,000 to the capital sum he provided, and committed itself to meet one-third of the total cost of maintaining and educating within Christ's Hospital all the children admitted under the terms of the Foundation, but to him even richer satisfaction came his way when the serving-officers of 617 (Dambusters) Squadron volunteered their intention of taking some active interest in the boys and girls of the Foundation. This promise their successors continue to honour.

There is another and visible link between the Foundation and the Squadron, between the Royal Air Force Foundationers Trust and its senior, the Royal Mathematical School, and, as Wallis would have had it, between him and Isaac Newton, his great predecessor both in the Royal Society and the Christ's Hospital Court. Wallis himself designed with great care a shoulder-badge for his Foundationers which is, in its masculine version, the same size as that worn by Mathemats; its central theme is the crest of 617 Squadron.

Wallis's call that his Foundation should serve for "the benefit of his Majesty's Dominions" was one that had been answered by many Old Blues since the earliest days.

We have noticed already in passing a few, lawyers and those many boys who, throughout the seventeenth and eighteenth centuries, moved from Newgate Street to the plantations of Virginia.

In that context it may be remarked that, already in the very first years of the Virginia Colony and 370 years before the notion became a fact, C.H. came close to receiving its first "exchange scholars" from America. Then it was that an "unknowne Messenger" representing an anonymous benefactor signing himself in gloriously romantic terms D and A [Dust and Ashes] appeared before the Court of the Virginia Company with the offer of £550, and more to come, "to see the erecting. . . of some waye whereby the Children of the Virginians might have bin taught and brought up in Christian and Religion". D and A insisted that these "Virginians" must be Indian boys and that they "be brought over into England here to be educated and taught in Christ's Hospital. . ."

The scheme came to nothing but D and A has been tentatively identified as Patrick Copland, Aberdonian, minister, traveller, merchant, and protegé of Sir

Thomas Dale, a Governor of C.H.. Soon after the collapse of the philanthropic scheme proposed by Dust and Ashes, Copland was appointed first President of British America's first college.

The century which saw, close to its beginnings, the frustration of D and A and the successful initiation of the enduring scheme which sent Blues as clerks to the Virginia Colony saw also, close to its end, the first acts in the long drama of association between C.H. and that "other India in the East".

A minute of the Court of the Honourable East India Company for 13th April 1694 preserved an arrangement that, as can be seen, was even then well-established. Then it was that the Court responded to a motion presented, on behalf of the Governors, by the Treasurer:

that the Company would please to accept in their service ten Hospital youths to be bred up in the India as their apprentices, the Court was pleased, out of their charity and respect for the foundation, to entertain them to serve the Company for the salary usually given to the Company's writers, and whereas all other their servants do pay their passage outwards, the Company are pleased to bear that charge themselves, the Governors allowing the £4 a head, as was formerly due, towards their transportation unto the captain of the ship to make fresh provisions for them on their voyage.

Service with the Company was often the high road to great influence, huge riches – or an early death – and in that service, as later in the Indian Civil, in the Indian Political, and in the mercantile houses of the Raj, many Old Blues came to fame and some to fortune.

If, in these pages, one stands for them all, it is not from any wish to under-value the Mathemats who became gallant captains of East Indianers, the several clerks who ended their days as nabobs, the Blues who governed districts or provinces, nor yet with any intention of ignoring the fact – by no means insignificant both in the history of C.H. and of India, or of the relationship between the two – that it was a Blue who passed out at the head of the list in the first competitive examination for the Indian Civil in 1856. Nor is it the rich resonance of his name, Louis Napoleon Cavagnari, that forces his selection, but rather is it that Cavagnari had qualities – and came to a fate – which made him fit representative not only for Old Blues in India but also for that whole exotic and devoted tribe which, over the centuries, created the unique relationship between Britain and India; love and despising, hate and admiration compounded; his own the epitome of that perverse contrast of high hopes, courage, deep knowledge, application and tragic consequence which was the life-story of so many who gave up Britain to serve Britain-in-India. Perhaps, too, he earns his special place because he has two monuments, one in the brutal loneliness of the Khyber

Pass, the other in the calm of the corridor to the Dominions Library at Horsham.

Cavagnari's father was a general in Napoleon's army, his mother an Irishwoman (their son did not become a British subject until after he had left C.H.)

After short service in the Army he transferred to the Indian Political Service to play what later Kipling called "the Great Game" on the Frontier. There he became very quickly the confidential agent of the Viceroy, Edward Bulwer Lytton. Lytton, the son of the author of *The Last Days of Pompeii*, was himself something of an eccentric, a poet, an adventurer – and anathema to Simla society because of his monstrous habit of smoking between courses. The dash and ambition of Cavagnari matched his own, and Lytton, the very Viceroy who proclaimed Victoria Empress of India, certain that Cavagnari would act with verve and decisiveness, chose him to preserve the frontiers of the Raj by dealing successfully with the ever-troublesome Afghans.

Cavagnari, in his turn, chose his adjutants well – and treated them much better than did Lytton treat his. Sir Robert Warburton, who worked with him for several years, wrote of Cavagnari that he was "a beau-ideal of a chief, and it was a great feat and honour to serve under him. . .!" And Warburton told how Cavagnari would spend a whole day in the saddle chasing raiders and then, back in his office, "without having taken or made any notes, he would sit down and write his report of ten, fifteen, twenty pages of foolscap, all in the best English, in a most beautiful clear hand, without a single blot or erasure".

That exquisite literary style and immaculate calligraphy is testimony to Cavagnari's schooling in C.H., as also, it is hoped, is his endurance, his energy and his courage.

What seemed to be Cavagnari's greatest achievement was, in truth, his undoing. He alone was responsible for the treaty concluded at Gandamak in 1879 with the Amir Takub Khan. Disraeli hailed it as securing "a scientific and adequate frontier for our Indian Empire" but triumph soon turned to disaster and the victim of the disaster was the architect of the triumph, Sir Louis Napoleon Cavagnari. In Kabul as Britain's first envoy, he was besieged in the Residency by hordes of Afghan soldiers – mutineers, perhaps, but more likely acting under orders from the Amir. And there Cavagnari was murdered.

Old Blues have thrived elsewhere overseas from the beginning of the seventeenth century, and still to-day, as merchants, industrialists, legislators, as rulers of districts and provinces. Both the Sudan and Borneo had Governors from C.H. The last British Governor of Sierra Leone added that eminence to his already substantial status as Senior Grecian. But it could well be that the Hospital's greatest contribution to the expansion of England lies in the record of Blues as explorers.

Many who in the seventeenth, eighteenth and early nineteenth century pushed back the frontiers of civilisation came, as might be expected, from the Royal Mathematical School. It was a Mathemat who, in 1727, assisted William Byrd of Westover in his survey of the Dividing Line between Virginia and North Carolina. There are (at a quick count) 12 Old Blues in the *Dictionary of Australian Biography*, all but one Mathemats, and only two not explorers; the best-remembered of them all J.S. Roe, and W.E.P. Giles, who more than any other single individual opened up Western Australia. The most adventurous of all these Mathemats was David Thompson, who left C.H., at the age of 14, in 1784, went straight to Canada, and within a very few years began a series of journeys of exploration as seismic to the development of Canada as the travels a few years later of Lewis and Clark to the development of the United States. He it was who explored the Columbia River and thus made practicable the settlement of British Columbia. And he, too, like so many from C.H., wrote so well that extracts from his journals appear again and again in anthologies of Canadian literature.

There were Mathemats with Captain Cook as companions and assistants to the man who was to become the most famous of all Masters of the Royal Mathematical School, William Wales, but not all Old Blue explorers had learnt their craft in the R.M.S. Former Grecians, too, moved sometimes from the placid professions appropriate to their scholarship into the unknown continents. E.C. Baber, for example, Consul-General in Korea in the mid-nineteenth century, added significantly to Western knowledge of the interior of China.

For four centuries (but perhaps no longer) a majority of Blues moved from Newgate Street, and later from Horsham, into City offices. Their achievements were many but their names seldom appear in the reference-books. Richard Thornton, of course, and our three Lord Mayors of London (C.H. has produced also a Lord Mayor for Manchester and, but recently, another for Westminster); but there can scarcely be an insurance company, a bank, a firm of Lloyds underwriters, a pension fund or a stock-brokers which has not had an Old Blue at or close to its head.

There have been, too, those Old Blues whose names are well-remembered but whose careers do not fit easily into any conventional category. Sir Henry Cole, for instance, who, virtually single-handed, established the Victoria and Albert Museum and who is said by some to have been responsible for another and less certain achievement, the introduction of the habit of sending Christmas cards, and his three successors who have been at various times high in the service of the British Museum.

Another Victorian Old Blue earns without question his place in the pantheon not for the work by which he earned his living but by the labours of his spare-time. G. Rowland Hill was from 1881 to 1904 the Honorary Secretary of the Rugby Football Union (and the last before the business of sport demanded a paid Secretary) and President from 1904 to 1907. More than any other individual he engineered administrative processes of the greatest of all games. To him, more than to any other in any sport, must be set the credit for creating the structure of his chosen game and for ensuring its future health. He was, writes the official historian of the Rugby Football Union:

A man of such obvious sincerity that he swayed every kind of meeting that he attended by an emotional appeal peculiar to himself and certainly most unlike the stolid characters he normally addressed. His personality addressed. His personal ability was only partly indicated by his conduct of affairs as Honorary Secretary. . . That he did not become President until 1904/5 was solely because he was satisfied that he could serve the game best as a secretary whose every wish was law.

This vigorous personality, this fervour and lucidity, was almost uniquely responsible for one of the most seismic events in the history of modern sport. It was Rowland Hill himself who introduced into the meeting called in 1893 to consider payments for broken-time, an amendment to the effect:

That this meeting, believing that the (principle of paying players) is contrary to the true interest of the game and its spirit, declines to sanction the same.

And it was Rowland Hill's vehement oratory which swayed the meeting, saved Rugby Football for the amateurs – and thus led to the foundation of the schismatic Northern Union, subsequently the Rugby League.

Just as careers in politics and at the Bar were in the past generally closed to Blues because, by definition, they could not carry with them the advantage of family fortune, so also was it difficult for them to make their way in the Armed Forces, and there they faced for almost three centuries the additional inhibition imposed by the custom of purchasing promotion.

Nevertheless, and largely because of the compensatory advantage conferred upon them by their unique early training as navigators, some Mathemats did rise to high rank in the Royal Navy. One at least, in the eighteenth century, Michael Everitt, achieved flag-rank. Blunden, who was rarely wrong about anything connected with Christ's Hospital, claims also Nelson's beloved Troubridge, but, alas, though Troubridge may have been for a brief enlivening period a non-Foundationer, the reflected glory of the hero of the *Culloden* must be conceded to St. Paul's School. The poor navigation and inglorious end of his predecessor Cloudesley Shovell, was certainly no fault of the Royal Mathematical School but Shovell was, it would seem, almost certainly a private pupil. Most Mathemats shrugged-off parental impecuniosity by

placing their rare professionalism, not at the service of the Royal Navy, but instead to the unfettered Merchant Marine, to the ships of the Company and of the Bombay Buccaneers, or else ignored sea-service and built upon their early training careers as surveyors and explorers.

Save only in the technical and specialist arms (which themselves were mostly developed in the second half of the nineteenth century) the Army did not shake off the imperative of a private income even when it gave up the practise of purchasing commissions, and it was not until the First World War that the land-service benefited considerably from the presence of Old Blues. There had been even before that time an occasional Old Blue general and there was one who made his way by ability alone – without buying one step in his promotion.

Field Marshal Sir John Colborne was a Foundationer (and also, it must be admitted, later a Wykehamist). He it was who led the charge of the British cavalry against Napoleon's Old Guard at Waterloo and later, as Governor of Upper Canada, he proved himself to be no less bold as administrator and proved also his dedication to education, as one of the founders of the University of Toronto and as prime mover in the establishment of what was to become Canada's leading public-school, Upper Canada College. For these efforts, and for his firm handling of the 1837 Rebellion in Lower Canada, he stands high among the famed in Canadian history. In the Christ's Hospital record he remains to this day the ranking officer, but has his place also as the first Old Blue elevated to the peerage – as Lord Seaton.

In more recent times, there have been many Old Blue admirals and generals (even one in the United States Army) but it is the Royal Air Force, a service which has never known the dedication to wealth which, until very recent times, clung vestigially to the other two Services, which has enjoyed most whole-heartedly a connection with C.H. For almost 60 years the *Air Force List* has boasted more than a fair share of Old Blue Air Commodores, Air Vice-Marshals and Air Marshals. Even there is one Air Chief Marshal – and he happily still very much alive and an Almoner – second only to Colborne in the Christ's Hospital order of seniority of service officers.

Service records cannot be measured exclusively by rank. The length of the Rolls of Honour for the two World Wars stands also as tragic testimony to the readiness of Old Blues, both professional military men and volunteers, to fight when fighting was necessary. And so, too, do the three Victoria Crosses and one George Cross won by men educated in Christ's Hospital.

If, in the past, some careers were too often closed to Blues by the financial circumstances which had allowed them to enter Christ's Hospital, there were two professions, the ministry and teaching, that just because they called for no equivalent support to entry from family wealth, were in that same period the most-favoured territory for the more academically advanced Blues.

In the professional service of the Almighty, Christ's Hospital's record was for several centuries more multifarious than glorious. St. Edmund Campion, it is true, and also Fathers David Baker and Hugh Greene (known as Ferdinand Brookes) were by any standards divines of high quality, but they practised their vocation in the service of what the Founder King would have regarded as the 'wrong Church'. So also, but for other 'wrong Churches', did several notable Nonconformist preachers of the seventeenth century. For Christ's Hospital's own communion, the Church of England, the School produced in every generation from the first godly parsons and goodly preachers, but promotion in the hierarchy came their way rarely. Old Blues occupied distant *cathedra:* in Calcutta (Middleton), Lebombo (B.W. Peacey) and Nova Scotia (F. Courtney), in Clonfert and Killala (Mordecai Carey), which must almost be considered *in partibus paganorum* and in Sodor and Man (Rowley Hill) which sounds as if it should be, but it was not until this century that C.H. produced an apron-full of home-settled bishops, E.C. Pearce at Derby, his brother, E.H., at Worcester and one (the author's friend, contemporary and fellow-Almoner) at Bradford and latterly as Episcopal Chaplain (Chief of Staff) to the Archbishop of Canterbury. In this century, too, at last an Archbishop, of West Africa and, another bishop in Africa, who must be entered in the text for the exotic quality of his episcopal signature, Lucien Upper Nile, even if by so doing the author breaks his self-imposed rule of holding the living anonymous. In this century, too, there has been an Old Blue Chaplain-General (F.U. Hughes) and another leader for a communion that is not Christ's Hospital's by tradition or charter: Newton Flew, President of the Methodist Church.

Deans, Archdeacons, Canons and Prebendaries have come from C.H. in plenty over four centuries. One only will be mentioned; and Richard Colfe not because of his ecclesiastical distinction but because he demonstrated his gratitude to the Hospital by establishing on C.H. principles a school in South East London. (So also did another Old Blue, Edward Colston, in Bristol, but Colston was not a cleric.)

In education at large Old Blues have been largely successful (if, by the very nature of the profession, few of them can be said to have prospered). Two – Sir Henry Maine at Calcutta and Sir Langham Dale at Cape Town – became Chancellors of universities, but Chancellors have not often been educators. There have been Old Blue Vice-Chancellors at Cambridge, Wales, Queensland and Adelaide. For the innumerable Old Blue heads of Oxford and Cambridge colleges two names two centuries apart, William Moses of Pembroke, Cambridge, and A.L. Smith of Balliol, Oxford, may speak for the distinction of the rest.

Professorships have come to Old Blues with such regularity and such frequency since the seventeenth century that the title seems hardly a distinction and a recital of names would be as monotonous – and as meaningless – as Old Testament rehearsals of begettings. For those twentieth century Old Blue academics three may serve as representatives for the rest. Sir Arthur Bowley, the eminent statistician, Sir Cyril Burt, the father of educational psychology, and Sir John Beazley, one of the greatest of all classical archaeologists. Between them they collected more than 30 honorary degrees and, in Beazley's case, it says much for C.H. training, and for his genius, that within four years of leaving the school with an Open Scholarship to Balliol, and before even he began the career which won for him international fame, Beazley had added to his Double First the Ireland, Craven, Derby and Hertford Scholarships and the Gaisford Prize.

These are but three of the grandest names among Old Blue professors. There are others of distinction almost as magnificent and in this century the river has become a flood; in British universities alone there are to-day something over 20 Horsham Old Blues settled in Chairs – and one from Hertford. As Bowley, or for that matter Burt, would have had it, "the representatives of Christ's Hospital considered as a proportion of the total British professoriate is a statistic that carries educational implications beyond dismissal as coincidence".

As schoolmasters, even more than as dons, Old Blues have proved themselves. For several centuries Christ's Hospital itself turned always to an Old Blue as Upper Grammar Master or Head Master. Each generation of Old Blues considered its own Head to be the greatest (or at very least the most ferocious) in any school in the country, but the laurels for fame outside the Hospital must go where they were placed by Coleridge, Lamb and Leigh Hunt, on James Boyer.

Poor J.B.! – may all his faults be forgiven; and may he be wafted to bliss by little cherub-boys, all heads and wings, with no bottoms to reproach his sublunacy infirmities.

The custom of appointing Old Blues was broken when the school moved to Horsham but was revived in 1955 when the late George Seaman became Head Master and again with the appointment of the present Head.

As with professors so also with headships of the great independent schools a list of names must be monotonous. In Britain alone there have been Old Blue Headmasters at Westminster, Charterhouse (twice), Radley, Marlborough, Sedbergh, Bedford, Blundell's, Edinburgh Academy and one Hertford girl as Headmistress at Leeds High School. Recently Old Blues have extended the influence of C.H. to the State system of education. There are now several comprehensive schools which can boast Old Blue

Heads and the most revolutionary experiment in secondary education, the new I.L.E.A. Community school in Westminster is being directed by one of our number.

It is a fallacy, but one that is common among those of other professions, that teaching is an unadventurous profession, and with it goes the misapprehension that teachers are, like parsons, timid and unworldly. Already in the seventeenth century, and from that day to this, Blues who took to pedagogy demonstrated that, no less than their more obviously bold contemporaries, they were prepared to go out into the still-mysterious continents, there to practise their craft. And, if it were truly possible to compare the influence on national and even world civilisation exercised by men of different generations and various professions, the prizes both for immediate potency and lasting effect might well go to two sturdy Calvinists who, in the mid-seventeenth century journeyed to New England; to Elias Corlett and Ezekiel Cheever.

Corlett left C.H. in 1626 for Lincoln College, Oxford and after a neophyte period schoolmastering in East Anglia he sailed for New England where he became Master of the Boston Latin School, newly-established to supply scholars for Harvard College. There he remained for 45 years.

Cheever, Corlett's younger contemporary, left C.H. in 1637 and took the more usual route for a Puritan scholar or divine, to New England by way of Emmanuel College, Cambridge. In America he taught in New Haven and Ipswich before he too reached Boston, the Mecca of Puritanism. His teaching career lasted for 70 years. Almost without exception every New England-born leader of New England thought, religion, politics, mercantile life and the arts in the seventeenth century was taught by either Corlett or Cheever, and many by both:

'Tis *Corlett's* pains and *Cheever's* we must own
That thou, *New-England*, are not Scythia grown

So wrote Corlett's greatest pupil, Cotton Mather, but even Mather could not foresee the enduring significance of the long careers of these two *alumni* of C.H. for, though Mather would have had it so, he had no way of telling that in time not so very far off the *mores* which Corlett and Cheever had done so much to instil into the minds of their charges would be largely responsible for creating the ideology and the cultural conventions of a great new nation, or that eventually the modes of thought which they had done so much to establish in New England would overcome the spirit of the only competitor, Virginia, and so would form a substantial part of the foundations for what has come to be called "the American way of life".

These are notions on a vast scale but there is a pleasing – and, it is believed, hitherto unnoticed coincidence – which carries the personality of Corlett into the intimacy of Horsham. One of Frank Brangwyn's paintings in the Chapel represents John Eliot bringing the Bible to the Indians. When Eliot worked on his translation he had as collaborator Elias Corlett. (Of his Indian Bible, published in Cambridge, Massachusetts between 1661 and 1663, 20 presentation copies were sent to England and one was for many years in the possession of C.H.) It is almost unthinkable that the artist knew of the connection, and so the inspiration to offer at second-hand tribute to a great Old Blue must be set down to subliminal forces.

In dominions beyond the seas other than New England the influence of emigré Old Blue pedagogues has been more ephemeral. It is true that there have been several such at the head of Australian and Indian independent schools, and there presumably their achievements endure, but in South Africa, where by statistical measure Christ's Hospital had its greatest success, political prejudices over which neither the individual Old Blue nor yet Britain had any control, have almost erased the mark once made by men from C.H. Not so very long ago, and at one time, three of the four leading schools established in South Africa on the British pattern had Old Blue headmasters. All three men gave up the unequal struggle against Anglophobia and two were driven back to Britain.

As foot-note to this roll-call of alumni and as symbolic statement of the enduring capacity of Christ's Hospital's products to outstrip the disadvantages of their birth, it is notable that, in 1981, three of the most patently establishment offices in the British Establishment – Chief of Staff to the Lambeth 'Curia', Director-General of the BBC and Secretary of the MCC, were filled by Old Blues. One of these has since moved to another of the Establishment's most dignified offices, as Chairman of horse-racing's Levy Board. Were it not a matter of public knowledge, it would be fascinating to make a book on which of the three achieved this extraordinary double.

CHAPTER NINE

The Brotherhood

Ending thus on a whimper the chapter on heroes would be misery indeed but, in truth, these cannot be the last chords in a paean to past grandeurs and present glories. Any recitation of the contribution of luminaries such as that presented in the last chapter is inevitably the eccentric product of the author's prejudice and is, no less inevitably, limited by his knowledge and by the records which are available to him. Others would devise other and essentially different lists, no less eccentric and equally limited. But all added together would but enhance the reputation which the Hospital has earned over almost four and a half centuries. And all would, of necessity, omit the greatest glory of Christ's Hospital, the vast congregation of Blues, men and women in all generations, who have served well and sometimes with great distinction, but who have left behind them nothing but the fruits of their labour and the intimate benefits that they have conferred on family, business, profession or community; men and women who have no memorial.

There is, too, a post-script that must be written. Current in the world at large and most vehemently articulated in Britain, there is a suspicion of great men and, most often expressed in Britain, a specious contention that extraordinary achievement is, more often than not, a consequence of family influence, inherited privilege, or bequeathed wealth. In our new perfervidly egalitarian society this suspicion and this contention have been used frequently as one powerful line in the fashionable attack on public schools. The Establishment, so runs the argument, is an evil; the Establishment is filled from the public schools; therefore the public schools are an evil.

As has been said already, Christ's Hospital is not a public school. The privileges that undoubtedly it confers upon its Scholars are the privileges of education, fraternity, community, but they have nothing whatsoever to do with wealth or family influence, and the greatest of the privileges which come from the Hospital is the privilege of service. So it is that Christ's Hospital could stand as a unique case-book for the study of the benefits which this type of education has, in the past, and can still, offer to society, and so it is that the roll-call of Old Blue worthies is evidence of the grandeur of the concept.

That there is an Establishment in Britain is beyond denying but so also is there an Establishment in every nation – even in the Soviet Union. And, at the last, it must be admitted without apology but with pride, that since the Second War probably as never before, Old Blues have been eminent – even pre-eminent – in that Establishment. Think only of this: in the last two decades there have been Old Blues as Secretary of State for Foreign Affairs, Director-General of the B.B.C. (and also its Controller of Music), Secretary of the M.C.C. (and also Assistant Secretary), "Chief of Staff" to the Archbishop of Canterbury, and President of the Royal College of Surgeons (and Vice President). What could be more Establishment? And is this not a matter for pride rather than apology?

Yet, even with this said, there is still more that, though it is understood by Blues, is not generally appreciated by those outside the fraternity. In a sense that is unusual and perhaps unique, C.H. is a continuing community. Blues do not have the benefit of family influence or fortune but they do have – and have always had – at their disposal the vast influence of the Hospital itself and, most potent of all, of the unflagging interest of their fellow-Blues. The outward and visible evidence of this – but not by any means the totality of advantage – is the long history, the continuing and world-wide strength, of Old Blue associations.

"Gentlemen educated in Christ's Hospital" have been celebrating their fraternity by dining in each other's company and by meeting together to listen to sermons since the first Blues became Old Blues. In this book, written by one President of the Amicable Society, revised by another and published by a third, some unaccustomed modesty measures the antiquity of that Society only from a dinner on Tuesday, 15th September 1629. Even so, the Amicables is the senior of all C.H. associations, the oldest of all "old boys clubs", and, so far as can be discovered, of all dining-clubs anywhere in the world the one with the longest unbroken history.

The name now used appears in the records for the first time in 1775 but was almost certainly in use some decades earlier, and the Society is a direct descendant of the Friendly Meetings and the Society of Blues of the seventeenth and early eighteenth centuries. From its parent-bodies it has inherited many of its esoteric customs, its mysterious rules, its mottoes, *Via Unita Fortior* and *Let Brotherly Love Continue*, the regularity of its festivals (three in each year), its prized *chaffs* (treasures) and the regulation whereby the number of Brethren is severely limited: to 40 and six Honorary Brethren, generally those who have passed the Chair.

Until the twentieth century, the Amicables, which now meets invariably in a Livery Hall, dined generally at City taverns or inns in rural Tottenham or bucolic Richmond. Twice, however, dinners were called for Canonbury Towers, the family home of Bishop Compton, the author of the C.H. Graces.

As some compensation for its exclusivity, the Society has been in the habit of receiving as guests distinguished persons, many with C.H. connections. Coleridge was dined when still a Grecian. Lamb honoured the Society with his only recorded after-dinner speech – almost certainly the finest because certainly the shortest ever heard by the Amicables. He rose to his feet, stammered out the one word "Gentlemen", then, overcome by the awesomeness of the occasion, sat down again.

The Society was "instituted for friendly intercourse and convivial and social engagement" and such remains its prime purpose, yet it is, beyond question, at once a power-house for the Foundation and evidence to that unique quality in Christ's Hospital which persuades Old Blues to pass on to children not their own the benefits they themselves have received. Of the current 46 Brethren, 14 are Almoners of the Hospital, 38 are Governors (most of them Donation Governors) and three are debarred from being Governors because they are Officers of the Foundation.

It was the Amicable Society which established in 1824 the second Christ's Hospital's association, the Benevolent Society of Blues, and it remains a rule of the Amicables that no candidate will be considered unless he is a subscriber to this charitable organisation and has subscribed for a year for the assistance of their fellow-Blues who have suffered misfortune, their widows and orphans. The Amicable Foundation (another off-shoot of the Amicable Society) maintains also Presentations to C.H.

The Old Blues Rugby Football Club was founded in 1873, only two years after the Rugby Football Union itself. Football of a sort had been played at C.H. already for decades. Superficially it was not unlike the Rugby game. A spherical ball was kicked or carried out of mauls, the ball-carrier could be tackled, and a score was made when the ball was grounded in goal.

But, had they been translated into the middle of a game in Newgate Street, William Webb Ellis or Tom Brown would have felt like Olympic fencers thrust suddenly into a bloody battle between savage tribes. The Housey game had few rules and many and widespread boundaries. The surface of the 'field' was asphalt (where it was not brick or stone) and a powerful or elusive ball-carrier (dressed, like all the scores of other players, in Housey uniform with coat tucked into girdle) burst through door-ways and archways and swerved around cloister-pillars.

The more gentle and genteel rules of the Rugby Football Union were introduced into C.H. in 1874 by two Old Blues, the one none other than Rowland Hill and the other Christ's Hospital's first Blue of that other upstart kind – the representatives of Oxford and Cambridge.

Already however, on 8th November 1873, C.H. had played its first school game, against the Old Blues, and already in that season, 1873-4, the Old Blues RFC had a full fixture-list and thus established its seniority over all other Old Boys still playing a century and more later.

The move of the school to the grandeur of West Horsham, with its vast array of good pitches, reared for the Old Blues new generations of players who added skill without losing for the Club the reputation it had earned from training in the hardy days in Newgate Street. Even more significant to the thrust of this chapter and against all gloomy predictions, the exodus served to heighten the will of Old Blues to retain their sense of community.

Then and for the next 50 years Old Blue rugger was the epitome of Old Blue enthusiasm and loyalty. These, and particularly the years between the wars – years which began with Sir Rowland Hill, the greatest of Old Blue men of Rugby Football and the first man to be knighted for services to the game, as President of the Club, and with the purchase of a fine ground at Fairlop in Essex – were the years when the Old Blues First XV had its internationals, Barbarians, trial caps; when there were County players even in the A XV. But it was not so much the great men of the Club as its remarkable depth which in those days made the Rugger Club significant in Housey history. For decades, without benefit of easy transport, plush dressing-rooms, crowd support, or publicity, the Old Blues put as many as ten XV's on various fields each week-end in the season.

The Club survived the Second War and it seemed that the old glory would not vanish. An Old Blue in a Victory International, another in the first post-war Varsity Match, more trial caps, the seemingly unending promotion of superannuated players to the panel of International referees – and still every Saturday several XV's – all encouraged the Club to improve the facilities at Fairlop and to look to a future as happy as its past.

But times had changed and were changing ever more

The new uniform for girls.

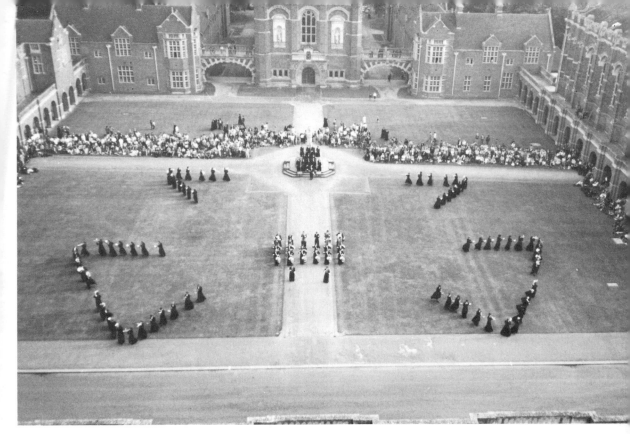

March and counter march seen from the Water Tower, Beating Retreat, 1982.

drastically. Of the Old Boys clubs playing first-class football only one other than the Old Blues was based upon a boarding-school, and the Old Blues in particular had in the past been compensated for this practical disadvantage by the fact that so many C.H. boys took up careers in the City. Even the academic élite (which at C.H. had never been, as at so many conventional public schools, separated from or antipathetic to their sporting brethren) moved generally to the 'suburban' universities, Oxford and Cambridge, from which they could come with comparative ease each Saturday to play for the Old Blues.

By the early 'Fifties, however, "the City" was no longer the inevitable haven for a majority of Old Blues, The "City" itself had shifted; business-houses were no longer concentrated in the Square Mile. Saturday morning work was now a rarity. What hitherto would have been regarded as a phenomenal proportion of boys moved on to higher education, but at universities all over the Kingdom and indeed all over the world. So the reservoir of talent began to dry and the attractions of community activity at Fairlop lessened. The process of decline was hastened by the administrators of the Rugby Football Union – a debilitating influence felt not only by the Old Blues but by all Old Boys clubs.

Even so the courage and obstinacy of playing-members held the Club together. Neither in Rugby Football nor in the sodality of Christ's Hospital is it as powerful as once it was but the cry of 'Housey' is still heard on the touch-lines.

The history of the Old Blues RFC is in certain limited senses mirrored by the history of the largest of all C.H. societies, the Christ's Hospital Club. Younger than the Rugger Club, when compared to the Benevolent Society a stripling; and by the standards of the Amicables scarcely out of the womb, the Club was founded in 1891 at a time when change was in the air and when it was not only the President of Christ's Hospital, the Duke of Cambridge, who predicted that a move from London must destroy the awareness of continuing community that had for centuries bonded together Old Blues in fraternity which – in this unlike 'old boy' sentiment of other schools – transcended school generations; the C.H. Club soon developed into what it remains to this day, a vast and world-wide organisation.

What has largely vanished in the years after the Second War – and what gives the appearance of similarity with the Old Blues RFC – is the centrality to the C.H. Club of its headquarters at 26 Great Tower Street in the City of London. For three decades of this century Christ's Hospital was unusual (if not quite unique) in the possession of Club rooms and there, particularly in the years between the wars, each working-day Old Blues (and C.H. Old Girl Associates) came to lunch, to play billiards – and to talk, as Old

Blues do incessantly, about C.H. Those same demographic influences which reduced the strength of the Old Blues RFC made the Club as meeting-place less convenient and, in addition, if but recently, economic and other practical difficulties associated with employing efficient labour have made it impossible to continue the practise of serving meals. The Club rooms exist still but too often they are empty.

Happily, this decline in the use of its most obvious facility has not affected the significance of the Club as a whole. The Club, and its slightly younger sister-organisation, the Christ's Hospital Old Girls' Association, remain the principal vehicle whereby news of the schools and of fellow-Blues is disseminated to the vast and widespread constituency which is Christ's Hospital. Happier yet, long before adverse circumstances reduced the significance of the Club rooms, the C.H. Club had established or fostered a number of subsidiaries; Masonic Lodges, the Dramatic Society, Regional and Overseas Sections, clubs for cricket, athletics, shooting, swimming and cycling enthusiasts. Of these the Dramatic Society, in the 'twenties and 'thirties, of all save perhaps the Rugger Club, the most active (and the least 'sexist') has succumbed to similar extraneous influences to those which reduced the importance of the Old Blues RFC and the Club rooms. Some others have disappeared in the wake of changing fashions but their place has been taken by new and energetic sections.

An habitual wanderer must see as the most blessed of all C.H. Club by-products the development of what long ago some wag called *Le Cordon Bleu* – a term which has now taken on the respectability of formal usage. All over the world there are corresponding secretaries, all over the world Old Blues join together in local groups. And, wherever he may go, the emigrating or visiting Old Blue finds a welcome and a helping-hand from resident Old Blues and their wives. (It is one of the marvels of Christ's Hospital, and as much to be remarked on the Council of Almoners as in distant places, how often and with what incomparable generosity and enthusiasm the wives of Old Blues allow themselves to be bombarded by their husbands into affection loyalty and service for Christ's Hospital.) Nowhere in the world is that emigrating or visiting Old Blue allowed to remain for long a stranger. (Two of the Australian sections, in Victoria and New South Wales, have also established corporate Donation Governorships.)

It was the Benevolent Society which first recognised that C.H. Old Girls were truly part of the total community but social equivalence was granted to them first by Overseas Sections, then by Regional Sections and at last, if hesitantly, by the Club itself. Although three times in their long history (the most recent for their 350th Anniversary Dinner in 1979) the Amicables have entertained lady-guests, there is as yet no sign that this most austere (if also paradoxically most frivolous) of Old Blue societies will concern itself with the provisions of the Equal Opportunities Act.

So one comes to the most formal of all Old Blue community gatherings, the celebration of Founder's Day, the 23rd October, the birthday of King Edward VI. The London Dinner is organised, not by the C.H. Club as such but by the self-perpetuating Stewards of Founder's Day, and it is they who select each year an Old Blue for the honour of occupying the Chair and for the ordeal of delivering what in other places would be called the key-note speech.

The Stewards, too, have at last recognised Hertford. C.H. Old Girls now attend the Dinner and the Head Girl is a guest-of-honour, as has been for many years the Senior Grecian.

London stages *the* Founder's Day Dinner, but in late October Old Blues of both sexes gather together in many places to dine, to demonstrate devotion to the Foundation and to each other, and to drink a toast to "The Pious and Immortal Memory of Kind Edward the Sixth". There is a tale of a Founder's Day Dinner during the First World War during which four Old Blue prisoners-of-war planned their escape by using the arcane Housey slang to confound their eavesdropping Turkish captors. During the Second War three Old Blues and one C.H. Old Girl joined together in a Founder's Day celebration in Changi Gaol, and the author of this chapter remembers with pride and poignancy the Dinner he attended in 1944 when five Old Blue officers from one Infantry Brigade sat down together in the midst of some of the harshest fighting of the Italian campaign; pride because we managed conviviality, and poignancy because in the next two months two of the five were killed and another lost a leg.

Then, as at the London Founder's Day, at all Founder's Day Dinners everywhere, we drank to the Founder King and then, as at all Old Blue celebrations, we drank our unique Loyal Toast, "Church and Queen".

Now, as then, and as at all gatherings, the Toast is called that somehow embodies all the traditions, all the achievements, and all the aspirations of Christ's Hospital:

The Religious, Royal and Ancient Foundation of Christ's Hospital; may those prosper who love it and may God increase their number.

CHAPTER TEN

Administration

The acceptance of the 1890 Scheme brought about a fundamental change in the constitution of the Hospital but it also initiated some shifts in emphasis which, important though they appeared to be at the time, are to the historian more fascinating and symbolic than truly consequential.

Of these the most intriguing was the Commissioners' decision to put a definitive end to the ancient wrangle between the Hospital and the City Corporation over the use of the Hospital's Seal. Although the Seal had always been held by the City and although the Corporation had consistently argued that its possession gave to the City over-riding influence in the Hospital's affairs; so much so that, at least once in the seventeenth century, the Corporation had insisted that all documents drawn by the Hospital must be examined by them and not sealed until they were satisfied as to the expediency of the transactions communicated therein; the Governors had remained adamant in their contention that in this context the Corporation was no more than a custodian, powerless to direct that the Hospital's activities were in any way subject to the City's scrutiny or that its writings must be drafted in comformity with the City's wishes.

The Commissioners found for the Governors. By the authority of Clause 50 of the Scheme the City still holds the Hospital's Seal but now all appropriate documents – leases, transfers, conveyances – require only the signature of two Almoners and the Clerk. They are then sent to Guildhall together with a document giving a summary of the contents and certifying to the resolution of the Council of Almoners. Thereafter, at its very next meeting, without amending or even reading the document, the Court of Common Council is bound to affix the Seal.

The significance of other and far more momentous changes wrought by the Scheme, like this nice resolution of antique conflicts, needs prefatory exposition of what had gone before if their importance is to be grasped.

The qualifying donation for a Governor had been increased from £400 to £500. All Governors were automatically members of the Court, the Hospital's supreme body, and the Chair at meetings of the Court was almost always taken by the President – by the Duke of Cambridge himself.

It was, however, necessary to delegate detailed duties to a Committee of Almoners. This body had no plenary powers but could only recommend to the Court. Inevitably this led to the suspicion, at times expressed with some vehemence, that the affairs of the Hospital were in the hands of a tiny cabal and though no serious charge of maladministration was ever substantiated relations between the Court and the Committee were often strained.

Donation Governors had the right of presenting children for admission and as a body they formed almost the only means of supplying entrants to the schools. Children thus presented were subjected to a simple educational test and to a medical examination which was far from stringent. There was some kind of means test on parental income but it was, by subsequent standards, notably elastic and, once passed, whatever the financial situation of the parents no charge whatsoever was levied as contribution to the cost of housing, feeding, clothing and educating the child.

Nevertheless, the election of a Governor was no easy matter. First he must be proposed and seconded, then his benefaction was accepted and finally he was called before the assembled Court to receive his charge; mercifully an edited version of the 1557 oration, but still solemn and weighty. Thus the original preamble as read to the newly-elected Governors from 1557 for almost three centuries:

That every of you endeavour yourselves with all your wisdoms and powers faithfully and diligently to serve in this vocation and calling: which is an office of high trust and worship; for you are called to be the faithful and true distributors and disposers of the goods of Almighty God to the poor and needy members. In the which office and calling, if you shall be found negligent and unfaithful you shall not only declare yourselves to be the most unthankful and unworthy servant of Almighty God, being put in trust to see to the relief and succour of His poor and needy flock; but also you shall show yourselves to be very notable and great enemies to that work which most highly doth advance and beautify the common weal of this realm, and chiefly of this City of London.

So it continued to the moment of cracking doom:

And to the intent that every of your worships may better understand what in this government you have to do during the time you are in office, now shall presently be read unto you the letters patent and grant from the King, with the indentures of Covenants.

As the documents referred to take up some forty closely-printed quarto pages the new Governors were left in no doubt that their duties were onerous. Their staying-power, the vocal athleticism of the Clerk (who read .the Charge) and the endurance of the previously-elected Governors (who had to listen to all this yearly) were beyond question.

Already charitably shortened by 1850 the Charging-ceremony went forever when the Scheme took away from the Governors even the pretence that they governed.

That prerogative is now unassailably in the possession of the Council of Almoners. The Court survives, and meets twice a year, but its principal function is to appoint the President, the Auditors, Donation Governors and the Council of Almoners – and to present to vacant benefices of which the Hospital has the advowson. The Court also receives a report from the Council on the condition of the schools and of any material changes introduced into the administration; a statement of receipts and expenditure; and of all dealings therewith, showing all accretions thereto and diminutions thereof, together with a statement of all sales or other alienations, and acquisitions, or real estate. It does not appear that the Governors have any authority to question the accounts or the reports. They must receive them; that it all. But the right of Presentation remains – and is still coveted.

However, one other substantial privilege remains with the Governors: 20 of the 46 Almoners are their representatives. The other 26 are nominees of the Universities of Oxford, Cambridge and London, of the Lord Mayor and Aldermen of the City of London, the Charity Commission, the Royal Society, the Inner London Education Authority (formerly the London County Council), the Ministry of Defence (formerly the Admiralty) and, in consequence of the particular requirements of the Wests Gift, the Boroughs of Reading, Newbury and Richmond (formerly Twickenham). Sad experience culminating in a lost case in Chancery has taught the Governors that they

have no will or pleasure in the appointment of nominees; whosoever is put forward by the nominating body must be accepted.

The Scheme proposed to reduce the number of presented children to 300 and to restrict the rights of Governors to the presentation of one child: that is, each Governor was only to have one child in the school at a time. This was the rock on which the waves of litigation broke, and which was successfully removed by the resistance of the Governors and their eventual bargain over the excepted endowments, whereby they regained in 1896 their privilege of presenting two children at a time, and the number of presented children was increased to 450. Certain rights of nominating boys for competition were given to the Governors in compensation for reduction of presentations, but these later lapsed in favour of corporate nomination by the Council. The Clause providing that there shall be not more than 150 places, nor more than one place to every two Donation Governors, ends thus:

Places capable of being filled under this clause shall not be filled except in so far as the number of such places for the time being is more than the excess of the number of foundationers for the time being admitted on the presentation of Donation Governors over the number of three hundred.

It is unlikely, but just possible, that some rarely erudite person unusually accustomed to legal phraseology can make sense of this verbal and arithmetical maze.

As the Scheme limited the number of places in the schools open to presentees so did it automatically restrict the number of Donation Governors. For some time the number of presentees exceeded the maximum imposed by the Scheme and eventually the Council accepted that it had too many Governors. In 1923 presenting privileges, previously held by a Governor for life and for two children at a time, were reduced to a period of 20 years and then, because still candidates for governorship came forward in droves, to one child at a time and, when even this out-ran the availability of places, to only two presentees consecutively. Most recently Donation Governors have been reduced to presenting only one child in the term of their Governorship.

The qualifying donation has been successively increased but never enough to match inflation and it remains to this day the best of charitable bargains. For an Old Blue, his or her immediate family, it stands now at £3500; and for other individuals at £5000. There have been, in recent years, a growing number of institutions, charities and business-houses taking Donation Governorships; from them the donation required is £8000.

It remains to be said that there is an implacable regulation which prevents any Governor from presenting his own child, grandchild or from entering into any deal which involves an explicit or implicit arrangement to exchange a Presentation with another Governor. Presenting rights, not the increase in the qualifying donation, have reduced the flow of candidates for Governorship.

The titular head of the Foundation is the President. Proud though Christ's Hospital remains of its long association with the City it cannot be other than delighted that the office of President has been for more than a century removed from the Aldermanic Bench into the care of the Royal Family. The installation of a new President is fortunately no frequent occurrence but when the need arises for this, too, Christ's Hospital has its long-established ceremonial.

The Lord Mayor, as is still his privilege and duty, takes the Chair at a meeting of the Court. The Treasurer proposes the election of His Royal Highness as President, the motion is seconded by the Deputy-Chairman and is carried (always *nemine contradicente*). Lord Mayor, Treasurer, Deputy-Chairman and Clerk then go to the main entrance of the London Office to greet the new President who is escorted to the Court Room and seated on the right of the Lord Mayor who then informs His Royal Highness of his election and invites him to take over the Chair. They change places; the President returns thanks for the honour done him by the Hospital and announces his intention to go to the Schools as soon as possible (no empty promise, as frequent visits from the present President, H.R.H. the Duke of Gloucester, bear witness). The Clerk then steps forward and reads the Charge to the President:

Agreeably to very ancient and laudable custom, you have been nominated, approved, and appointed President of Christ's Hospital, in succession to your royal predecessor.

You are therefore confidently expected faithfully to act in that station, which is of the highest importance and of great trust.

And whereas the President of every Royal Hospital is the chief Ruler and Governor of the House whereunto he is chosen, your authority as President of this Royal, Religious and Ancient Foundation shall be, from time to time, at pleasure, and for any reason that may seem sufficient, to cause the Governors to be called together to a full Court, or the Almoners to a special meeting of the Council, and to preside over their deliberations.

And may Almighty God grant you health and strength to discharge the duties of your high Office with satisfaction to yourself and to the advantage of the House.

(Christ's Hospital is unswervingly loyal but never obsequious; not even royalty is allowed to forget that service to Christ's Hospital is an honour and a responsibility.)

The Clerk then hands to the President an engrossed copy of the Charge and, the Clerk announcing their names one by one, all in the Court Room are presented.

The *de facto* head of the Foundation is the Worshipful the Treasurer who, since 1957 has added to his estate the seemingly lesser but all-important title of Chairman of the Council. In him are invested many prerogatives, responsibilities and onerous duties. He takes the Chair at all meetings of the Council, is *ex officio* a member of all its Committees and is implicitly granted by the Council the right to act on its behalf in all matters, whether great or small. The right man – and there have been few occasions since the days of Nathaniel Hawes in the late seventeenth century when the Treasurer was the wrong man – takes to himself full responsibility for all emergency decisions, in the certain knowledge that the Council will support him *ex post facto*. He is the Hospital's representative at all official occasions – and there are many such both within the Schools and without.

Since the passing of the Scheme every Treasurer has been an Old Blue and the devoted service given by the Treasurers – and their wives – amply justifies Allan's contention that "the gain to the Hospital in sympathetic consideration of its needs and to the Schools in an understanding knowledge of its conditions is incalculable".

Each year at its first meeting the Council elects four standing Committees: A Committee of Women, Education, Renters and House and Finance.

The Committee of Women, not altogether to the satisfaction of its members, though charged to assist in the management of the Girls' School, now deals only with changes in the uniform of the Girls' School.

With the Head Master and Head Mistress as its advisers the Education Committee has responsibility for all academic, extra-curricular and social aspects of life in the Schools. It is entrusted with enquiry into the qualifications of all children presented for admission, with framing regulations for their admission and eventual discharge and for receiving and considering, in the first instance, "all Reports and recommendations made regarding the Schools by the Head Master or Head Mistress". Grants from the Exhibition Fund and the Advancement in Life Fund (of which more later) are also recommended at the discretion of the Education Committee.

As its name implies the Committee of Renters has the management and care of "all the estates and properties of the Foundation not required to be retained and occupied for the purposes thereof" – and they are many. In the days when members of the Committee were in the habit of visiting the Hospital's widespread properties – and by stage-coach – their duties were arduous indeed. To-day their role is largely managerial; intimate inspections are carried out by the Hospital's professional Surveyor.

The House and Finance Committee takes on board

almost everything that is not educational or concerned with the Hospital's estates. It recommends to the Council on appointments of officers, is responsible for accounts and estimates, for repairs and improvements to School buildings, for all matters relating to clothing and boarding, and, above all, for the Foundation's investments. It is in the performance of this last responsibility that the Foundation has been notably blessed. Its close association with the City and in particular the perennial success of Old Blues in the world of finance has given to the House and Finance Committee a regular supply of shrewd and experienced Chairmen and Committee members and has made the manipulation of its portfolio a model which many would covet could they but uncover it. Were it not for this generous cunning the Hospital's financial state, made perilous by the hideous circumstances of the last two decades, would by now be parlous.

Almost from the first page of this book there have been references to the Clerk and any descriptions of the Administration of the Hospital which do not attempt to define his status, duties and influence would be empty indeed. Yet such definition is far from easy. He is not, as some would have it, Christ's Hospital's equivalent to the Bursar of other schools. Though he and his staff include in their tasks many that would be performed by a Bursar – the collection of dues, the maintenance of accounts, the care of buildings – the Clerk is a personage much grander than a mere Bursar, his role much more like that of Clerk to a City Livery Company. Better still as simile he is the Hospital's Permanent Secretary; with the Head Master and Head Mistress he makes up the trinity of senior paid officials. He, with his staff, arrange and minute all meetings of Court, Council and Committees and he, with his staff, organises most of the ceremonies of the Hospital. He (and not the two Heads whose responsibilities in this are limited to purely academic matters) advises the Council on admissions-policy. He is the Hospital's financial officer.

The Clerk is the administrator of the Hospital's estates, including those at Horsham and Hertford, and of the Hospital's several charities.

Even to some who are intimately concerned with the affairs of the Hospital it comes sometimes as a surprise that it cares for almost as many pensioners as children and that in every year it pays out under charitable trusts more than £63,000.

The smallest of these charities is that of Dame Mary Ramsey which provides pensions of £12 a year to "three poor widows and three poor old maimed soldiers". Many charities of a similar kind were combined in 1909 into 'the Consolidated Charities of Barnes and Others' and this fund provides pensions of £15 a year, principally to poor widows of 60 years and more living north of the Thames in the County of London. In addition to their gifts destined for the education of children John and Frances West gave money and lands to provide pensions for poor relatives, specifically

for their respective, proper and personal use, to prevent their perishing by want, to be expended in meat, drink, clothes and other necessities, and not to be assigned to any other person, or subject to their creditors, or debts.

Allan wrote feelingly:

A ceaseless flow of applications is our portion but there is only sufficient income to pay pensions of £100 a year to eight hundred members of this family, each of whom has to prove relationship to the founders by documentary evidence. We keep a genealogical record of this extensive race in four large volumes, and fresh entries are being made almost daily.

In 1774 the Rev. William Hetherington gave a sum of money to establish a pension fund for poor, old and blind men and women, in the hope that others would follow his example. He was not disappointed; many other benefactors came forward, among them Charles Lamb's friend, Thomas Coventry, and some gave handsomely so that the income is now £14,344 a year and provides pensions of £20 to 225 blind persons.

It might be thought that the arrival of the Welfare State has removed the need for these subsidiary charities and certainly the pensions cannot march with inflation but there is no shortage of applicants and the business of dealing with them and with recommendations from Local Authorities and Voluntary Bodies adds considerably to the work of the Clerk's office.

The relationship of the Clerk *vis-à-vis* Court, Council and Governors is clear enough. Far more ambiguous is the imposed stance in his dealings with the other two members of the Trinity, the Head Master and the Head Mistress, though it is in this that the distinction between the office of Clerk to Christ's Hospital and the Bursar of most other schools is most obvious.

Because he is the Officer responsible for estates, the Stewards at Horsham and Hertford and the estate staffs are answerable to the Clerk and not to the respective Heads. Because he is administratively responsible for maintaining the Hospital's charitable purposes he deals with all matters of admission policy that are not definitively educational. Because he is the Hospital's senior servant in all matters financial he acts for the Council in all that involves emergency expenditure. The arrangement gives to the Clerk great power but it also relieves the Heads of many onerous duties which must be exercised by those in charge of other schools and leaves them to concentrate on their academic and pastoral responsibilities. Nevertheless, from time to time but happily no longer, the magisterial significance of the office of Clerk has been the cause of suspicion and even contention.

There is yet one more duty imposed upon the Clerk, subtle, never written down and yet implicitly accepted by every Clerk for several centuries. More than any other individual, more even than the Treasurer or the Heads, he is the custodian of the Hospital's traditions. Perhaps because every Clerk has lived virtually his whole life within Christ's Hospital, as boy, as junior in the Office and finally as one of its three senior paid Officers, no Clerk has ever failed in this responsibility. All who know C.H., whether as Scholars, Governors or Almoners, know also how much the Hospital owes to its succession of loyal, shrewd and dedicated Clerks.

Since 1915 the Clerk has had his headquarters and houses his fifteen-strong administrative staff at 26 Great Tower Street in the City of London close to the Tower of London, the same building which houses the Christ's Hospital Club. To the sorrow of some (including the author of this chapter) only a few devout traditionalists now call it the Counting House but the mundane name, the Christ's Hospital Office, demonstrates no change in purpose.

And eventually whether he sits in Office or Counting House, the Clerk, like the President, the Treasurer, Court, Council, Governors, Head Master, Head Mistress, clerical, service and teaching staff are all combined to further a cause that, though it has been adapted in detail, has not altered in principle since 1552: the education of needy children.

So one comes to the question that, more often than any other, is asked of almost anyone connected with C.H.: "How can I get a child into Christ's Hospital?"

It is a question which denies a succinct answer. "By Presentation or by competition": so far, so good but still not good enough to explain the steps that must first be taken or to give even a hint of the diversity of modes of entry.

The supervening regulation which applies to all methods of admission save two, Non-Foundationers and New Foundationers (both minimal exceptions) is that no child will be admitted whose parent or guardians are not, at the time of the child's admission, in the opinion of the Council of Almoners, in need of assistance towards the education and maintenance of such children. In this connection, the Council's "opinion" has been codified into a scale by which need is measured in terms of annual income and number of dependent children. The same scale – a confidential document – is employed to assess the parental contribution, if any, payable for each child. No contribution at all is charged where the income falls below the minimum prescribed by the scale, but contributions up to £1341 a year may be imposed where the Council considers that the parents are able to contribute. After the child's admission, a contribution, or an increased contribution, may be required from parents whose circumstances have so improved as to

warrant such requirement. But this must not be taken to imply that it is open to a parent with means to secure the admission of a child by offering to pay higher contributions or full cost or more.

It is consistent with the charitable spirit of the Hospital that, once a child has been admitted, he or she is not removed because his parents' fortune improves so much that they go "out-of-scale".

All candidates for admission must be between the ages of 10 years 3 months and 12 years. Parents must demonstrate that their children are in good health – sufficient to sustain boarding-school life – and, though it is not required of them that they prove their offspring to be saints the Hospital holds to itself the right to exclude those who are patently sinners.

For presented children the academic qualifications were formerly minimal and even now they are by no means severe but no child is accepted who, in the opinion of the Head Master or Head Mistress, is not likely to achieve eventually a satisfactory performance at O Level.

No attempt was made by the Commissioners, and none has been made since, to shift the Hospital's allegiance to the Established Church and it remains to this day an explicit condition of admission that all children will attend acts of corporate worship (which are considered to be important almost as much because they are corporate as because they give opportunity to worship) but archaic dogmatism has in this century virtually disappeared. Boys and girls of all faiths and, indeed, of many races, have been admitted, have been allowed opportunity to go to services of their own choosing, have prospered in C.H. and, many of them, in adult life have repaid the charity of Christ's Hospital by devoted participation in the governance of the Foundation.

The Scheme preserved for certain City Livery Companies – Cooks, Drapers, Fishmongers, Grocers, Ironmongers, Mercers and Skinners – rights of Presentation held under ancient benefactions or trusts but these are customarily used for children of liverymen or of others closely associated with the Companies, as also are the Presentations of other Livery Companies which have acquired their rights in more recent times. Similar restrictions in purpose are generally practised by other institutions and businesses – and even some wise Local Authorities – which have given donations in order to acquire Donation Governorships. Also by antique arrangement, Guy's Hospital has the right to four places in the Schools.

There remain the individual Donation Governors – some 500 in number. Every one of these becomes accustomed to the arduous task of selecting one from several hundred applications and to the sadness which comes with rejecting many worthy and even tragic cases.

One of the Commissioners of 1866 had the brilliant notion of setting-aside some of the Hospital's funds to make places available for the children of distinguished persons – those who had done "something more than common for the good of their neighbours, their country, or mankind" for the labours of such as these, he urged, are "not unfrequently brought to a close whilst their families are still young and inadequately provided for". It was his suggestion that many parties up and down the country, learned societies and trade associations be invited to testify to the merits of "deceased persons associated with them" and to nominate their children "for reception into this national college". His fellow-Commissioners were not easily convinced of the practicality or propriety of this proposal but it was eventually accepted, adapted and incorporated in the Scheme as Clause 100. 60 places are reserved for "children, as nearly as may be in equal shares to boys and girls, being sons and daughters respectively of persons distinguished in literature, science, or art, or in the service of the Crown, or for services rendered to the public or to Christ's Hospital". The possibility of admission under this provision, Clause 100, was later extended to the grandchildren of "distinguished persons".

The selection process for Clause 100 is delegated to a sub-committee of the Education Committee and is one of the most difficult and invidious of all duties performed by any Almoner for there can be no easy method of comparing the right to a Clause 100 place of the grandchild of an Air Marshal with that of a child of an Associate of the Royal Academy, and no nice arithmetical measure which can make equitable preferring a poet's son or daughter to the grandson or granddaughter of a Permanent Under Secretary.

The Royal Mathematical School was duly preserved under the Scheme by the maintenance of 40 places for the sons of commissioned officers of the Royal Navy, the Royal Marines, or the Royal Naval Reserve. Already before the Scheme the R.M.S. had lost its status as an independent kingdom within the Commonwealth of Christ's Hospital, though the title Master of the Royal Mathematical School survived and survives still, and is conferred on the Senior Mathematics Master. And already before the Scheme, by Letters Patent granted in 1858, it was no longer expected of Mathemats that they go to sea on leaving school However, boys who do intend to enter the sea-service, even if they have not come into C.H. as Mathemats, may volunteer for the R.M.S. and, if accepted, like all Mathemats, are entitled to wear the R.M.S. badge and to the generous grants that are available from the R.M.S. fund. Until very recently on leaving school every Mathemat was given money for his uniform, a box of compasses, 17 shillings as "Her Majesty's Bounty" and a silver watch. Now the Hospital's generosity is limited to the gift of a watch – and that only to boys specially recommended.

In the century and more since the introduction of the Scheme there have been added benefactions which, being not unlike those previously committed, allow to the Council new exercises in patronage by Presentation.

In 1904 an anonymous donor gave £20,000 and in

Below: The Counting House Yard, London, c. 1901.

Above: The Treasurer's House, London, c. 1901.

Below: The Ditch, c. 1901.

the next year another £10,000 to form the Girls' School Additional Endowment Fund. Under this headway 15 places are reserved for girls, preference being given to orphan daughters of commissioned officers in the Armed Forces, civil servants, clergymen of the Church of England and members of the legal and medical professions. In these days when there are so many broken homes and single-parent families it is fortunate that the regulations of this gift allowed that the term "orphan daughters" be defined as "girls, one or both of whose parents are dead, and may include girls whose fathers are not contributing to their children's support through insanity, failure of health, or *other similar causes"*.

The Brodribb Trust, established in 1927 to benefit members of the family of that name, has proved less useful; very few Brodribb siblings have become Blues.

The Royal Air Force Foundationers Trust, established after the Second War by Barnes Wallis with funds received from the Royal Commission on Awards for Inventors as tribute to "the men who had gone in jeopardy of their lives" to carry his bombs to the enemy was by him proudly modelled in part on the Royal Mathematical School. The money that he provided, together with monies given subsequently by the RAF Benevolent Fund and other donors, allows for admission by Presentation of children of Air Force personnel.

Even more recently the Hospital has taken over some small part of the charitable function of other institutions that could not sustain the huge burden of maintaining their own schools. When the Masons closed the Royal Masonic School for Boys at Bushey the Craft so arranged matters as to allow for places to be made available at C.H. Similarly, when the Royal Commercial Travellers School at Hatch End was closed, its Governors gave money to the Hospital to establish rights of Presentation. So did the Governors of the Oliver Whitby Trust of Chichester and of the Sheffield Bluecoat School.

Certain other benefactions ensure that there are always two places in the School filled by sons of Freemen of the City of London, two by boys whose names are submitted by the Ministry of Defence (Navy) and three by children of poor clergymen.

All these and the places reserved for City Companies, for the R.M.S., for individual and corporate Donation Governors, for the RAF Foundation and the rest, though some are of ancient origin and some recent innovations, represent no significant change in the manner of admission to C.H. for, whether they be the creation of individuals or of institution and whether the right is exercised by the Council, by a representative of the institution serving as a Donation Governor or by the Governor himself, all are utilised as Presentations.

The Scheme, however, did introduce into Christ's Hospital an entirely novel mode of admission: entry by competitive examination.

Not even the most revolutionary of the Commissioners could have dreamed of instituting within C.H. a system of scholarships such as is common in public schools for none would shift from the premise that not even the most brilliant child had the right to a Christ's Hospital education unless his parents or guardians could prove need but, with this proviso accepted, certain highly significant clauses were included in the Scheme which allowed for the addition of methods of admission which were tantamount to scholarships.

A Council of Almoners' Nomination was for many years, in academic terms, the most advanced and it remains among the most competitive. Its title may deceive and undoubtedly it is not difficult to obtain a nomination but this means no more than permission to sit an examination more strenuous by far than that given to Presentees and whereas the Presentation examination tests no more than the Presentee's ability to come eventually to O Level and whereas in that test if the candidate satisfies the examiners he or she is automatically accepted, the Nominee must compete against other bright children and there are only a limited number of places available to C.A.N. candidates.

The benefactions of John and Frances West have already been noted, if briefly, in the record of bequests received by the Hospital over the centuries but they deserve some extended attention here because (if by a later scheme, instituted in 1911) admission by West Gifts – one of the regular trusts administered by the Hospital – became subject to competitive examination.

John West was born in 1640, Frances his wife in 1643. Both lived from the reign of Charles I, through the turbulence of the Civil War, the two Protectorates, the Restoration, the Plague, the Fire, the Glorious Revolution and on into the reign of the first Hanoverian monarch. John was an eminent scrivener who lived most of his life near Stocks Market, the site of the Mansion House. He became Master of the Clothworkers Company, Deputy of the Walbrook Ward during the mayorality of Sir John Moore, and a Governor of the Hospital and, with portently his greatest honour was that he was witness to the will of Samuel Pepys. The Wests amassed a fortune and even before they died (John at the age of 83 and his wife at 80) they transferred much of it to the Hospital. In addition to large gifts for the provision of pensions (of which more later) the Wests conveyed to C.H. valuable lands in Westminster and in the Central London parishes of St. Giles, and St. Andrew, Holborn, for the maintenance and education of children, both boys and girls, from three parishes in Reading, from Newbury and from Twickenham, and of children whose parents could establish consanguinity with the Wests.

Since 1911 36 places have been reserved for children from Reading, 36 for Newbury, 18 from Twickenham (now, after the re-organisation of Local

Authorities, Richmond). Candidates must be and must have been for no less than two years resident in the appropriate borough or, in default, in any contiguous parish. In each of the three areas preference must be given as to one-third of the places to kin of the Wests and, within that one-third, in the proportion of two boys to one girl. (It is seldom, if ever, possible to meet these two requirements.) Within another third of the total preference is demanded for children who have been for two years or more in attendance at a local Primary School.

The Education Authority in each area selects candidates by competitive examination and, because the constituencies are limited, Blues who have entered by more severe competitive process sometimes insinuate, with less charity than should be their custom, that this is the least stringent of all competitive routes into C.H. It is, however, in academic terms, more selective than the mode of admission open to children from certain "country parishes" – Princes Risborough, Sherborne, Swinbrook, Cowley, Hertford, and four parishes in Essex. These places are also limited to children from Primary Schools but in this case they are required to have attended for three years.

The most sensational innovation under the Scheme – a recognition both of the Hospital's close connection with the capital and of the rapid growth in elementary education – was the allotment of 179 places for children educated in the Elementary Schools of the Metropolis. The right to conduct the examination for selection was left with the London County Council which in practice used for this purpose its Junior County Examination, designed for selecting children for secondary education, which took from the top of the list of those picked-out by that process the top candidates for recommendation to the Hospital for further oral examination.

The L.C.C. examination was also used by the Reeve's Foundation to select candidates to fill its places. Reeve's Foundationers must have attended an "Elementary School" for two years and their parents must reside or have their occupation in the parish of St. Sepulchre's, Holborn or in the adjoining parishes of St. Andrew's or Clerkenwell.

For almost a century by way of the L.C.C. and later the I.L.E.A. examination, loosely and inaccurately called a Christ's Hospital Scholarship, was the most coveted of all awards open to children in London's schools. Any school that produced a 'scholarship' winner took the glory of the triumph to itself. The whole school was given an extra holiday and, in due course, the photograph of the winner, in Housey uniform, was hung in the School Hall.

For Christ's Hospital itself the L.C.C. entry provided an incomparable reservoir of talent. A majority of Grecians had entered the School by this route, of those Blues of the last 100 years mentioned in this book in the chapter "On Heroes", well over half were L.C.C. scholars, so were more than half of the

Old Blues in the current edition of *Who's Who*. One more example of the significance of the L.C.C. entry: of the Old Blues on the Council of Almoners one-third came to C.H. by way of the L.C.C. examination, among them the Treasurer (a Reeves Foundationer), the Deputy Chairman, the Chairman and Deputy Chairman of the Education Committee, and the Chairman of the Finance Committee.

When the London Country Council became the Greater London Council and when its educational function was taken over by the Inner London Education Authority, the process survived – but only for a while. Then vicious political prejudice swept away this wondrous opportunity for London's children. What could not be granted to all, so ran the argument, must be denied to any. Christ's Hospital was creaming the brains of London (an accusation that the present author is not sufficiently modest to deny). Competition was, to the new legislators, an anathema. All London's children must move from Primary to Comprehensive Schools. The mean-spirited legislators in County Hall would no longer allow to Christ's Hospital even the limited privilege of circulating information about the places available by way of ILEA mailings.

The provision exists still; and, perversely the ILEA keeps its places on the Council of Almoners. Christ's Hospital does its best to continue to fulfil its obligations to London by advertisement in the Press but newspaper announcements of this kind are most often noticed only by middle-class parents and consequently the effect of political malice is perverse both to the purposes of Christ's Hospital and to the jealous intentions of those who have so ruled. It is no longer as common as once it was for children of the truly deprived section of the Metropolis to be transformed by the magic of Christ's Hospital into equals of what Lamb and Coleridge both described in almost identical terms as products of "lesser public schools, Eton, Harrow and Westminster".

The consequences for the academic standards of Christ's Hospital itself cannot yet be judged. Optimism born of four centuries of experience persuades that somehow C.H. will master the difficulties created by others, but realism forces the admission that no method has yet been discovered by which this victory can be won.

There are two aberrant modes of admission that must be noticed. Aberrant – because neither is subject to the generally over-riding principle of need.

The children of some staff at the schools are allowed in as Non-Foundationers on condition that they do not fill boarding-places. In all other respects; in matters of clothing, education and affiliation to Houses; they are treated precisely as are "Scholars of the House".

In 1977 the Council decided to reserve, in any one year, not more than 45 places at the Boys' School and 15 at Hertford for New Foundationers, children of parents whose incomes are above the scale. This

125

shattering conclusion was reached only after much debate and conscientious hesitation and is still regarded by many with suspicion for is not this the slippery slope on which so many formerly charitable foundations slithered into the mire of privilege that is the dwelling-place of most conventional public schools? The decision was forced by the damning realities of finance; to-day it costs the Hospital almost £4000 a year for every child in the Schools. The Hospital's investment portfolio bulges still but, like all other investors, it suffers for the debilitating effects of national economic sickness. Its properties are many and bring in handsome revenues but every time a property is sold to meet mounting deficits by that much do the Almoners deprive their successors of the ability to continue the Hospital's benevolence.

There were, too, other and generally telling arguments in favour of this innovation. The comforting notion that it was not an innovation at all but merely a revival and modernisation of the old custom of admitting private pupils – the loop-hole which allowed the young Warren Hastings into C.H. – could be dismissed as special pleading but not so the case that in the latter half of the twentieth century "need" is no longer synonymous with "poverty", that there are to-day in truth many parents who would wish to see their children educated in a school like Christ's Hospital who cannot afford the full fees that are charged by any school that is even remotely like Christ's Hospital, but who are willing and eager to pay to Christ's Hospital fees equated with their means.

It has also salved the consciences of the many Almoners who mislike the novelty that New Foundationers are selected by competition (within the examination for Council of Almoners Nominees) and that, therefore, they may provide some academic high-fliers to fill the places once occupied by LCC and ILEA Scholars.

Most comforting of all: because some minimal advantage is allowed to the children of Old Blues of both sexes the New Foundationers' scheme may ameliorate one of the hitherto persistent tragedies of C.H., that no Old Blue who was in worldly terms, even modestly successful could arrange for his children to enjoy the same great privileges from which he himself had benefited.

It is as yet too early to judge whether the institution of New Foundationers will make a significant contribution to the solution of the Hospital's financial problems or to the maintenance of its academic excellence. All that can be said for certain is that the Council watches the scheme with care, that it is not likely to be enlarged, and that, without exception, Almoners are determined that Christ's Hospital will never become "just another public school".

All these various methods of securing admission to Christ's Hospital – and a few more arcane and more limited than any of these – are listed in a pamphlet that is sent out, every day by the dozen, from the Christ's Hospital Office. Also from the Office, and also by the dozen, there goes out a list, published each January, of Donation Governors who have Presentations available.

To the aspiring parent this list can be a disappointment for, as many Governors have previously committed their Presentations or else have their own sources from which to discover deserving cases, it contains few names. It can also be a delusion, for even of those listed, many have made their decision within weeks of the publication-date.

There is no decline in the number of parents who look hopefully to C.H. Indeed, in the last decades Donation Governors have noticed an increase in the number of supplicants – and a recurrent plea that was never voiced in the past, when local Grammar Schools provided an alternative of a sort for caring, ambitious but indigent parents: "I cannot submit my child to education in a Comprehensive". There is, however, no easy answer to that perennial question "How do I get my child into Christ's Hospital?" All that one can advise is, study the literature, see if there is some qualification available to parent or child that will allow him a chance to secure one of the pre-empted places and, if the only possibility is a Presentation for a Donation Governor, start the quest early. Tales are told (and are true) of parents who wrote hundreds of letters over three or four years – and succeeded just weeks before the child was due for admission.

Allow then that, by one means or another, a place is secured, that the child has passed whatever examinations are appropriate and that all the formalities are completed. What next?

In the past the process was after this fashion: each September and January a Committee of Education met in the Clerk's Room at the Hospital's Office in Great Tower Street. One parent was summoned to attend with each child. (At the September meeting when there was something of the order of 120 children to be admitted the Court Room was used as a waiting-room.) In turn parents and children were ushered into the Clerk's Office, and informed by the Committee's Chairman "Your child is admitted into Christ's Hospital and you will be required to contribute £x in every year" or "your child is admitted free of charge". Nervous parent and mystified child were then bustled into another office, given labels allotting the child to a House, handed railway-tickets and packed off, the boys to London Bridge Station and the girls to Liverpool Street.

The ceremony has been abandoned. All instructions are now sent in advance by post, including the list of games-clothes (the only clothing that a parent is called upon to buy for his own child). Scholars of Christ's Hospital now join their respective schools in a manner that is scarcely more dramatic than the arrival of new boys or new girls at some conventional boarding-school.

Yet there is hidden in that qualifying adjective 'scarcely' a subtle but, to-day for boys in particular and tomorrow perhaps also for girls, a significant exception. When they leave their homes and even when they arrive at Horsham they have not yet experienced the symbolic metamorphosis. Still they are ordinary little boys dressed in ordinary clothes that are common to their kind. At Horsham each new boy is taken over by his "nurse", a boy only a little older than himself yet by the life-time of a year already sophisticated in the ways of C.H. and therefore qualified to guide the new boy through his neophyte days. With nurse as companion the new boy goes to the Wardrobe. There he is fitted out with yellow stockings, bands, shoes, breeches, shirt and blue-coat.

Dressed for the first time in this treasured uniform the boy is truly a Blue, a Housey boy, a member of a world-wide and age-old community, possessor of a promissory-note on a rich future and heir to four-centuries of tradition.

The routine that fills the daily life of present Blues in the five, six or seven years after that day of initiation must remain in many respects mysterious to an author whose school-days ended before the Second War and it would be impertinence beyond excusing were he to breach the privacy of Hertford. Though there is good reason to believe that the substance and depth of the Housey experience is unchanged but for this age as for all that have gone before the validation of that conviction must wait upon the autobiographers – and, because the very act of autobiography is itself eccentric, even then will not be entire.

Some of the superficial alterations of C.H. custom, and some more substantial, have been noticed either implicitly or explicit in this book: the abolition of swobbing, for example, and of corporal punishment, the decline in the use of Housey slang, the virtual extinction of the superannuation system, the enlargement in the number of Grecians and of the number of boys (and girls) going on to higher education, and the sensational development in the variety of sporting facilities.

An observer who has been closely involved with C.H. for much of a long life may dare one generalised comment even if he expects to have it immediately and indignantly rejected by others whose association is even more intimate. The observation involves a paradox: the Blue of to-day is more wordly-wise and noticeably more competent in the company of adults than was his predecessor of even 30 years ago but, also much more than those who went before he is dependent upon the adults in the community, for the organisation of his extra-curricular activities and for the structure of his social life.

A few changes are worthy of notice, even though they have been forced upon C.H. by factors beyond its control and even though they have not in any way affected the essential character of the Hospital or the timeless qualities in the character of its boys and girls.

There is, for instance, the matter of prizes. For more than a century C.H. has been well-endowed with the means of rewarding excellence in scholarship and prowess in sport. It has received also from generous benefactors funds for the establishment of prizes that are given, as is the Master Mariners Prize, for reasons that remain mysterious even to the recipient: for qualities that can only be described loosely as gifts of character.

Already in the 1930's C.H. was ahead of most other schools in its policy with regard to prizes. Not for us a morocco-bound, crested edition of Macaulay's *History of England* or Palgrave's *Golden Treasury*. Instead each prize-winner was told the monetary-value of his prize and thereafter allowed to select books to this value without advice or censorship. (How else could this author have acquired so early in his life an edition of *Sanctuary*, William Faulkner's most patently pornographic book?)

This liberal attitude has been largely frustrated by inflation. From time to time prize-funds have been supplemented by grants from the Council but it would cost a fortune that the Hospital does not have to compensate for the hideous increase in the price of books. It is no longer conceivable that any boy can follow where some few went before and lay the foundations of an excellent adult library exclusively upon prizes won at C.H. and it is no longer thinkable that any notably successful or cunning Grecian will win for himself so many books that he must take his swob with him to the platform in Big School to carry back the heavy fruits of his endeavours. (Unthinkable, even if any Grecian had a swob.)

Similarly, the stupendous increase in the value of precious metals has removed from the C.H. scene all the elegant gold medals that were formerly awarded to the best Classical Scholar, the best in mathematics and to the author of the finest set of Latin hexameters. As has been said, the Charles Lamb Memorial Prize exists still and is competed for each year by every Grecian, of whatever academic discipline, but gone the exquisite silver medals. (Sir Cyril Burt was so proud of his Lamb Medal that he included it in his *Who's Who* entry with all his many honorary degrees!)

Lamb has his Memorial Medal, Coleridge his Memorial Trophy which is held each year by the House which, measured by the number of prizes won by its members, stands first in academic excellence. And the Coleridge Trophy, established in 1872, the centenary of birth of the greatest of all Blues, merits a place as a work of art among the Hospital's treasures. A bronze by Thomas Woolner R.A., it is a group of three boys, Coleridge, Middleton and Lamb, and is said to represent an incident in Coleridge's school-days (an episode which other more substantial evidence makes unlikely). When he was a boy in the lower school, Middleton (who was then a Grecian) found him sitting by himself reading Virgil, not as a lesson but for pleasure. Middleton reported this to Mr. Boyer the Head Master, who on questioning the Master of the Lower School about Coleridge was told that he was a dull scholar, could never repeat a single rule of syntax, but was always ready to give one of his own. Henceforth Coleridge was under the Head Master's eye and soon passed into the upper school to be under his immediate care. The third member of the group, the little Charles Lamb, has stopped his play to become an interested spectator.

The Hospital's care for its children, which is virtually entire during their school-days, does not end when they receive their Leaving Bibles. In the past many Blues had cause to bless the benefactors who had given so generously to its Exhibition Fund for without them not even those who won Open Awards to British Universities (until the 1930's generally Oxford or Cambridge) would have been able to take up their places, and during the 1930's the generosity of the Exhibition Fund was extended to a few eccentrics who chose to go to institutions of higher learning beyond the seas, to universities hitherto undreamed of by C.H. Since the Second War more liberal grants-policies of Local Education Authorities have made the use of the Hospital's own Exhibition Fund largely unnecessary.

However, C.H. still recognises distinguished achievements by graduating Old Blues. Any former Scholar of the House who gains a First Class Honours degree is rewarded with a cash-prize of £100.

Contemporary enlargement in the beneficence of Local Authorities and Central Government has not reduced the importance of the Hospital's Advancement in Life Fund for there are many careers open to the young which, though they make considerable financial demands upon aspirants, are not susceptible to governmental monetary support. Calls for help come regularly from Old Blues of both sexes seeking to qualify as barristers, solicitors, farmers, nurses, accountants, surveyors, and even from some who, though not involved in the pursuit of any formal qualification, must first go abroad if they are to make a success of their chosen careers.

"I give you my mature and unshakeable conviction that Christ's Hospital is the best school in the world". So said Sir William Hamilton Fyfe. Bishop Middleton called it "the noblest institution", and in 1867 the Schools Inquiry Commissioners said that it is "a thing without parallel in this country, and *sui generis*". There are some in the land to-day who reject and resent the implications of such praise, who insist that in the Utopia which is the Welfare State, where poverty has been legislated out-of-existence and where secondary education is uniformly excellent and universally accessible, Christ's Hospital has become an anachronism. Richer in venom that in logic, their antagonism bred of envy out of brutish dogma, they are apt to confound their own cause by confusing distaste for the Hospital with dislike for independent schools in general and for boarding-schools in particular.

Though it is inconceivable that prejudice can ever be conquered by sensibility or sense it is possible to refute the claims of these antagonists, in part at least, on their own terms.

Christ's Hospital is an independent school, and in a manner that is not true for most public schools for it is free not only of the State but of the need to sell itself to the wealthy. In that freedom it has acquired over the centuries both the will and the ability to experiment, to lead, to pursue excellence in all things.

No less because it is a Christian community, in every aspect of their school-life and in their life after school caring for its Scholars and teaching them to care for each other, its appeal to parents, many of them not by obvious definition themselves Christian, has not been diminished but rather has been enhanced by the growth of a society whose standards are at best uncertain and at worst non-existent.

As for the myth that poverty has vanished: any Donation Governor can bear witness to its emptiness. Pleas for Presentations for the children of one-parent families come with every post to the Hospital and its Governors and so also do prayers for aid from many parents who are loath to see their children subjected to an education less assured and, in moral terms, less complete than that which they themselves enjoyed – but who are financially incapable of purchasing the equivalent for their young.

There are, it is true, few beggars on the streets but thousands beg still for the chance that only Christ's Hospital can provide; so many indeed that to satisfy them all we would need several dozen Christ's Hospitals.

There comes again to mind that venomous outburst by a canting opponent "I hate Christ's Hospital more than I hate Eton. Eton merely perpetuates privilege; Christ's Hospital creates it".

It is a condemnation – if condemnation it be – which many thousands of Old Blues of both sexes and all generations, and with them hundreds now in the Schools, would accept, with gratitude to their benefactors and pride in Christ's Hospital.

CHAPTER ELEVEN

Epilogue as Prologue

Christ's Hospital is unique. That claim has been reiterated, by the authors of this book, by Old Blues in all generations, and by those, not of the fraternity, who nonetheless honour the Foundation. Repetitiousness may be wearisome but it does not reduce the authority of the boast. Through four-and-a-half centuries the Hospital has held to the intentions of its founders. Enduring crises and resisting the lures of triumph Christ's Hospital has remained consistently true to their charitable purpose.

Even so, and though in spirit Christ's Hospital has little in common with those other institutions which (as has been said already) in times not inhibited by polite convention, both Lamb and Coleridge dismissed as beyond sensible consideration, though its methods of financing its educational and social endeavours are, like its criteria for admitting children, out-of-step with the practices of other great schools, and though it is only by the meanest and most legalistic definition, that Christ's Hospital can be classified as a public-school, in the last two centuries it has come to be regarded as in essence one of the great public-schools – by the generality of those well-informed about education and even by Blues themselves.

And, in some important respects – in its internal organisation by houses, in its enthusiasm for *ludi viriles*, in its conviction that the Chapel is central to the life of the community, and in the manner of career adopted by its products – Christ's Hospital looks to be not so very different from any other great public-school a century and more after Thomas Arnold.

It is, above all else, its undimmed charity which sustains the uniqueness of Christ's Hospital.

There are also, of course, unique traditions – the handsome Tudor uniform, the private language (still surviving, if only just, despite the conformism engendered by radio and television), the frequency of State and stately occasions – but it would be both impertinent and erroneous and beyond the capacity for chauvinism even of Old Blues to claim that dedication to tradition is eccentric to Christ's Hospital. Many a noble and ancient institution, and even some that are by no means noble and which create their own traditions "starting next Monday", draw vitality from rare customs and idiosyncratic habits.

Yet, though tradition and traditionalism are not unique to Christ's Hospital, it is nevertheless true that tradition is the most sonorous and compelling word in the Christ's Hospital vocabulary and that, within the community of the Foundation, traditionalism is more potent than it is in most other schools.

It is possible that this assertion will be misunderstood for there is, abroad to-day, a miserable suspicion that tradition implies reaction, that traditionalism is synonymous with conservatism. Against this, the true traditionalist knows that tradition can never be used as an excuse for slavish dedication to antique precedents and that it is not unchanging or unchangeable. This is ritual – and even so, not to be despised for ritual enhances the sense of community – and ritual Christ's Hospital has, in abundance. The true traditionalist knows too that the past was not always golden and from that knowledge derives the comfort of knowing also that he faces tribulations and challenges no more daunting than those met, endured and overcome by his predecessors.

Those men and women who are devoted to Christ's Hospital are deeply conscious that tradition has been the mainspring of change, the driving-force that has impelled development. Those who work most strenuously for the future of Christ's Hospital are generally the very same men and women who are best-informed about its history, for it is from understanding of the fact that the Foundation has faced many crises and has invariably been improved by the need to surmount the immediate consequences of crisis that they gather the optimism which allows them to believe that the resolution of immediate difficulties must produce a Christ's Hospital better and stronger than it ever was in the past. For them it is no paradox that Christ's Hospital is at once immutable and ever eager for change.

It is with this sense of certainty that the Hospital to

its next sensational adventure: the bringing-together for the first time in three centuries of its boys and its girls; this time at Horsham.

The feeling of confidence that the Merger (so it has come to be called, though perhaps Re-unification would be a better and more accurate word), will benefit the Foundation as a whole and all future generations of boys and girls is made undeniable by circumstances that are, in the Christ's Hospital folk-memory, freshly-remembered. When the great migration of boys from Newgate Street to Sussex was proposed many prophets, gloomy but sophisticated and benevolent, foretold the end of Christ's Hospital. The heirs to that decision have no doubt but that Christ's Hospital has remained true to itself and yet immeasurably improved by the move.

So it must be after Christ's Hospital's girls have joined Christ's Hospital's boys at Horsham.

And it is the sentience which springs from experience of the progress engendered in Christ's Hospital by fidelity to the over-riding tradition which allows to the author of this chapter an occasional shift in stance, from that proper to a chronicler or to an observer of the current scene which has been generally his (and that of his distinguished forerunner) to that of soothsayer.

Even prophets cannot ignore the past. The Merger has its own history.

It is a delightful myth that the first child entered into Christ's Hospital was a girl, but certainly there were girl-children in Christ's Hospital in its founding-days and for this reason there is cause for claiming that Christ's Hospital is the oldest girls' school in the country and perhaps in the world. But, as must have been palpable from earlier chapters, though from its beginnings the Hospital gave to its boys an education beyond the expectations implied by their poverty, as a girls' school in the modern sense Christ's Hospital is not yet a century old.

However, already in the last years of the nineteenth century, when controversy was rampant over the proposed exodus from Newgate Street, a few brave and far-sighted individuals saw already the possibility inherent in amalgamation – of a kind – and, when the Horsham site was acquired some, the boldest of these few, proposed that advantage be taken of the spaciousness of the property by building a new Girls's School at Horsham; of course decently chaperoned from the Boys' School by vast playing-fields which no juvenile seducer (or seductress) could cross without being noticed and intercepted by his (or her) vigilant seniors. Even this suggestion, by the standards of 1983 modest, unacceptably modest, was castigated by a majority of the Council and its apostles were laughed out of the Court Room.

Thereafter the two Schools went each its own way, the Girls' School growing in numbers, strength and quality so that, by the end of the First World War, Hertford no less that Horsham stood high among its peers. And, throughout this century, the two Schools have moved ever, in C.H. spirit, each closer one to the other, linked by mutually-held traditions (that word yet again!) by joint participation in grand occasions, and, above all, by acceptance entire of the underlying purpose of the Foundation: to give the best possible schooling and the most hopeful start in life to children who could not possibly acquire anything of comparable standard elsewhere, not even in the best schools fathered by an increasingly benevolent and insistently meddlesome State.

As symbol of their growing concern for the girls in their charge, during the 'thirties, the Council accepted as *lex non scripta* that whenever something especial was done for Horsham – a grand new Science School, for example – some similar benevolence must be allowed to Hertford.

Nevertheless, it remained true that for the public at large and, it must be admitted if with shame, also for the majority of male Old Blues, the words Christ's Hospital conjured-up immediately and inevitably only Horsham. The Boys' School was famous, its reputation nation-wide, even world-wide. Excellent though it had become Hertford went largely unrecognised, except by those who were its products. Governors, at that time given always the choice of presenting either a boy or a girl, showed themselves generally committed to the well-worn fallacy that, somehow, the education of a boy must take precedence over the education of his sister. Proud though undoubtedly they were of the heritage which they shared with the boys, even the girls themselves were often convinced that the share doled out to them was out of all proportion the lesser part of the legacy, and that Hertford stood as poor relation to Horsham.

The word co-education was not uttered in Christ's Hospital circles until after the Second World War, and even then only in a whisper. As late as the early 'sixties, Sir Barnes Wallis, a man who in other activities worked always for the twenty-first century and who, as Treasurer of Christ's Hospital was in all else percipient and adventurous, made emphatic his birth as a Victorian by dismissing peremptorily – and as a recipe for encouraging in C.H. boys and girls the amorality, common among their contemporaries – the notion that the time must come and must come soon, when Christ's Hospital would accept the logic of its own history and rear all its children in one community.

Only a few years later co-education became a cause, though as yet a cause propounded only by a vocal minority on the Council. Their immediate predecessors had themselves been raised at a time when there were few co-educational boarding-schools anywhere in the world, when the colleges at Oxford and Cambridge had not yet fallen to co-education, when even the most progressive civic universities were still pretending that it was possible to enforce regulations which preserved the myth that, for all purposes except those of the lecture-hall, young men and young women could be held to the proprieties of segregation. By the 'sixties it was obvious to some of the successors to these generous but blind men that the new, and by now generally-accepted, principles of equality could not be given practical expression unless boys and girls were educated together. By that time some admittedly great public-schools had added their weight to the examples of the few, and admittedly less than great, pioneering co-educational establishments which had been founded in the previous decades. And, though the experiments in many of the grander schools were often timid, being generally confined to admitting girls into the Sixth Form, these, and evidence from abroad, gave heart to Christ's Hospital's own revolutionaries. At very least, these examples proved that co-education disadvantaged neither girls nor boys. At least these examples tended to establish that there were inherent in co-education some benefits to both boys and girls. At least, from the study of these examples, it could be argued that morals in co-educational schools were no more lax than in one-sex educational institutions. (Some even dared to suggest that such breaches of morality as did occur in co-educational schools were preferable to the lapses into turpitude that were not uncommon where boys grew up in an exclusively male environment and girls came to puberty surrounded only by other girls and spinster-teachers.)

Despite the urgency with which they pressed their case, and in contradistinction to Christ's Hospital's receptivity to new ideas – for example in the teaching of science, in which throughout the century it had led the nation – little heed was paid to those who clamoured for this particular advance. And so it must have been for many years to come had it not been for a desperate situation which, in itself, had no bearing on the rights or wrongs of co-education.

Not for the first time in its history Christ's Hospital faced financial disaster and, not for the first time, Providence (and the worldly wisdom of those who govern the Foundation) wrought advantage out of crisis.

To any superficial observer, as sometimes to those who serve it, Christ's Hospital is the re-incarnation of Croesus. The Foundation owns properties all over the country and notably in London. It has a vast portfolio of investments. It is, indeed, in all probability potentially the richest school in the country. But not Providence (or the collective wisdom of its Council) could hold Christ's Hospital free from the effects of the economic ills which have battered England since the Second War. Indeed, that war itself added to the financial problems, for Christ's Hospital, like many another owner of property, suffered bitterly at the hands of Hitler and his bomb-aimers. Buildings in its possession were destroyed and with their destruction went the decimation of rent-income.

There followed inflation, virulent and ever-rising. As has been said Christ's Hospital's ancient connection with the City of London has for centuries settled many Old Blues into careers in high finance and so, in turn, has given to the Foundation the benefit among its advisers some of Britain's most experienced and shrewdest financial experts, but no manipulation of investments, however deft, could match the galloping RPI. Christ's Hospital is an employer on a substantial scale (the Foundation has on its pay-roll more than 400 men and women). Rates-of-pay accelerated even faster than inflation and the Hospital, always proud of its reputation as a good employer, could do no other than accept each new pay-award. (Often it did better.) The annual cost for maintaining every child in the Schools, which in 1914 had stood at £69 for a boy and at £62 for a girl, and in 1950 at £203 for a boy and £171 for a girl, had by 1970 risen to £649 for a boy and £611 for a girl.

So it was that by 1970 it was hideously obvious to those in charge, as it would have been obvious to a financial illiterate, that nemesis was not far off.

Benefactions stayed at a high level. Men and women – a majority among them, as always, Old Blues responding in middle-age to the Charge pressed upon them in youth – continued to offer donations to secure the right of presentation. But benefactions could not bridge the chasm between income and expenditure and the "price" of a Donation Governorship represented, as it had always done, but a small contribution to the actual cost of a child's school-life.

Raising fees, the response to the problem of inflation available to other schools, was denied to Christ's Hospital save only in the form of a minimal enlargement of the scale of parental contributions, fixed according to a means-test. Hesitantly, even with great reluctance, it was accepted that the category of New Foundationers be admitted, but all who conceded this innovation agreed that this could well be the first step on that icy slope down which many another ancient and originally charitable foundation had slithered. Only one voice was raised (and that voice from without the Council) in support of the proposition that Christ's Hospital's future could be secured by filling it with fee-paying pupils. That voice was silenced; to the majority a public-school financed by conventional means would no longer be Christ's Hospital at all. And because the number of New Foundationers was deliberately kept small and their parents, though liberated from the upper income-bar in place against the parents of all other candidates for admission, still subjected to a means-test to decide the contribution that they would pay, even the most optimistic projection of parental enthusiasm for the New Foundationers mode of entry did not forecast that it would contribute hugely towards the financial salvation of the Hospital.

Some property was sold (happily for a rich return) and some investments, but, though it was clear to all that pillaging of the Foundation's endowments might solve current difficulties, it was no less obvious that it would serve only to postpone the inevitable. No

Almoner was prepared to meet the hazards of the moment by betraying his heirs to the privilege of governing Christ's Hospital.

Some other measure must be adopted, no less drastic but blessed by unquestionable integrity.

That measure was obvious; at least to a few. Christ's Hospital must close its Girl's School. The obvious was cried down as a heresy.

An alternative was suggested. Christ's Hospital could follow the example by then in vogue in all but a few major public-schools. It could continue to educate girls, at Horsham, but only in the Sixth Form.

One Almoner, more given to acerbity than his colleagues, asked immediately the question that was in the minds of many. 'Since when did Christ's Hospital Boys' School have a Sixth Form?', but reasons more powerful than captions and parochial semantics persuaded all to dismiss out-of-hand the mean compromise put forward by the heretics.

As so often in the past, traditionalism proved to be the bulwark which defended the future of the House. Christ's Hospital had always cared for girls, if sometimes, in the light of afterthought, not as generously as it might have done, but always, by the measure of the times, as best it could. By the measure of the latter-half of the twentieth century this must mean giving to Christ's Hospital's girls, in number proportionally consistent with the ratio developed during this century, an environment and an education no less rich than that offered to its boys. Any panacea that involved sacrificing one part of the whole must be corrosive to the other half.

And, glory be, careful prognosis suggested that the amalgamation of the two schools on the Horsham site might well cure the financial disease which had seemed likely to be terminal.

At that moment the advocates of co-education came, at last, into their own. They could now argue that what was expedient in financial terms was also socially and educationally right. The days of segregated schooling were past; amalgamation of the two Schools was now the one way in which the Foundation could fulfil its responsibilities, to girls and to boys.

On 2 April 1980 the Council of Almoners accepted a resolution as momentous and as brave as anything in its history: 'This Council resolves to bring together the boys and girls of the Foundation on one site at Horsham'.

The Resolution was passed unanimously but there was still some hesitation about its implications. Some, though only a small minority, slipped back to the 1890s (it may be that they had not heard that Queen Victoria is dead) and advocated, as an interpretation of the Resolution, the building of a new Girls' School at Horsham distinct from the Boys' School both in situation and organisation. This speciousness satisfied neither the financial intentions nor the educational philosophy by then general to the Council. What Christ's Hospital does it cannot do with half its heart.

Nothing short of Merger would suffice.

Because Christ's Hospital is a continuing and indivisible community in which no cabal, not even the Council, has undisputed authority to make decisions as dramatic as those involved in accepting the notion of Merger, there remained the necessity to win the approval, expressed when possible, tacit when overt acquiescence was not practicable, of a vast and wide-spread constituency. A programme of consultation was instituted: with the Governors at large, with Old Blues, with the boys and girls (who would themselves be Old Blues before the Merger was completed but whose experience was by definition more immediate than that of any member of the Council).

The process of consultation is not yet finished, and in all probability will not be ended even long after the Merger, like the founding of the Royal Mathematical School, has become no more than a glorious event in the record, but it was soon clear that, in principle certainly, most of those consulted endorsed the decision of the Council.

There were, of course, reservations, many of them no more than rehearsals of doubts that had previously exercised the Council.

Not all these reservations are peculiar to Christ's Hospital. Every school that has turned from segregated to conjoined-educational has heard dire predictions that the change must be preface, at worst, to immorality, at best, to excessive attention to the attractions that one sex exercises on the other. Every school which has committed itself to this metamorphosis has been asked to pay heed to what is said to be a difference in the rates of academic progress of boys and girls. (Because in the last three or four decades Christ's Hospital Boys' School has become noticeably more gentle than it was in the past and in the last few years, with a few notorious and censured exceptions, corporal punishment has been abandoned – though not outwith the law it was therefore, unnecessary for Christ's Hospital to follow the example of two overseas public schools which on moving to co-education and in pursuance of equality, decided that, when called for, punitive chastisement could be applied without deference to conventional gentility.)

There were, there are, and there will persist until fact makes speculation redundant, many uncertainties and of these some are aggravated by the especial characteristics of Christ's Hospital and by the liveliness of the Christ's Hospital folk-memory. As example: whenever the Merger was discussed with those older girls who would not themselves go to Horsham they expressed concern lest the move deprive their younger sisters of those policies which they took to be evidence of Hertford's greater liberalism. Hertford girls, they pleaded, are allowed into the town to mix freely with the community. Similar privilege is not often conceded to the boys and, at all events, the

Girls' School is in the middle of Hertford, the Boys' School a mile or more distant from Horsham. Above all they worried lest the Merger be taken as reason to deny to the girls their regular Leave Days – whole holidays which present to them a chance to visit London or to go back to their family and friends.

Though most of these kindly if pessimistic young critics accepted the force of the counter-argument that Horsham's plenitude of opportunity for sport, entertainment and social concourse would compensate for some loss of Hertford freedoms, and though all, as was proper to their age, regretted that – in this unlike their contemporaries at Horsham – they had never enjoyed membership in the Grecians Club serving wine and beer, none knew that the very same gloomy forebodings had been voiced in the 1890s when the move from Newgate Street to Horsham was imminent, or that they had never been heard again once the generation of the Great Migration had left the School.

More even than their seniors the young look at the past through the well-nigh impenetrable fogs of recent events. Their folk-memory is lively but of short span. It is so even in traditionalist Christ's Hospital and it cannot be expected that girls now in their schooldays will remember that, for more than two centuries, Leave Days were a comforting feature of otherwise harsh life in Newgate Street. In his *Autobiography*, published in 1851, Leigh Hunt looks back over 60 years and recalls with undimmed enthusiasm the delights that were his in his school days when, in the company of Thomas Barnes, he was granted the liberation of Leave Days.

What pleasant days have I now passed with him, and other school-fellows, bathing in the New River, and boating on the Thames! He and I began to learn Italian together; and anybody not within the pale of the enthusiasts, might have thought us mad, as we went shouting the beginning of Metastasio's Ode to Venus, as loud as we could, over the Hornsey fields.

Appeals in this kind based on the evidence of distant history are commonplace to an historian-advocate; they carry no conviction for a young if judicious jury; it has served little to reduce the apprehensions of Hertford that the Leave Days they hold in such affection are, in the term of Christ's Hospital's history, no recent innovation, that, at the Boys' School the privilege fell to desuetude 80 years ago, and that almost immediately thereafter, the very term disappeared from the boys' vocabulary, without protest or regret.

More cogent, in the view of the planners, was the expressed fear that, as they must form a minority within the combined school, the girls would find themselves overwhelmed by the power of Horsham custom – as by the obsessive interest of their male peers.

Meanwhile, as the business of consultation has continued so also has the planning. In this, too, Council, its Committees and sub-committees, and Staff, boys and girls have been intimately involved.

Some sad but undeniable decisions were taken at the very highest level.

If Christ's Hospital were to continue to educate the number of children present in the Schools when the idea of Merger was accepted almost all those costs would remain that had prefaced the resolve to amalgamate the two Schools. Therefore, if with reluctance tempered only by hope that times would improve and thus allow the Council to rescind its disagreeable if unanimous decision; it was decreed that at the moment of re-unification there would be 820 in the School, 620 of them boys and 200 girls (a ratio minimally more favourable to girls than was the ratio before planning began). The Clerk and the two Heads were set to the arduous task of legislating an appropriate rate of rundown; a process considerably more complex than it would be for other schools. The age-range in the conventional public-school runs from fourteen to eighteen. Christ's Hospital has for many years cared for children from the age of eleven to the age of eighteen. This unique generosity the Council did not intend to reduce. Indeed Almoners took prospective pride from the knowledge that, of the great schools, Christ's Hospital would be the first to introduce co-education at once for young children and for young adults.

Yet more burdensome to those responsible for the programme of rundown: the process must be engineered with the least-possible disturbance to the Hospital's much-cherished, intricate and honoured associations with great institutions, to the more recent but no less cherished connections with those few Local Education Authorities which, unlike the Inner London Education Authority, had not sacrificed the advantage of their children on the altar raised in honour of some specious egalitarian creed, and, if possible, without discommoding that large number of charitable individuals who offered themselves and their money for Donation Governorships.

Nevertheless, some amendment in this kind was inescapable.

Once more with reluctance the Council agreed that, as was within its power, the Presentation rights of Governors must be reduced. It says much for the benevolence of Governors of all kinds that not one protested, much for the affection in which Christ's Hospital is held, both by institutions and by individuals, that the Foundation continues to receive in plenty qualifying donations, and much for the sense of loyalty and obligation of those who have been educated in the Hospital that of this number of donations the majority was made up of Old Blues and their families.

Once the decision had been taken to merge the two Schools into one undivided entity detailed strategic planning began. After preliminary but sensitive studies and consultations with the Hospital's architects, and on the advice of the Clerk in respect of the acceptable and practical rate of run-down, a date was set for the completion of the Merger.

On the first day of the Michaelmas Term in 1985 there will be again, as there was in 1552, just one Christ's Hospital and then, all bias having been removed that for almost four-and-a-half centuries (if with decreasing virulence) has tended to favour boys more than girls, for the first time in its long history the Foundation will have honoured the dimly-perceived intentions of its Founders.

In the years since the adoption of the Merger Resolution several sub-committees have set about the interwoven, arduous but intriguing tasks involved in preparing for the integration of the two Schools – and their work must continue even into 1985. Overall responsibility was given to a small but powerful Ways and Means Committee and there were set up smaller working-parties of Almoners, Staff and professional advisers, each designated to organise and supervise some especial activity essential to the Merger, such as building, and educational and social re-adjustment.

From the outset, the planners were sensitive to the need to resolve immediately practical conundrum that were well-nigh beyond resolution and to excise some of the philosophical paradoxes in their brief which, had they been allowed to remain until 1985, must then make the Merger unsatisfactory and incomplete.

It was the unambiguous intention of the Council, and one that was forcefully expressed, that processes essential to re-unification be effected with the least possible deleterious consequence for the school generations of the Merger but, especially for Hertford, the acceptance (and implementation) of this benevolent fiat was inhibited by the realities.

By the measure conventionally acceptable to boarding-schools Christ's Hospital, Hertford is a small school. As preface to that moment when the girls will enter the 'lovely garden' at Horsham, the girls must

Right: East Lodge 1983.

Left: The Library, Hertford — exterior.

Below: The Library, Hertford, interior.

Left: Main Entrance, Hertford 1983.

Above: The Library and Dominion Library, Horsham from the Quarter Mile.

Left: The stairway, Assembly Hall, Hertford.

Above right: The Organ Loft, Assembly Hall, Hertford.

Right: The Science Block, Hertford.

Left: Coleridge.

Below: Barnes.

see their school shrink until, by the end of the academic-year 1984-5, there will be 'hardly enough left. . . to make a respectable. . .' school. The implications for pastoral and educational well-being were terrifying.

At Horsham, too, and even in the years preparatory to the Merger, well-established loyalties must be sacrificed, valued customs abandoned, and some comforts denied to the boys if builders were to be admitted to the site to begin work on the adaptations and the new accommodation required for the eventual reception of the girls.

For several years Hertford has worked to a four-term year Horsham to the conventional three-term calendar. At A and O Levels the two Schools are examined each by a different Board.

Again particularly for Hertford, it was imperative that presentiment among the teaching-staff had to be assuaged. In some senses, the very first decision made by the Council, though in itself probably inevitable, did little to reduce their worries. If Christ's Hospital is to be in reality indivisible there must be only one Head for any other arrangment would incite confusion and encourage schism. The decision to give this role to the Head Master was made somewhat easier by a circumstance that in any other situation would have been tragic: by the departure to another post of the lovable, loved and honoured Head Mistress, her place being taken by a senior mistress, also loved and respected, who is due to retire soon after 1985, but the strident voice of feminism was only momentarily silenced by the Council's assurance that this decision should not be taken as unimpeachable precedent. More persuasive to acquiescence, if notably amongst the girls themselves, was the pledge given by the Head Master that he and his successors would not reserve for boys the chance to rise to the lordly rank of Senior Grecian.

It was clear that many of the Hertford Staff either could not or had no wish to migrate with the girls to Horsham. Among those who thought to make the move, as also among the women-teachers newly-appointed to Horsham (extensions to a long and distinguished line that stretched back to the First World War) there were occasional rumblings of fear that, in the predominantly masculine atmosphere of Horsham, they might find themselves ill-considered as somehow underprivileged citizens.

Everything that can be done has been done to treat with generosity those Hertford mistresses who either cannot or will not move to Sussex, and both Council and Head Master have promised that all women on the combined Staff will be given opportunities for careers at least as rich as those presented to their male colleagues.

There remains, insistent at Hertford, a question that can be given only pragmatic answer. What to do about vacancies in the Staff that occur in the period of run-up to the Merger? Such vacancies there must be, whether they are created by what has come to be called, without elegance, natural wastage, by retirement, mobility or by pregnancy, the most natural of all causes – and one that is happily more common among the staff at girls' boarding-schools today than it was in the days when most mistresses in such schools were spinsters. Fill these places always with teachers eager for the move, with elderly staff destined for retirement by 1885, or with temporaries, and the corollary must be that, immediately, the generation now at Hertford will not have the benefit of tuition from the most competent staff that is available, and that, eventually, the girls who go to Horsham will be deprived of some of the advantages inherent in continuity and familiarity.

All in any way involved with planning strain to guard both Staff and boys and girls from the disturbances of the preface to the Merger and, to a not inconsiderable extent, their efforts are assisted by the utility as a prophylactic – against the *malaises* rife in periods of revolution – of the excitement inherent in speculation and the thrill of participating in an enthralling adventure.

Even so, as the planning-committees set themselves to the vital business of logistic management, well-intentioned members of the extended community thrust before them new and hitherto-unconsidered puzzles. Had it been recognised that girls' schools are accustomed to playing games against each other on a midweek half-holiday whereas it is customary for boys' schools to play inter-school games on Saturdays? Or, almost as antiphon (if always from male Old Blues) a question loaded with pessimism: in its (numerically) diminished state, will the Boys' School ever again be strong enough to face and defeat its traditional sporting-rivals?

Such questions are by no means frivolous but an answer to them can be postponed. No similar hesitation was possible when faced with the need to make a decision about the eventual disposition of the girls on the Horsham site. Until that was settled the architects could not begin work on their designs, houses could not be made ready for the builders, and nothing could be done to prepare for integration and social re-organisation.

There were still, even on the Council, a few who favoured a modified version of the notions advanced by some of their nineteenth century predecessors. These few argued, with some vehemence, that the cause of simplicity would be served best, and with it the cause of maintaining the cohesiveness and identity of the Girls' School, if the girls were settled at the most Easterly end of the Avenue.

A few others looked at the example of the universities and pleaded for mixed houses in which all social accommodation (except, of course, dormitories) is mutual to boys and girls.

The majority favoured neither the reactionary nor the brash modernist solution but was resolute in its view that, if integration is to be real it must be demonstrated by geography; that Christ's Hospital cannot risk the possibility that after 1985 it will still have two schools, if two schools on one site. It was decided, therefore, that two blocks, Coleridge and Barnes be emptied of boys and adapted for the reception of girls.

Coleridge boys have always prided themselves on their proximity to all that is the very heart of Christ's Hospital – and for this superlative centrality have been derided by their envious schoolfellows and by their masters (''Members of the Coleridge houses have less distance to walk than do any others. It follows that they are late for everything.'') The Chapel, the Dining Hall, the Tuck Shop; all are closer to Coleridge than to any other block. Barnes, on the other side of the Quadrangle, is nevertheless central to the Eastern Avenue.

It says something for the dedication of Almoners to the principles implicit in the Merger that, of the Committee which recommended the transmogrification of Coleridge and Barnes more than half had ancient loyalties to one or another of the four houses of those blocks.

At the end of the Summer Term 1982 Coleridge A and Coleridge B ceased to exist as boys' houses. Immediately the builders moved in to begin conversion. The end of the school year 1983-4 will see also the end of masculinity in the two Barnes houses.

Meanwhile the staffs at Hertford and Horsham work together to prepare for the co-ordination of the syllabus and, so that the shock of re-adjustment be not too seismic either for staff or Scholars of the House (the generous term it must be re-iterated, that, Christ's Hospital, prefers 'pupils' or 'students', the term that has, in Christ's Hospital's official usage only one synonym, 'children of the Hospital' – and that less acceptable to the generation of the 1980s) a series of exchange-visits is in progress. Hertford staff teach at Horsham, Horsham staff teach at Hertford. Girls go to Horsham and boys to Hertford to live, work and play with their fellow-scholars of the opposite sex.

Such activities are deliberately engineered but even more significant as giving reason for optimism about the smoothness of transition is the potency of that sense of a conjoined tradition which has always existed in Christ's Hospital; as much as Hertford as at Horsham. At Hertford in particular this has been enhanced during this century by participation in the great occasions of the Hospital. In the earliest days of the Foundation the mutuality of panoply was evident. It disappeared in the eighteenth and early nineteenth century. (Not one of the great writers produced by the Foundation in its literary golden generation so much as mentions the existence of a girls' school.) Even when, early in this century, the girls were returned to their proper status, still, perhaps, the presence of girls on St. Matthew's Day or Speech Day at Horsham, was regarded by some as an aberration.

After the Second World War, however, the unusual became a commonplace, and the certainty that girls shared equally with boys the entirety of Christ's Hospital tradition was, from that time on, made more evident by the fact that the number of grand occasions seemed to increase.

There were, for example, the celebrations of the Quatercentenary – a dinner in the Mansion House and a service in St. Paul's. There was that other magnificent service in the magnificence of Westminster Abbey when the Hospital presented to the Abbey a stone in honour of its Royal Founder. At these, as in many other public events, the girls were present with the boys and C.H. Old Girls with male Old Blues. On 27 February 1980, when, again in St. Paul's Cathedral, the whole Christ's Hospital community joined 617 (Dambusters) Squadron, the City of London, the Services and representatives of the nation and the Commonwealth, led by the Prince of Wales, in a Service of Thanksgiving for the life and work of Sir Barnes Wallis, it was borne in on many present that boys, girls and Old Blues of both sexes were aware that they were doing even more than salute the memory of one of the great originals of this century, their much-loved Treasurer. This was a glorious and moving demonstration of the essential unity of the House, and when, after but a few hours of combined rehearsal, the two School Orchestras and the two School Choirs entranced the congregation, there was clear in the miraculous music both an anthem resplendent with the confidence of one undivided Foundation and a prayer that, at the last, the Merger would be no more than the physical consequence of an inward sensibility that is already beyond doubt.

There are still many difficulties that must be overcome but most seem tractable. However, there remained to be definitively answered one question which long-since, at the very beginning of the Merger debate, one Jeremiah had prophesied would create more dissension than all else: what to do about the Girls' School uniform?

Tudor bluecoat and yellow stockings are precious to the Boys' School, and to all who have ever worn them of much more significance than aliens will believe possible in the wearing of a uniform, however noble, however eccentric. They are (and it cannot be said too often) the prime symbols of continuity, the most immediate evidence to the equality of all Blues, and among the most compelling influences which assure every boy in the school that equality is beyond challenge, that, from wheresoever he comes, however deprived his background, however disadvantaged his family or miserable his home-circumstances, he is settled with all his contemporaries and with all their predecessors in the aristrocracy that is Christ's Hospital. (There are many who believe that it was no trifling error of judgement which allowed boys to go home at the end-of-term in *mufti*. Previous generations had accepted with general good humour an occasional shout of 'mustard-pot', complacent in their conviction that what seemed to be a jeer was in truth an expression of affection. And those who criticised the decision hold still to the opinion that by it Christ's Hospital was deprived of some of the comfortable familiarity it had previously enjoyed, especially with the people of London.) No boy, no Old Blue, no Almoner, not even the most impudent outsider and, in all probability, no girl, has dared the heretical suggestion that, for the sake of conformity, the boys be asked to abandon their traditional dress. But, even in the earliest days of the Hospital, its girls did not wear the bluecoat and, already a century back, they exchanged their own attractive uniform for a pattern of dress much after the example of that worn in other girls' schools. Since then the Girls' School uniform has changed frequently but always according to the fashion of the day – or a little behind it. Certainly, to the eye of a male observer not entirely unsophisticated in such matters, the uniform at present worn by Hertford girls is notable only for its ordinariness.

It cannot be that the boys will be allowed to stride as peacocks around the Horsham site whilst the girls are noticeable only for their dowdiness for this of itself would undermine the purpose of integration and would deny to the girls the sociological benefits conferred on the boys by their uniform.

Already in the years when the girls have joined the annual march through the City of London on St. Matthew's Day the incongruity of their uniform has been apparent. How much more so must it be when the Schools are merged and how much more depressing the shame of unequal grandeur?

And there is the Band.

For many years the School Band has contributed much to the pride of the Boys' School. It plays superbly for the daily Dinner Parade. On Speech Day it is the Band (and, a recent addition to Christ's Hospital traditions, the small boy who marches, alone, erect and solemn, before the admiring audience assembled in the Quadrangle to present a bouquet to the Lady Mayoress) with the remarkable feat of composition and memory demonstrated each year in the Senior Grecian's English Oration, which makes the day much more resplendent than are most similar occasions in other schools. The Band blasts its harmonious way through the City of London at the head of the Schools as they march on St. Matthew's Day to St. Sepulchre's Church and the Mansion House. In recent years, at the invitation of incoming Lord Mayors, it has added a popular and colourful dimension to the popular and colourful Lord Mayor's Procession. In recent years, at the invitation of the Dowager Duchess of Norfolk, the Band has welcomed touring Test teams when they come to play their first game in England on the lovely cricket-ground at Arundel Castle. At the end of the summer Term hundreds come to watch the Band Beating Retreat.

When first the idea of Merger was mooted even those most eager for co-education held it to be unthinkable that there could ever be girls in the Band ("next we will have prancing drum-majorettes!") but gradually good sense, and conscience stirred by the high quality of Hertford music, have worn down male chauvinism and at the last it is appreciated that unity cannot be real if girls are not included in this, among the most public and most triumphant of school-activities.

Nonetheless, the rejection of *apartheid* in the Band has added force to the argument that some uniform must be designated for the girls which will not strike discord where there should be harmony, which will not shame female musicians by placing them, a gaggle from St. Trinian's, amidst the masculine Tudor elegance of the Band.

The task of finding a mode of dress which will be appropriate both to policy and to the delectable qualities of feminity the Treasurer remitted to the Council's hitherto generally-unused and ungallantly-named Committee of Women, but to the Committee of Women strengthened (if that is the word) by the addition of a few male Old Blues who, for one reason or another but always, it is hoped, for good and respectable reason, have especial experience in matters relating to female clothing, and strengthened also by the inclusion of two recent Head Girls. As the Treasurer said, with his customary percipience and habitual (and justified) lack of confidence in the wisdom of his friends, had he put this issue to the whole Council for decision he would have received back as many designs as there are Almoners.

The Treasurer's *fiat* could not still controversy. The girls' uniform is subject for debate in Wagga-Wagga, Hackensack, Wigan and wherever two or three Old Blues of either sex are gathered together. At Hertford, as was to be expected, it is, in all probability, more than anything else connected with the Merger, the prime topic for discussion, and there resolution is made even more difficult than it is elsewhere because it is clouded by what Hertford sees as a threat to another of Hertford's freedoms, the right, when out-of-school and on all but formal occasions, to discard uniform in favour of privately-owned dress. But, if the matter of uniform excites Hertford, the cause of this excitement is not always that which arouses argument elsewhere. The girls, and particularly the older girls, are fearful lest their seniors make obscure what is to them obvious and by so doing settle generations of young women is some garb that is ludicrous and unbecoming. For there is, to many of these girls, no occasion for controversy. The girls, they say, are persuaded that they and their successors can think of no uniform more attractive than Housey dress – if Housey dress were minimally if suitably adapted to show off the notable advantages of femininity. Buckle-shoes, perhaps, as the boys used to wear?

This simple answer from the girls to a question which has exercised the minds of adults for several years is in its turn made complex by a rider. Housey dress for school, for public occasions and invariably for the Band *but* for 'private times', and *both* for boys and girls, private clothes, even jeans.

Were it not for the addition of the word jeans; a word which, to most of their seniors carries with it a terrifying vision of uncouthness utterly out-of-place in the well-ordered society of Christ's Hospital; this sensible and sensitive suggestion from sensible and sensitive young women might have won immediate acceptance.

The fateful decision has been made:

The brief given to Peter Rice, one of Britain's most skilful theatrical designers, was direct enough.

He was to produce for the girls a uniform harmonious with that worn throughout the centuries by the boys and yet neither self-consciously archaic nor antipathetic to delicious femininity. He must attempt to substitute for the multiplicity of conventional schoolgirl modes previously in use at Hertford, a system of variations on the theme suggested by the boys' uniform that would meet the many needs of school-life and the seasons and that, even so, could be without difficulty adapted for use when the girls take their proper place alongside the boys on the ceremonial occasions which are so much a part of Christ's Hospital life.

The brief was direct, its fulfilment far from easy, but Peter Rice's solutions (when this book goes to press not yet finally agreed by the Council but in principle almost certainly acceptable) are brilliant and exquisite.

He has proposed a flannel jacket in the same colour as the boys' coats and fitted with the same silver buttons – six small and one large for all but Grecians, fourteen large for Grecians – and for girl-Grecians as for boy-Grecians velvet cuffs. This will normally be worn with a short, permanently-pleated skirt in the same colour and material, and on more formal occasions a long, flared skirt. The girls, as the boys, will wear the Housey girdle, 'narrowy', or 'broadie' with a silver buckle, according to their station.

Two blouse designs are projected: one short-sleeved with a wide-centre front shirt-opening, and one with long sleeves and a side-fastening mandarin collar, allowing not only for seasonal variations but also for the girls to adopt what has now become the Boys' School custom of wearing 'half-Housey' (the uniform without the coat).

In the place of the boys starched bands, girls will wear an attractive lace jabot, Grecians a jabot more elaborate than that sported by lesser beings.

For daily wear: dark-toned stockings with black medium-heeled shoes and (as used to be for the boys) silver buckles but with long skirt, and as must be, yellow stockings.

Peter Rice has also designed an all-weather hooded cloak of proofed gabardine with a yellow lining which is already coveted by all who have seen the prototype, girls, adult women – and men.

The decision has been made but the controversy is not yet at an end nor is it likely to be silenced until that time comes when the dress worn by the girls is accepted as an essential, admirable and virtually immutable part of the Christ's Hospital tradition, blessed with that same immediate and generous recognition that has been granted the boys' uniform for more than four centuries.

There are other problems still to be solved and questions that remain as yet unanswered. Almost every week some complexity is raised which, even in their wide-ranging and generally far-sighted preliminary planning, had never before occurred to the Council, some new inhibition to the smooth management of the logistics of the Merger. When that days comes in 1985 when Hertford is emptied there will be much sadness for the loss of the oldest and some of the finest buildings in the Hospital's possession. But at Horsham the builders are busy. The boys and girls have for the most part slipped apprehension and taken on enthusiasm for the Merger. The two Staffs are beginning to work as one. Old Blues and Governors are learning to relish the prospect of seismic change. The Council is unanimous in its optimism.

The Merger will not, of itself alone, serve as answer to all Christ's Hospital's financial problems. For that the Foundation looks to the hard currency of the gratitude of Old Blues and to sustenance from those sources of practical beneficence, both institutional and private, that have always cosseted its activities. On both counts, there is no reason for doubt. But the certainty, general in the C.H. community, comes also from the knowledge that what was born out of financial necessity will in the last accounting stand as monument to courage and wisdom, as fulfilment of an obligation inherited from the centuries, and as a rich and useful gift to posterity.

The Christ's Hospital sodality is united in the belief that it owes it to the past that it preserves Christ's Hospital's uniqueness and to the future that it hands on an enlarged inheritance.

The Merger completed, and then all who take their part in this glorious revolution will have the right to echo the words of a man – the greatest, perhaps, of all the many great men reared by the Hospital. In 1813, when Christ's Hospital was burdened, as it is to-day, with financial problems and, as it is to-day, threatened by some political animus, Samuel Taylor Coleridge wrote, "I say solemnly and on my conscience, that we can hardly imagine a larger sum of goodness struck off at once from the ledger of useful benevolence."

INDEX

Numbers in italics indicate illustrations